IN PLAIN RUSSIAN

VLADIMIR VOINOVICH

IN PLAIN RUSSIAN

STORIES

TRANSLATED BY RICHARD LOURIE

FARRAR STRAUS GIROUX

NEW YORK

Printed in the United States of America

Designed by Cynthia Krupat

First edition, 1979

Library of Congress Cataloging in Publication Data

Voĭnovich, Vladimir / In Plain Russian.

Translation of Putem vzaimnoĭ perepiski. / I. Title.

PZ4.8955In / [PG3489.4.I53] / 891.7′3′44 / 79–11980

The open letters to Comrade Pankin and to the Writers' Union were
first published in *Index on Censorship;* the letter to the
Minister of Communications, in *The Washington Post*

CONTENTS

AUTHOR'S FOREWORD

A certain émigré critic recently stated that everything I had written before *Chonkin* could have been published in any Soviet journal including *Molodaya Gvardia* and *Krokodil.*

That is not quite true.

Even in *Novy Mir,* the best and bravest journal of its time, my stories, with the exception of "We Live Here," barely squeaked by, and sometimes, as in the case of "From an Exchange of Letters," they did not squeak by at all.

The former story (published in *Novy Mir,* No. 1, 1961) received an altogether favorable critical evaluation. But even then the more vigilant critics pointed out that the young writer not only depicted the progressive movement of harvesters and other agricultural machines but, as one critic put it, also "adhered to an aesthetic, alien to us, of representing life 'as it is.'" But a certain A. Ivanov (now, incidentally, editor-in-chief of the journal *Molodaya Gvardia*) called the completely inoffensive story "Two Comrades" ideologically harmful, anti-socialist, and pornographic, and quoted the song sung by one of the story's heroines as an example of that pornography:

Mama, I love a pilot,
Mama, I'll marry him.

> *A pilot flies high*
> *and earns good money.*
> *Mama, I'll marry him.*

I have no desire to repeat what was written in the newspapers concerning the story "I Want to Be Honest" or what Ilyichev, then secretary of the Central Committee of the Communist Party of the Soviet Union, said of it from his lofty tribunal. It is hardly an accident that to this day Russian readers can find this story, which has been translated into many languages, only in the journal where it was originally published (*Novy Mir,* No. 2, 1963).

This present volume consists of pieces written at various times but never published together in a single volume. Wishing to acquaint the reader with various aspects of my work, I have included material published both in the Soviet Union and abroad, as well as material never before published. I have also included what I consider the more successful of my open letters.

As the discerning reader may notice, the story "Skurlatsky, Man of Letters" is in fact a reworked chapter from my novel on Vera Figner, *A Degree of Trust.*

In manuscript, the story "I Want to Be Honest" was entitled "What I Might Have Been." The change occurred due to the insistence of one member of the editorial board of *Novy Mir,* who felt that the new title would be less likely to be censored. The title "I Want to Be Honest" attracted many readers by its directness and also caused some irritation among the bureaucratic critics. I, too, never liked the title and am now returning to the story its original title—not, of course, to satisfy the bureaucratic critics, but purely on aesthetic grounds.

1978   V. V.

TRANSLATOR'S INTRODUCTION

The history of Russian literature and the nature of the Soviet experience had prepared us for the somber trage- dies and harrowing testimonies that have reached the West in the twenty-five years since the death of Stalin. But really very little in Russian literature and, it would seem, practically nothing in the Soviet era could have foretold the coming of Vladimir Voinovich's comic master- piece *The Life and Extraordinary Adventures of Private Ivan Chonkin*. Chekhov's distant smile, Gogol's peculiar, jangling laughter, Dostoevsky's mean and caustic satire can hardly be considered Voinovich's spiritual ancestors. Zoshchenko, and Ilf and Petrov, the principal Soviet comic authors, may have taught Voinovich a thing or two, but hardly much more than that. Genius finds its way alone—not alone in the convolutions of the author's own personality, but alone in the world, alone with the world.

In the stories which comprise *In Plain Russian* we see the route Voinovich's genius took in discovering its own strength and mission. This is not to say that these stories can only be appreciated as a prelude. On the contrary; they are vigorous and tender, scathing and impartial, and they reveal not the extremes of Soviet Russian experience but its middle, its daily life, its common people, their common cares and fates. Voinovich's experience of Soviet society is vast; he has first-hand knowledge of the collective farm, the village, the drab railway-crossing provincial town, the construction industry, the army, the world of workers' hostels and cheap cafeterias, not to mention the other social sphere, the offices of the KGB, which is all too familiar to many Soviet intellectuals.

Not a great deal is known about Voinovich, but even the barest outline of his life suggests the same integrity that marks his stories and his novel. He was born on September 26, 1932, in Dyushambe, in Soviet Central Asia. His father, Serbian by background, translated Serbian literature and worked as a journalist. Voinovich's mother was Jewish. Thus, right from the beginning, he was given something of an outsider's viewpoint, of value to the writer and especially to the writer of comedy. His vision is entirely free of that peculiarly constraining Russian chauvinism.

Voinovich himself said, in jest: "I came to literature because I lacked education." This is hardly an exaggeration. His school years coincided with the war and, all told, he reached the level of fourth or fifth grade. After that, it was the collective farm, work, the army, the gaps filled in by books and evening classes. This fact, coupled with Voinovich's innate modesty, accounts for the lovely plainness of his prose, especially in these early stories, examples of plain truth and plain speech.

Voinovich said of his early attempts at writing: "I felt a great need to say something, but I myself didn't yet know what that was." Clearly, this is a statement any young writer could make, which only subsequent substantial achievement renders of interest. The young Voinovich believed in his own strength of will, and was determined to write a poem a day for one year, as if he were a one-man Soviet poem-producing enterprise with a verse quota to fill. In time he published stories in magazines and worked in radio. He wrote the lyrics for the song "Fourteen Minutes to Go," which became the unofficial anthem of the Soviet cosmonauts and which, in one of those ironies that characterize the Russian experience, Khrushchev himself sang from the top of the Lenin Mausoleum to greet the cosmonauts Nikolaev and Popovich on their return from space. In fact, Voinovich was developing into a model Soviet writer—at least, at first glance. There was, however, one slight problem. Soviet society, like every other, has its approved virtues; and Voinovich, as we can see in his autobiographical stories and from the record of his own behavior, was "fool" enough to have accepted the basic human (and official Soviet) virtues and located their point of origin and ultimate authority in the person. This can prove very inconvenient. This can cause a good deal of trouble. No rewards are given to inconvenient troublemakers.

It is thus entirely fitting that his first major story, "What I Might Have Been" (formerly entitled "I Want to Be Honest"), which concerns a construction supervisor who refuses to yield to political pressures and turn over a building before it is entirely safe and ready, was also the story that first brought Voinovich under attack (by Leonid Ilyichev, Khrushchev's advisor on cultural affairs: the singing was over; the shouting had started). The drama that would lead to Voinovich's expulsion from the Writers' Union ten years later had begun. It was nothing that Voinovich himself desired. He said of himself: "My character is absolutely not that of a dissident. I am a completely apolitical person. I have never held literature to be a part of politics." So, Voinovich, like his construction supervisor and his Chonkin, creates commotion without meaning to, having perhaps forgotten, or never having been corrupted enough to accept, that in a political ocean every gesture makes political waves and sometimes one is expected to drown in silent obedience.

Even though Voinovich felt that "in Khrushchev's time the degree of freedom for literature was sufficient for me personally," future developments would cause him to reassess that statement, as well as his own place in Soviet society. Further honorable acts (the support of Andrei Sinyavsky and Yuli Daniel) would cost him increasingly more (books, plays, film scripts, canceled) and would at the same time expose the nature of the struggle between personal integrity and social tyranny with increasing severity and clarity. Ultimately, Voinovich's gift for hearty, sane, and exaggerated comedy would be revealed to him as well. There is little trace of it in these early works, except for a certain standard Soviet Russian brand of grim sarcasm.

The process of Voinovich's forced alienation from his society was accelerated by his open support of Alexander Solzhenitsyn, whom Voinovich called at the time "the greatest of our citizens." It was, however, no single action that led to Voinovich's expulsion from the Writers' Union but a series of steps, acts, and statements. And the underlying cause, the matrix from which all the acts and statements arose, was Voinovich's hard-won yet natural integrity, coupled with his gift for plain speech. Invited to a meeting of the Writers' Union in which his own behavior and positions were to be discussed, Voinovich replied: "We have nothing to discuss and nothing to argue about, because I express my own opinions, while you say what you are told to." The entire relationship between the Soviet intelligentsia and the cultural bureaucracy could hardly have been stated more precisely. Solzhenitsyn was deported from the Soviet Union on

February 13, 1974; Voinovich was expelled from the Writers' Union on the twentieth of that month.

I think it worth a moment to hazard a guess as to how the author of realistic stories came to create a grand epic comedy. To my mind, the key lies in Voinovich's integrity, which maintained the purity of his vision. He didn't fall for anything. There are no "ideas" in his works, no "theories," no exhortations. He knows how people are—wonderful, ridiculous, dangerous—and he knows about the great mysteries, too, but is either too smart or too modest to go on about them. The death in "A Distance of Half a Kilometer" is as mundane as a death can be (one minute Ochkin is alive, living his shabby, unadmirable life; the next moment he's dead, his face in his soup) and yet we also feel the sting of the reality: a person is no more. Ultimately, Voinovich's inner stability, his clear eye, his plain and direct approach led him to a great truth about the world—by the very nature of things, the great villains of history are the true fools of the world. They do not live the human life given to us all (even to Chonkin, the simplest of men; even to Ochkin, the shabbiest). Voinovich presents this view most clearly in the story "A Circle of Friends" (a chapter withheld from *Chonkin*), which depicts Stalin and the members of the Politburo on the shortest night of the year, June 21, 1941, the eve of Hitler's invasion. In this story Stalin is called by his revolutionary nickname, "Koba," the others by puns on their own names (e.g., Khrushchev = Borshchev, Beria = Aria). This nightmarish Kremlin get-together, resembling those in Milovan Djilas's *Conversations with Stalin*, portrays a private moment in the lives of the "great." All of the men are revolting, pitiable, grotesque, boot-licking, fear-ridden specimens. They are boobs, idiots, jerks. Of course! How else could they be if they act the way they do. There is no great mystery here. In fact, it is *they* who thrive on mystery, spectacle, false appearances (even Stalin's moustache turns out to be the paste-on variety). The remark that Nixon and crew were everyone you hated in high school applies, *mutatis mutandis*, here as well. But neither does Voinovich spare the enemies of authority. In the story "Skurlatsky, Man of Letters," the hero is also pitiable, ridiculous, and grotesque, because he chooses self-importance over self-respect. Occasionally, though of course quite rarely, pompous authority can be transformed by moral confrontation, as we see in the story "Captain Kurasov."

Since Voinovich's expulsion from the Writers' Union his isolation has been forcibly increased—his telephone has been disconnected, the KGB has invited him in for a "philosophical" discussion which turned out to concern mortality, his mortality. Nevertheless, working in solitude like a medieval alchemist, Voinovich manages to create a rare, clear, and marvelous elixir, which, when imbibed by a Russian, returns the gift of laughter to him, that great restorer of sanity and enemy of tyrants everywhere. *Chonkin* had a similar though inevitably less liberating effect on readers outside the Soviet Union and its success has provided Voinovich with a modicum of safety. One must hope, and really one must assume, that Voinovich's good spirits, resilience, and courage, which have taken him so far, will carry him through the writing of the further extraordinary adventures of Ivan Chonkin, and beyond.

R. L.

IN PLAIN
RUSSIAN

WHAT I MIGHT HAVE BEEN

HAVE BEEN

(I WANT TO BE HONEST)

But you, my friend true-hearted—
God keep our friendship green!—
You know how I was parted
From all I might have been.

—Henry Lawson

The alarm clock on my table goes off every morning at quarter to seven, reminding me that it is time to get up and go to work. Naturally I don't want to get up or go to work. It's still dark outside and I can barely make out the rain-spattered window against the dark wall. I pull the chain on my lamp and for a few minutes I lie with the light on, experiencing that age-old desire, to sleep just a little bit more. Then, one at a time, I lower my feet to the floor. The slow process which transforms me back into a modern man has begun.

At first I sit on my bed and stare without a thought in my head at some indefinite point on the wall opposite me, scratching my head and sighing, my mouth wide open. My mouth tastes terrible. My heart knocks in my chest from smoking too much. My heart hurts. It's not that it hurts so much but that I feel it there. Like a cobblestone under my skin. If some stranger happened to observe me at this moment I think the sight would afford him some little pleasure. What in the world could be more absurd than my face, my body, my posture at this moment. Then I begin curling my bare toes, waving my arms and making other gestures vaguely reminiscent of calisthenics. The dumbbells I bought last year are on the floor under the radiator; covered with a thick layer of dust, they seem larger than they really are. It's been a long time since I've used them and the fact that they're covered with dust and would make my hands dirty helps me justify not touching them. At one point I could both perform my calisthenics and be outside and ready, with my submachine gun and all my ammunition, within three minutes after reveille. Sergeant Shuldikov, who was my first instructor in these things, used to say: "I'll teach you to get ready in three minutes even when you're a civilian. That's my purpose in life."

If he had no purpose other than that, Sergeant Shuldikov's life passed with little effect.

Mulling over thoughts like these, I ran my hand across my cheek. A shave might not be a bad idea. My beard grows astonishingly fast. Anyone seeing me in the evening would never believe that I'd shaved myself clean as a whistle that morning. I started shaving at sixteen; in high school my nickname was the "Hairy Ape."

My Neva electric razor buzzed so loud that the pensioner in the next room, Ivan Adamovich Shishkin, woke up and began coughing lightly, hinting that it was shameful for a man of my age to behave with so little consideration. But there was nothing I could do for him and I stuck courageously to my task. I must admit that the sight of myself in the small circular mirror with its metal frame hardly thrilled me. Staring back at me was a man red-haired and balding, fatter than he should be, with large ears overgrown with fluffy gray hair. When I was a child my mother used to tell me that Beethoven had the same kind of ears I did. For a while I comforted myself with the hope that I might become another Beethoven. Though I was ashamed of my ears in my early youth, now I've grown used to them. In the final analysis they haven't been that much of a hindrance to me in this life.

After shaving I walked to the bathroom and carefully washed with water so cold it left my fingers red and stiff. Then I put on my rubber boots, sweater, jacket, rubberized raincoat, and a ragged hat. There was a letter for me in the mailbox by the door. From my mother. I'll read it at work.

2

It was the beginning of November. The sky was one mass of clouds. Dawn had not yet broken and it didn't look like it ever would. It was hard to believe the sun's rays could ever pierce that impenetrable grayness. But the city had already come to life. Thousands of people, collars up or umbrellas open, were running down the streets boarding buses that gleamed with rain, surging into the entrance of the tobacco factory. There was something terrifying about the sight of them—where did they all come from?

A large crowd had gathered at the crosswalk, ready to dart through the first break in traffic. The cars seemed endless, too. I crossed the large street with the crowd and ended up in a half-glass, half-metal, hood-shaped building, a cafeteria. Inside there was a food counter and several small tables with long iron legs. The cement floor was covered with a thick layer of sawdust. There was a long line stretching back from the counter. People were stamping their feet, huddling up, rubbing their hands—steam rose from their sopping overcoats and raincoats.

Zoya, a tall girl with neatly cut hair, loomed behind the counter. She tossed small coins onto a plastic plate, made change, and manipulated the shining levers of the coffee machine with some style. Maybe she thought she was at the helm of a spaceship.

Catching sight of me, Zoya smiled, revealing beautiful, even teeth. But she was hardly smiling because she was fond of me. There was a simpler explanation. I was a regular customer.

"The usual?" she asked.

"The usual," I answered.

In return for the fifty-kopeck piece I handed her, she served me sausages and kraut, coffee with milk, and a poppy-seed roll. This upset the people in line, who began grumbling, but Zoya soothed them by saying with a smile: "He works here."

Maybe she really did like me. There was nothing surprising in that; many women liked me, because I was tall, strong, earned a good living, and didn't drink too much.

3

Not far from the last bus stop there was a large area partitioned off by plank-board fences. On one of the fences there was a large plywood plaque with the inscription:

Construction Project-II
Construction Supervisor—Comrade Samokhin

Next to the plaque there was an advertisement for the singer Helena Velikanova.

Comrade Samokhin, that's me. Helena Velikanova bears no relationship whatever to me, it's just that the ad office decided to make good use of free space.

The singer's concerts were over and she had left our city the day before. The plaque with my name on it will disappear as well. The building I'm constructing will soon be ready to hand over. Right now it still stands empty behind the fence, its silicate brick walls darkened by the rain.

The·long neck of a tower crane stretched across the murky autumn sky. I had no further use for the crane, I ought to call the construction-machines department and have them send some men over to dismantle it.

In the right wing of the building, on the first floor, on one of the doors of the fourth section, there is a paper sign reading: "Work Superintendent's Office." This is where I am usually to be found from seven-thirty till five. Quite often I can be found there at ten o'clock, eleven o'clock, even midnight, because there's no set limit to my workday.

The office was one cloud of cigarette smoke. I could barely see the light through the dense layers of smoke. Some of the workers had found places on stools or on the long benches; others were simply squatting by the wall or near the iron stove. Babaev's entire plastering team was lying on the floor.

"You could've at least opened the casement window," I growled, making my way to my desk by the window.

No one paid the slightest attention as I opened the little window. The smoke gradually began to thin out. Raw air blew in from outside.

Everyone was spending the half hour before work in his own way. Brigade leader Shilov was sitting on a box of nails, drying out his cloth foot-wraps by the stove. Babaev was leafing through a book, preparing for his classes at the university. Katya Zhelobanova was telling her girlfriend Lyusa Markina that in the summertime the actor Roshchin was always at the beach and, guess what, it turned out he was bald and so he must wear a wig when he sings on television.

Deryushev, a big galoot in a pea jacket, was standing by the window, trying to bend a crowbar (and puffing from the effort), one end of which he'd set in between the sections of the radiator. Shmakov, who laid parquet and was nicknamed the "Writer" because he didn't wear a hat in the winter, was standing beside him.

"Come on, come on," he encouraged Deryushev. "The main thing is to brace yourself with your legs."

"What are you doing?" I asked Deryushev.

Deryushev twitched and smiled shyly. "Nothing really, Evgeny Ivanich. Just fooling around."

"Ach, Deryushev, Deryushev," sighed the Writer, distressed. "You can't bend a crowbar with blubber on you like that. Looks like we'll just have to cut you up for lard. Evgeny Ivanich here'll bend it just like that," he said, to egg me on.

There was too much familiarity in the way he spoke to me. I was about to straighten him out, but then I thought: "But really, why not test my strength? It's one thing I've still got to brag about."

"All right, give it here."

I took the crowbar from Deryushev, put it behind my

neck, and started forcing the ends downward. I felt a ringing in my ears as the veins in my neck swelled with blood.

I carefully set the crowbar, now U-shaped, down on the floor. I couldn't resist asking: "Now maybe somebody wants to bend it back out?"

"That's strength for you," sighed Deryushev enviously, stealing a quick squeeze of his own muscle.

Katya Zhelobanova was looking at me with undisguised admiration. Roshchin the actor certainly couldn't bend any crowbars around his neck.

But I was out of breath. My heart was knocking as if I'd just run several miles. I hadn't been feeling very well lately. To hide my shortness of breath, I sat down at my desk and pretended to be rummaging through some papers.

The Writer continued hectoring Deryushev. "So, Deryushev," he said, "what would you do if you were that strong? Join the circus? C'mon, tell me, would you?"

"Well," answered Deryushev thoughtfully, "I just might!"

"Here's an idea for you. They could show you to people for money. Anyone'd like a look at a swine like you, even if it did cost money."

The Writer laughed and looked around the room, as if inviting the others to join in his laughter. But no one gave him any encouragement, except Lyusa Markina, who made no secret of being in love with him.

"Shmakov," I said to the Writer, "was it you who laid the parquet floors in section 3?"

"Yes, what of it?" He looked at me with his characteristic insolence.

"I'll tell you what of it," I said. "The parquet's completely come apart."

"It's nothing, it'll go back together. Before we turn over the building, we'll sprinkle a little water on the floor and it'll go back."

"Shmakov," I said heatedly, "don't you ever take any pride in your work? Don't you ever want to do a job right?"

"We're ignorant people here," he said. "All we care about is chow and money."

He spoke without fear. Arguments and threats had no effect on him. At a construction site you prize every able-bodied worker like the apple of your eye. Not that it helps keep them there. We get recently discharged soldiers, peasants straight from the village—they work a little, have a look around, then they take off to a factory or a mill. The pay's better there and it's warmer working inside.

Matvey Shilov was sitting in front of the stove. He had taken off his shoes and was drying his foot-wraps, thinking his own thoughts. Maybe he was composing his resignation. But men like Shilov rarely leave. He'd already been in construction about twelve years. He was used to it and we were used to him.

I looked at my watch. Almost eight.

"Everyone in?" I asked Shilov.

He turned his head slowly to me, then just as slowly ran his eyes around the room. "Looks like everybody."

"Finish up the break, then get to work."

"In a minute," answered Shilov reluctantly, winding the cloths around his legs. He put on his shoes, stood up, stamped first one foot, then the other, and only then did he get the hammer from behind the stove and hand it to the Writer. "Go give the rail a hit."

The Writer obediently left the room and struck the rail. Suspended on a piece of wire from a utility pole, the rail rang like a church bell announcing the start of the workday. Gradually they all got up and left.

4

My Dear Son,
It's been two weeks since I've had any news from you
and I simply don't know what to think. Yesterday
I dreamed that you were walking barefoot through
the snow. I don't believe in dreams, but where you're
concerned, I can't help getting upset. Such terrible
thoughts come into my mind that it's painful even
to talk about them. I keep thinking you might have
gotten sick or, God forbid, been hit by a car.

A letter from my mother, a former schoolteacher, retired on her pension. She always liked getting letters, now more than ever.

But what could I write her about? Every day was the same. Up at quarter of seven. Start work at eight. Lunch from twelve to one. Five o'clock the workday ends. Five-thirty meeting with the head of construction administration. As far as getting hit by a car is concerned, the personnel department or the ORUD would have informed her; that's what they're paid for.

I have no news unless you count the fact that the day
before yesterday I was elected chairman of our
building at a tenants' meeting. I know you don't place
much stock in such things, but for me it was quite
a pleasant experience.
Recently I ran into Vladik Tugarinov on the street.
He was here on vacation with his wife. He's such an

*important person now. Recently he was appointed
head of some major construction project in Siberia.
He asked about you. He took your address and
promised to write.*

As they say, you have to read between the lines here.
Vladik is no more competent than I am. He always did
much worse in math, but now he's a big cheese. I could
have stuck it out in one place, too, and gotten myself a
good position, but I chose to fly from job to job.

Mama fails to take one circumstance into account—
Vladik received his diploma in 1944 (we'd started at the
institute together) while I was in the hospital in Boris-
oglebsk. Of course it wasn't Vladik's fault he wasn't sent
to the front; his nearsightedness had shown up in the
tenth grade. But it wasn't my fault either that I was a
student apprentice at the time Vladik was already head
of a construction project.

Of course I could have stayed in one spot after the
institute. But, instead, I worked on Sakhalin Island, in
Yakutia, the Pechora project, and even in the Virgin
Lands putting up adobe houses. Who knows, I might not
last here much longer either.

5

The telephone rang. I receive many calls and as a rule
I don't pay much attention to them. But this time some
sixth sense told me that this call was going to make
trouble. I had no basis for thinking that, I just felt it.
And so I didn't pick up the receiver. Let it ring, let's
see who can take it the longest. The caller won out. I
picked up the receiver and heard the voice of Silaev,
head of construction administration.

"Samokhin, what's the matter, don't you answer the telephone?"

"I was walking around the unit. I didn't know it was you calling."

"You've got to know. You should sense it when the boss is calling."

"I do," I said. "Only not right away. It takes me a minute."

"But that's the whole point. Learn how to sense it in time, that way you'll make something of yourself."

For some reason he was terribly playful today. I don't like it when the boss acts too jolly.

"Listen, Samokhin," he said, taking a more serious tone, "you ought to drop by. We need to have a little chat."

"About what?"

"You'll see. It's not something for the telephone."

"All right. But right now I'm inspecting the building."

"Go ahead, but make it quick."

What was the big rush? I left the office and went up to the fourth floor. Shilov was standing on the landing, running a spray gun along the wall. A light blue stream of paint was whistling from the brass nozzle, sending an even layer onto the plaster. Shilov himself—his cap, jacket, and boots—was covered with paint.

"Well, Shilov," I asked, "did you dry out your foot-wraps?"

"I'm drying them out on my feet."

"Why's the paint going on so thick?"

"There's no linseed oil to thin it. Will we be getting any?"

"We will," I said, "if Bogdashkin gives us some."

"Then there won't be any," remarked Shilov skeptically. "Bogdashkin won't give us any."

"Don't worry. With God's help, we'll get some."

"I doubt it." Shilov spat and looked out the window.

I popped into one of the apartments and had a look around. In general, everything looked pretty decent. Except the plaster wasn't drying and the doors had swollen from the dampness and wouldn't shut tight. If we'd received the linseed oil in time, it would have been a different story.

I went into the kitchen. Katya Zhelobanova and Lyusa Markina were sitting against the radiator, their legs stretched out in front of them. They were talking about boyfriends, ice cream, movies, nothing that was in any way connected with their job. The radiator wasn't throwing off any heat. The water hadn't been hooked up yet.

"Aren't you cold?" I asked.

They didn't answer.

"So why are you just sitting around? Nothing to do?"

"Smoke break plus nap," joked Katya in embarrassment.

"You've barely begun working and it's break time already? Go over to section 4, there's nobody to carry tile there," I said in an annoyed voice which I couldn't stand to hear myself. But that's how I am—the sight of people loafing rubs me the wrong way. If you come to work, then you've got to work and not hide in a corner.

No one got my goat more than Deryushev. He was welding railings with a gas unit. I noticed immediately that his seams were irregular and weak. I pushed on one and the seam split.

"What do you want, to get us both thrown in jail?" I asked him.

Deryushev turned off his welder and pushed his dark blue goggles, spattered with drops of metal, up onto his forehead. "The solder is weak, Evgeny Ivanovich, it doesn't hold," he said smiling, as if telling me good news. "We should have an arc welder here anyway."

"I know that without your telling me. But where am I supposed to get one? Reweld all the railings. I'll be back to check them. We'll get you some decent solder."

Everybody wants something from me and I promise them all something—solder to one, linseed oil to another, tarpaulin gloves to somebody else. But where, where to get it all?

6

When I was in grade school the teacher told us about James Watt. When he was a little boy Watt noticed a boiling tea kettle and, recalling it later as an adult, he invented the steam engine. When the teacher was through, I raised my hand and asked: "And who invented the tea kettle?"

That question still interests me. When I was studying at the institute various professors taught us innumerable complex theories of science, which I in the course of fifteen years have fortunately managed to forget. Neither Euclidean geometry nor the theory of relativity has been of much use in my life, even though our professors considered it obligatory for a construction engineer to know each and every one of these subjects. They knew a lot, those professors, but not a single one of them would have been able to solve the simplest problems—how to get a box of nails when the warehouse was out or when Bogdashkin was in a foul mood.

Bogdashkin is in charge of supply for our Constradmin. He's a total knucklehead. When we had a chief engineer there, the supply section ran fairly well. But the chief engineer retired, so now there is no one above Bogdashkin and he's gone completely to pot. Supervisors call him from morning till night trying to squeeze every sort of material out of him. Bogdashkin got himself so completely confused that he decided to simplify matters by sending out whatever was on hand. Someone requests alabaster, Bogdashkin sends electric cord; the person who needs electric cord receives door handles. A while back he sent me another gas welder. It took me quite a while to figure out what to do with it, then I swapped it with Limar for an electric motor.

Of course I could call Bogdashkin and ask him for linseed oil, but chances are it would be a waste of time. He didn't have any, and so no matter what you said or did, you'd still come up empty-handed. Better to work out a swap with somebody. I took a scrap of paper and made a list:

Construction Supervisor	Has	Needs
Filiminov	*Linseed oil*	*Roofing iron*
Limar	*Dutch tiles*	*Window frames*
Sidorkin	*Roofing iron*	*Dutch tiles*
Ermoshin	*Window frames*	*Tiles*
Me	*Tiles*	*Linseed oil*

Now, I could call up Ermoshin and swap him the tiles for his window frames and then get Dutch tiles from Limar. Sidorkin would give his roofing iron for the Dutch tiles. Then I could call Filiminov . . . No, it was useless. I had just remembered that Filiminov had given all his linseed oil to Ermoshin, I don't know what he got in exchange. What does Ermoshin need linseed oil for if he hasn't even started on the trimmings?

I looked at my list. A complete strategic plan. And all for one barrel of linseed oil.

7

Scene two, same characters plus Sidorkin. He opens the door and bursts into the office in all his splendor—tall, gaunt, wearing a crumpled green hat, a tattered dark blue raincoat, and incredibly wide trousers. His yellow boots are spattered with mud up to the ankles. And in boots like that he marches right up to my desk.

"You could have wiped your feet," I said. "This is a decent place, not a pigpen."

"In decent places they spread Persian rugs under your feet." He sat on a chair by my desk, pulled off one boot, and stretched out his leg. "My socks are wet clean through."

"Why don't you buy yourself a pair of rubber boots? You're too stingy."

"I'm not stingy," grumbled Sidorkin and crinkled up his eyes. "Those kind of boots give me rheumatism, I tramped all over Karelia in them, I should know."

He pulled a cigarette from my pack, lit up, then took some ragged cards from his pocket and began shuffling them lazily.

"Shall we play?"

"For what?"

"A sack of cement."

"No way. You cheat."

"So let's play with a piece of string." He took a piece of string from his pocket and folded it into two loops. "Fox, box, socks, the devil rode on an ox on a green wreath from America. Hit or miss, I'll pay money for this. Put it here, you win; put it there, you lose. Use your head, you'll make some bread. Where will you put it?"

"You know, Sidorkin," I said, "let me just give you a

sack of cement as a present. I'll even write something nice on it. Then just make sure that's the last I see of you."

"Come on now," objected Sidorkin magnanimously, "I couldn't deprive you of such pleasure for a mere sack of cement. But make it two, and I'll give it some thought."

How shameless can you get? While he was tying his muddy boot back up, I tried Bogdashkin's number. Somebody picked up the phone at the other end.

"Bogdashkin?" I asked.

"Not here," answered Bogdashkin, disguising his voice; then he hung up.

"Bastard," I said and looked over at Sidorkin.

Sidorkin looked back at me. "Is he joking around again?" he asked sympathetically. "Don't let it get to you. We'll play a little joke on him, too."

He pulled the phone over and dialed. A talented man, that Sidorkin! If he'd chosen a career in acting, he'd have made a bundle!

"Hello, is this Dima?" he said in a throaty feminine voice.

I could not see Bogdashkin but I could imagine his puffy face melting into a sugary grin. The old fool! He'll be on his pension soon and he's still chasing young girls. Neither his age nor the alimony which costs him half his salary could force him to his senses.

"Hello, Dima," Sidorkin cooed affectionately. "It's your little Pussycat. I've already told Papa what we decided and Papa wants to have a little talk with you. Here he is now."

I took the phone with malicious glee.

"Well, how about it?"

I could hear his heavy wheezing—Bogdashkin was thinking.

"Who is this?" he asked finally.

"It's your little Pussycat's Papa," I said, continuing Sidorkin's game.

"What do you want?" said Bogdashkin, displeased, having recognized me.

"Nothing special. A barrel of linseed oil."

"Linseed oil?" Bogdashkin took this as a personal affront. "What do you do, put it on your bread or something? I sent you two barrels last week. There's no more."

"Maybe you could find some more?" I asked without any hope.

"Find it how?" Bogdashkin grew angry. "Find this for that one, and that for this one. Everybody comes to Bogdashkin. This one needs Bogdashkin, that one needs Bogdashkin. There's not enough Bogdashkin to go around."

Finally I lost control and said a few blunt words to him. Bogdashkin took no offense, everybody spoke more or less the same way to him.

"Nice talk, nice talk," grumbled Bogdashkin amiably. "Nice talk from somebody with a college degree. I can give you a little alabaster if you want."

I could have told him where to go, but that's not what I'm paid for. Besides, the alabaster was at least something and maybe I could swap it for something else.

"The hell with you then," I agreed. "I'll take the alabaster. Even a mangy sheep's good for a little wool."

Sidorkin sat waiting patiently while I was talking with Bogdashkin. Now he rose to his feet. "So, I can take three sacks then?"

"You've lost all sense of shame," I said. "First it was one sack, then it was two, and now even two's not enough."

"That's right," said Sidorkin. "One for friendship, one so you won't have to see me again, and one for Bogdashkin. Fair enough?"

"All right," I said. "Take four sacks and get lost."

"No sooner said than done," said Sidorkin, imitating Arkady Raikin, the comedian. "I'll send a truck over right away."

Sidorkin and I were standing out front when Ermoshin arrived on a dump truck. He stood for a long minute on the running board, then hesitantly placed one foot on the narrow plank thrown across the mud, which he then began walking across like a tightrope walker. Sidorkin and I watched him eagerly, hoping he would slip and fall, but he safely negotiated the first plank, crossed over to the second, and appeared in front of us just as clean as if he'd been whisked through the air. His moustache, side-whiskers, and hat gave his face a certain intelligent look.

"You heard the news?" Ermoshin said, speaking to Sidorkin. "They're appointing him chief engineer." He nodded at me.

This came as a surprise not only to Sidorkin but to me as well. True enough, rumors about my being appointed chief engineer had been going around for quite some time, but rumors are rumors, there'd been no confirmation unless you counted two or three hints to me from Silaev.

"Go on," said Sidorkin in disbelief. "Did the manager confirm it or what?"

"Not yet, but he's had the order drafted. I was just at Silaev's. I heard their whole conversation on the phone."

"What did he do to deserve such an honor?" Sidorkin looked me over critically. "A fat redhead with a nothing-special mug on him. What did they do, bypass you or something?"

"I'm switching over to union work," said Ermoshin importantly. "They're letting Romanenko go. I'm taking his place."

"Good luck," said Sidorkin and turned toward me. "So you'll give me the tiles, right?"

"What tiles?" I said in surprise.

"Come on now. You know we just agreed that you'd give me the tiles and I'd give you a barrel of linseed oil. Or are you so happy now you've forgotten everything else?"

Sidorkin gave me an exaggerated wink. I realized he was going to play a joke on Ermoshin.

"No," I said. "I won't. Not for one barrel."

"What's with you guys?" asked Ermoshin with assumed indifference.

"Nothing really," I explained. "I just happen to have about a hundred and fifty tiles on hand and he wants them all for one barrel of linseed oil."

Would he fall for it or not? But what else could he do? The bait was too enticing. One hundred and fifty tiles! Just try and get tiles from Bogdashkin.

"I could give you a barrel and a half," Ermoshin said at last, trying not to look over at Sidorkin.

"What do you need tiles for?" said Sidorkin. "Your partitions are already up. You said so in your report at the meeting."

"Who cares what I said at the meeting," said Ermoshin and turned to me again. "So, how about a barrel and a half?"

"Are you kidding me? A hundred and fifty tiles for a barrel and a half of linseed oil? That's just about enough to grease down your hair with."

"That's all I have."

"So, go talk to Bogdashkin. Maybe he'll give you a hundred and fifty tiles."

"All right then," decided Ermoshin. "Take two barrels. Let's shake on it."

"Still not enough. Take your two barrels to Bogdashkin."

I didn't show him any mercy, even though I knew that was all the linseed oil he had. But linseed oil is not the only thing of value in this world. In the end we agreed that Ermoshin would also give me ten packs of parquet and a little solder for the gas welder.

We were both satisfied with the deal. He thought he'd twisted me around his little finger and I thought the same about him. And we were both right in our own way. We'd both used everything we had to squeeze as much as possible from the other. It all would have been so much simpler if Bogdashkin gave each of us what we needed.

As soon as Ermoshin left, the telephone started ringing. I thought it was Silaev again and told Sidorkin to answer it.

"If it's Silaev I'm not here."

Sidorkin picked up the receiver. "Hello. One minute. Chief Engineer Samokhin is busy but I'll try and connect you . . . It's her," said Sidorkin, handing me the phone, his eyes crinkling in delight.

I heard Klava's voice saying: "Is that you?"

"It's me."

"I didn't call for any reason, just to talk."

"You couldn't have called at a more convenient time," I said politely.

"Don't be angry. When will I see you? I waited for you all evening yesterday, then I went to see *Ivan's Childhood.* Have you seen it?"

"No."

All I needed was her to start telling me the whole plot. "I might stop by today," I said.

"Really?"

"There's a chance," I answered more precisely. "But, excuse me, right now I'm in a hurry."

Sidorkin and I left the office together. It was still drizzling.

"So I'll send a truck by and take five sacks," said Sidorkin, pulling up the collar of his raincoat.

"Ten," I said. "Take ten, you earned them today."

8

When I entered his office, Silaev was sitting at his desk taking his table lamp apart. At one time, quite a while back, he had worked as a handyman in a factory; he loved to reminisce about those days and to amuse himself repairing appliances. As a rule, these efforts were not crowned with success and Silaev would have to call in various repairmen, depending on what he had attempted to do himself.

"What took you so long? Am I supposed to send runners for you now?" complained Silaev, displeased, and without waiting for me to answer, nodded at the armchair by his desk. "Sit down."

I wasn't about to sit in that armchair. It was too soft. You'd sink so deep into it that even a man of my height would barely be above eye level with the edge of his desk. Perhaps those chairs are specially designed to intimidate. I took a chair from against the wall and pushed it over to his desk.

"How's life?" he asked, removing the shade from the lamp.

"Nice and quiet, thanks," I said.

"And the wife?" Silaev took the push-button switch from the lamp and began picking at it with a screwdriver.

"Fine, thanks." I was tired of telling him I wasn't married.

"All right," he said, laying the screwdriver down on his desk. "Of course you know why I called you in?"

I had some idea after my talk with Ermoshin, but just to play it safe, I said I didn't know.

"All the better," said Silaev. "Let it come as a surprise."

He pressed his buzzer and at almost the same instant his secretary Lyusya appeared in the doorway. She was a good-looking girl, except that she put too much mascara on her eyelashes.

"Lysusenka, please bring me the orders concerning Samokhin," Silaev asked without looking at her.

Lyusya disappeared just as quickly as she had appeared. Silaev watched the door closing behind her and, for some reason, sighed.

"How are things over there?" he asked after a moment of silence. "I haven't been over to your section for some time now, I don't know why. When do you plan to turn over the building?"

"By the first of the year."

"And when were you supposed to?"

"By the first of December."

He knew all this as well as I did, and I thought he was asking me these questions just to get the conversation going. The chief looked up at me, paused, and then said: "Here's the thing. Hand it over by the holiday."

"Before it's ready?" I asked.

"Why before? Get it ready, then hand it over."

Lyusya appeared in the doorway again. She walked over to the desk, her high heels tapping as she went, and placed a sheet of paper in front of Silaev.

"Is that all?" she asked, grinning as she always did when speaking to her superiors.

"No, it isn't," said Silaev sternly. "Inform all units that there'll be a production conference today at seventeen-thirty. No, make that at seventeen hundred. It never takes less than half an hour to get them all together."

Lyusya stood there, her eyelashes lowered expectantly.

"May I go?" she asked.

"When I say so," said the chief angrily. He was obviously in a bad mood and looking for someone to take it out on. "Why are you standing there like a dummy batting your eyelashes. Are you trying to seduce me, is that it?"

"Not you," said Lyusya softly.

Her reply enraged him. "I'll take a wet rag and wipe those lashes off your face."

"You have no right."

"I've got plenty of right. I'm like a father to you."

"I have a father of my own," Lyusya reminded him.

"That's too bad," said Silaev, then corrected himself. "I mean it's too bad he doesn't take better care of his daughter. You may go."

Lyusya turned and rapped her heels across the floor. During the entire conversation she did not once change her tone of voice, nor had her face shown the slightest emotion.

I realized that Silaev was in some kind of trouble. He always vented his anger on his secretary when things weren't going well for him, and she patiently endured these attacks. Maybe that was why he kept her.

"Who the hell knows," he said after the door had closed behind her. "She's a little fool."

He opened a pack of Kazbek cigarettes, and while he was lighting one up, he pushed the paper Lyusya had brought in over to me. It was the order stating that I had been appointed chief engineer.

"Read it yet?" asked Silaev. "You'll assume your duties after the unit is turned over."

"That means in December," I said.

"Before," said Silaev. "You'll turn over the building before the holiday, and you'll assume your new duties after it. You can consider this an order which must be obeyed."

"An order has to be within reason, Gleb Nikolaevich," I said. "We're still not done plastering over there. We still have to lay the parquet."

"You'll get everything done."

"But the plaster won't even have time to dry."

"That doesn't concern me. The building has to be turned over. Do you think this is some whim on my part? I got the word from the top." He ground his cigarette out on the edge of the ashtray and pointed to the ceiling. "The district committee has decided that Komsomol families should be given a present. The holiday celebrating the Revolution, drums playing, the keys handed over. You should be overjoyed that they gave you the idea."

"I'd be happier if I could swap the idea for a barrel of linseed oil," I said. "That's going to be some present for the Komsomol families, we'll give them a building and a month later it'll need major repairs. And what if I won't turn the building over?"

"If you won't?" Silaev looked me right in the eye. "Then we'll take any measures we have to, including firing you. So, the choice is yours. Either hand over the building on time and everything that goes with it or . . .

You choose." He rose and offered me his hand. "Excuse me, I have to go see the director now."

9

I'm a failure. Or at least my mother considers me one. I'm a failure because I didn't become a scientist or somebody big in management. All I am is a senior supervisor. Using the army for comparison—a senior supervisor is something like a first lieutenant. If you haven't risen any higher than that by the time you're forty, you might as well throw away the marshal's baton in your knapsack.

I'm already forty-two. And now, at forty-two, I've been offered the post of chief engineer. They could have done this much earlier. Fifteen years have passed since I graduated from the Construction Institute and for practically all fifteen I've held the same post of senior construction supervisor. In that time I've developed a bald spot and a paunch, I've grown nervous and irritable.

My work is no better or no worse than any other. I still don't know whether this is my calling or not, and to tell the truth, it's not a matter of much interest to me. A calling is tested in practice where certain specific skills are required. A supervisor has no need of any unusual skills; for him the ability to get hold of supplies, read blueprints, and make sure the workers are on the job on time is enough. I can't make a building any better than it was projected to be.

But sometimes I am forced to make one worse than I can, and this I don't like, even though my superiors dislike it when I object. I have already left two jobs "of my own accord." Maybe I'll leave this one, too. This isn't the only town where the sun shines; but I'm tired of this rootless life. I'm tired of living in tents and trailers or renting a bed from the "private sector." When you're past forty, you want to live a normal human life, to have a place of your own, maybe even a family.

There's a photo of a girl around eighteen years old under the glass on my night table: an elongated face, large dark eyes, dark braids wound neatly around her head. Rosa. I met her in Kiev at the beginning of 1941 when I arrived for my winter school vacation. Rosa was in her last year of high school (just to think that now I could have a daughter her age) and preparing to enter the history department of the pedagogical institute.

For some reason, she did not leave Kiev when the Germans arrived. The mass grave at Babi Yar is probably hers as well. She was young and beautiful, you can tell by the photo. But she was also smart and good, unusually sensitive and tender. Could it be that I no longer remember what she was really like and it is an image I've created myself that lives on in my memory? But, in all these years, I have not met any woman who even comes close to my image of Rosa. Maybe that's the reason I'm still not married.

10

Precisely at five-thirty the supervisors filed into Silaev's office. We took our places at a long table placed perpendicular to the chief's desk. Bent over his papers, Silaev paid us no attention while we were getting ourselves seated.

This was just the beginning of the conference, which could last for hours, and everyone was trying to put the time to some advantage. Limar was reading a book called *The Atom in the Service of Man;* Sabidze had a sheet of paper in front of him and was sketching someone. Tikhon Generalov, a gloomy man with a large family, was sitting to my left, drawing up a plan for bringing up his children:

PLAN
1. *Ivan—use corporal punishment (belt).*
2. *Natasha—stand in the corner thirty minutes for breaking the television.*
3. *Alla and Lyuba—buy tickets for puppet show.*
4. *Sergei—check his diary.*
5. *Have talk with wife about dirty clothes (perhaps take to laundry).*

Vaska Sidorkin was sitting on my right. He took a traveling chess set from his pocket. "Shall we play?"
"All right."
Sidorkin set the pegboard on the edges of our two chairs so that it couldn't be seen.
The chief nodded his head. "Everyone present?"
"Almost," answered Ermoshin, who always sat closest to the chief.
"Well, let's start."
Silaev pulled his cigarettes over to him. Everyone else got out theirs, except for Sidorkin, who never had any of his own and who reached for mine. In five minutes the room would be dim with smoke.
"Who'll give the first report?" asked the chief. "Ermoshin?"
Ermoshin, the glibbest, always went first. He rose and assumed an air of dignity, straightening his tie. "On this day, in the unit entrusted to my care . . ."
The chief closed his eyes in pleasure. His interest in what Ermoshin had to say was not a practical but a purely literary one: Ermoshin's words flowed as smoothly and

evenly as if he were reading a newspaper article entitled "On-the-Spot Reports."

"The unit's collective," said Ermoshin in his customary double-talk, "is taking part in the competition for the honor of celebrating the forty-fourth anniversary of the Revolution . . ."

"Forty-third," wheezed Sidorkin.

Taken aback, Ermoshin ceased speaking, his lips continuing to move slowly as he tried to figure out the dates. Confused, the chief kept looking from Sidorkin to Ermoshin, and then he, too, began trying to make the computation. Ermoshin got the answer first.

". . . . for the honor of celebrating the forty-fourth anniversary of the Revolution," he continued firmly, casting a contemptuous glance at Sidorkin.

"Hold on," Silaev interrupted him. "Sidorkin, are you playing chess over there?"

"Of course not!" barked Sidorkin, devouring the chief with his impudent eyes.

"Don't you dare, you hear me!"

"Yes, sir!" roared Sidorkin, moving his piece.

The others made their reports after Ermoshin. Everyone detailed their successes and only mentioned their shortcomings in passing. As usual, they railed at Chief of Supply Bogdashkin, who was sitting at a separate table near the wall and coolly entering their remarks into a thick cloth-covered notebook. This he did at all conferences, planning sessions, and briefings. If all Bogdashkin's notes were published, they'd make for quite a set of collected works.

Finally it was Sidorkin's turn. He made a quick move, not a very smart one, and then rose to his feet.

"Well, everything in my area's in perfect order," said

Sidorkin, hitching up his pants. "Except that Bogdashkin here's not giving me any radiators. Make a note of that, Bogdashkin."

And Bogdashkin obediently made a note of it.

The chief waited patiently, then turned his head to me. My report was the last.

No one listened to me, everyone was fed up and wanted to go home. Sidorkin reluctantly gathered up his pieces. Sabidze had broken his pencil and was sitting there bored. The chief was picking at his desk lock with a screwdriver. He was only waiting for the conclusion of my report so he could ask: "So, how about it, we'll hand over the building by the holiday?"

"I doubt it."

"Still singing that tune. Comrade Supervisors, Samokhin's unit must be handed over by the holiday. If it is, the annual plan will be basically fulfilled. For that reason I am suggesting that each of you send three men from your units to help Samokhin tomorrow. Bogdashkin, when you're distributing building material tomorrow, take care of Samokhin's needs first. Any questions?"

"Yes," said Ermoshin.

"Your question has already been decided," said the chief. "You'll take your vacation in the winter. I call this meeting closed. Take care, comrades."

11

We left the building around eight o'clock. The rain had stopped, but obviously not for long. The damp wind cut through your raincoat and went right through you, too. Sidorkin put up his collar and held it with his hand to protect his sore ear from the wind.

Someone proposed killing a bottle of vodka and nobody had any special objection. We bought three half liters in a store, then went to the cafeteria in a textile factory which we liked because they always had Zhigulovsky beer and because you could sit there without removing your coat.

While we were carrying over our beer, cutlets, and macaroni, Sidorkin was pouring the vodka into glasses under the table and coloring it with beer. He did this quickly so no one would see.

Marusia, who cleaned tables, walked over, took one look at us, and shook her head reproachfully. "Ai, boys, you've brought vodka in here again. The police have been by, they just took two away half an hour ago."

"That's all right, Marusia," said Sidorkin. "Don't worry, they won't get us." He put a fifty-kopeck piece on the table. Marusia wiped the coin into the palm of her hand with her rag and walked away, pacified.

"What shall we drink to?" asked Sidorkin.

"To friendship," said Ermoshin, looking over at me. "To us always being friends."

"You'll go far," said Sidorkin and was the first to drink down his vodka.

We drank ours, too. Sidorkin poured the second bottle into our glasses and set the bottle under the table as he had with the first. We drank again. Ermoshin, who was always up on the latest news, said he'd overheard a conversation in the main office that we'd be switching over to building apartment blocks in the new year.

"It's about time," said Filiminov, who'd been with us all of two months. He was fresh from the institute and a champion of the progressive approach. "That'll be great. A building a month."

"What's so good about it?" said Sidorkin. "You'll be running from one job to another. There's nothing worse for a construction supervisor than running from one place to another. Tell him, Ermoshin."

"I'm for progress," said Ermoshin.

"Good luck," agreed Sidorkin readily. "How about another drop? Who's got the bottle?"

I had the third bottle but didn't get to pull it out. Two policemen had entered the cafeteria. One was tall and broad-shouldered, with an all-knowing eye. The other was small, even puny. They stood by the door, looked around, and then headed straight for our table.

"What do you say, guys, have some beer with us," Sidorkin invited them cordially, filling his own glass with beer.

"Another time," said the tall one, pushing the tablecloth aside and glancing under the table.

I froze and looked over at Sidorkin. He took a sip of beer from his glass, then he, too, peeked under the table. Ermoshin suddenly jumped up from his seat and, saying he had to go get his tea, walked off toward the serving window.

Sidorkin and the tall policeman had bent over at the same time and ended up looking each other right in the eye. The tall volunteer's eyes were surprised and searching, Sidorkin's friendly and trusting.

"All right," said the tall volunteer. "Please excuse us."

"No trouble at all," said Sidorkin politely. "Drop by again."

"Excuse us," said the tall one once again. "Let's go, Oleg."

They'd reached the door when Sidorkin called out to them: "Hey, guys!"

The policemen walked back to our table. Ermoshin had gotten his tea, but seeing them return, he stayed where he was and read the menu stuck to the wall.

"Hey, guys," said Sidorkin to the policemen. "Want me to show you my trick?"

"What kind of trick?" said the small one, his eyes shining with curiosity.

"What kind? The usual kind, like in the circus," promised Sidorkin. "But it's just between us, okay?"

"Okay," the small one agreed at once and the tall one seconded him reluctantly. "Okay."

"All right then," said Sidorkin. "Look under the table." They looked. Sidorkin lifted his feet up. There were now two empty bottles on the floor.

"Now you see them," said Sidorkin, "now you don't." He lowered his feet and again covered the bottles with his huge pants legs. The policemen looked at each other, confused, unsure of how to act in such a situation. But evidently they remembered that they'd given their word.

"All right," said the tall one. "Next time we'll know. See you then."

They left. Ermoshin waited until the door had closed behind them before returning to the table.

"How's your tea?" asked Sidorkin. "Not cold yet?"

"It's cold," said Ermoshin, averting his eyes. "Hey, don't be sore at me. If something happened, I'd have been the worst off."

"And why's that?" asked Sidorkin.

"You know. I'll be working with the trade unions. People know me. They'll say: You get up and speak at meetings, then you go out and . . ."

"So do one of two things," said Sidorkin. "Either give up speeches or give up drinking. Zhenya," he said to me, "give me your bottle."

I don't remember why, but after the third bottle we started arguing about honesty. Ermoshin said that, frankly speaking, being a construction supervisor and honesty were as incompatible as genius and crime: you can play at honesty as much as you like, but when it comes time to squirm out of something, you'll fake invoices and you'll fake results.

"Take Samokhin," said Ermoshin. "Even he's no better than the rest of us. He's been ordered to turn over his building by the holiday and he'll do it like a good boy, no matter what condition it's in."

I probably wouldn't have said anything if it had been anybody but Ermoshin. But I suddenly got carried away and said that I'd hand over the building when it was one hundred percent ready and that I didn't give a damn for Silaev and all the rest of them. I was going to obey my conscience.

I bet Ermoshin a bottle of cognac that I would do just what I said I would. After that, we all split up and went home.

12

Returning home, I found my neighbor Ivan Adamovich Shishkin in the kitchen as usual, reading his favorite book. There was no way of ever finding out the author or the title. The cover was long gone; the pages were no longer in order and kept falling out. But it was from this book and this book alone that Ivan Adamovich learned all the simple wisdom of life.

Catching sight of me, Ivan Adamovich jumped up as he always did and followed me into my room. He held the book open with both hands.

"Zhenya, take a look at what's written here," he said

with his usual astonishment. "You think you exist. But in fact you don't. How can that be?" After a moment's silence Ivan Adamovich answered his own question. "Here's how. There's no you, no room, no table, there's nothing. Everything is just our imagination. It's a total vacuum. That's something to think about."

I didn't feel like thinking about it right at the moment.

"Ivan Adamovich," I said, "you don't have to overwhelm me all at once with discoveries like that. You should take a step-by-step approach."

"How's that?"

"I'll tell you. First imagine that you don't exist. But the table, the room, and I will stay where we are. A partial vacuum."

Ivan Adamovich looked at me attentively, trying to figure out whether he had understood me. He had.

"All right then," he said, his feelings hurt. "I'll be going."

"A pleasant journey."

13

I always fall asleep quickly but I'm a light sleeper. If they turn on a radio next door, if Ivan Adamovich slams the door, if a fire truck passes the house, I wake right up.

This time it was the telephone that woke me. "As long as it's not for me," I thought, holding my breath as if that could help.

Shishkin went to the phone.

"Hello. Who wants him? Klava? No, he's not sleeping. I'll get him right away."

He knocked at my door and, hearing no answer, knocked again.

"Zhenya, phone for you."

I wriggled my feet into my slippers and went out to the corridor. Shishkin was probably already preparing for bed; all he had on were his underpants and his glasses. He was standing by the phone, his face beaming with malicious joy.

"You couldn't say I wasn't here?" I hissed, flaring with hatred for him.

"No, I couldn't," said Shishkin. "How could I say you're not here when you are?" Ivan Adamovich has never deceived anyone, especially a member of the fair sex.

I took the phone.

"What do you think the hardest thing for a person to do is?"

"The hardest thing is to talk on the phone when you want to be sleeping," I said, feeling a quiet rage in me.

"Yes, that's true," she agreed as if I'd said something wise. "Listen, why didn't you come by?"

"I was busy."

"But you're not busy right now, are you?"

"Right now I feel like sleeping. It's already late."

"It's only eleven o'clock."

I looked at my watch. It was only eleven but it seemed much later.

"I really want to see you, you hear me? Really, really!"

While saying those words, she of course had closed her eyes and nodded her head. Her amateur theatrics irritated me, but I agreed anyway.

"All right, I'll come by."

I felt sorry for her.

14

Klava had been married once. She lived for seven years with a teacher who was also an amateur musician. Shortly after he was invited to play in the regional philharmonic, he left Klava, having decided that their interests no longer coincided. Klava then went off to Pechora, where I met her four years ago. She worked in our infirmary and everyone used to borrow alcohol from her when the stores were out. Our relationship began there and continued out of inertia.

Now she was working in the polyclinic as district physician. She lived at the outskirts of town in the rambling gray building where she had once lived with her husband. Her room was on the second floor, at the end of a narrow hallway with doors on both sides alternating like the squares on a chessboard. All the neighbors had known me a long time. Whenever I walked down the hall, the doors would open one after the other and I'd bow right and left without breaking stride, as if I were rocking from side to side.

I found Klava in her usual position, lying on a low ottoman surrounded by books. She devoured enormous quantities of books, which made me a little envious. But you can't just read indiscriminately. Everything affected and artificial in her came from books.

As soon as I arrived, our usual evening of questions and answers began.

"How did you get here?"

"By taxi."

"Is it cold out?"

"Not too bad."

"Remember how cold it got in Pechora?"

If I didn't cut this off in time I'd have to answer questions about changes in the climate and my views on the harvest, share impressions of the latest films, and state my attitude on the Algerian question.

"Listen, heat up some tea, will you," I asked, only to break her endless chain of questions.

"Oh, I'm sorry."

She jumped up quickly, wrapped her robe around her, and ran off to the kitchen. I pushed her books to one side, lay down on the ottoman, and tried to think of absolutely nothing.

A blissful state. I would have liked to lie there like that forever, but I knew that in seven hours my alarm clock would wake me, and once again cursing the world, I would have to drag myself to work, squeeze supplies from Bogdashkin, fight with the workers and the bosses, or sit bored to death at another pointless production conference.

But I could take all that if they weren't hurrying me to turn over the building. It could be turned over looking the way it does right now. But I was aching to do something real, something I didn't have to be ashamed of.

Of course I could refuse to turn it over, which I'd already done twice before. But I was a little younger and a little braver then. Moving from place to place was no big problem for me; I lived in tents or barracks, despising creature comforts.

Klava brought in the teapot, poured me a cup, and then slid over a plate of homemade cookies. She sat down across from me and, propping her head on her hands, watched me as I ate and drank.

"You just don't look right," she said. "I think you're sick."

"The cookies are good," I said. "How'd you find the time to make them?"

"Drink your tea, then I'll listen to your chest. I really don't like the way you look," said Klava.

"I'm not something to listen to," I said. "I'm not a pho-nograph record. And I'm not too crazy about how I look myself."

Klava took my hand in hers and held it for a moment. "Your pulse is terrible. It feels pre-coronary."

"You said the same thing last time," I said. "Every supervisor's pulse is pre-coronary. Especially before the holiday."

"If you don't believe me," said Klava offended, "go see another doctor."

"I would if I thought they'd put me in the hospital." Right about now, a stretch in the hospital wouldn't be bad at all. Let Silaev turn over my building himself, since he likes it so much.

"Good cookies," I said. "Where'd you find flour?"

"A good housewife can find anything. I'd be a good housewife, wouldn't I?"

"Don't brag. I'm not marrying you anyway."

She broke out laughing. "It takes two to make that de-cision. And, by the way, how's Zoya?"

"Zoya who?"

"You know, your sweetheart, the one that works in the cafeteria. I think you have a chance with that one."

She made a point of saying all this jokingly, yet at the same time she kept casting quick, worried looks at me. She was afraid there might be some truth in her jest.

While I was drinking my tea, Klava suddenly turned pale and put her hand to her chest near her throat.

"What's the matter?" I jumped up.

She didn't say a word. She closed her eyes and waved me away. Then, having caught her breath, she smiled. "It was nothing."

"You feel sick?"

"Just a little. Don't pay it any mind."

I looked suspiciously at her. This wasn't from her books. Klava sighed. "You big dope, I'm a doctor, I know how to handle these things."

"Because you're a woman, not because you're a doctor."

"Even so," she agreed. "I know."

Well, her age gave her the right to be experienced, but still I found such talk mortifying. Rosa would never have spoken like that.

I pushed my glass away and stood up.

"You want to go now?" she asked softly.

"Yes," I said.

Tears appeared in her eyes but she didn't start crying.

"If you're tired of it here, you can go," she said after a moment's silence. "I won't try and stop you. God, what an idiot I am. Why do I get on your nerves like this? You're a good, kind, talented person."

If she had started screaming or crying, I probably would have left, but now I couldn't.

"You're talking nonsense again," I grumbled, calming down. "I'm not the least bit talented. I'm just your ordinary man in the street. What do you need me to be talented for? You already had one talented man, wasn't that enough for you?"

It was almost twelve. Klava took a long minute thinking something over, then said: "Tell me, do you love me, even a little bit?"

"How many times can you ask the same question?"

"Don't be angry. I just think you come to see me out of pity. And pity is the most revolting human emotion."

"Not true," I said wearily. "That's something you read in one of your books. It wouldn't be so terrible if we pitied each other a little more."

I'd fallen off to sleep when Klava nudged me in the side. "You know what I was thinking?"

"No, what?" I was past being angry.

"I was thinking how good it is to know a man like you is always there by my side."

This she says about *me*. Those books of hers do her no good.

15

The weather was a little better the next day, the sun was out from morning on. The workers were sitting on logs and smoking near the solution mixer. Most of them were strangers to me; the other supervisors had sent them here on Silaev's orders. You could tell what each of them did by the tool he carried. Shilov and I dispatched them to the various work sites, then I inspected the building and went back to the office. Gusev, a reporter for the city paper, was sitting at my desk. His paper must have considered him a specialist in construction, because he was always hanging around our site. His articles were not distinguished by any variety of style and they all began more or less like this: "In the such-and-such construction project everyone knows Brigade leader so-and-so . . ."

Seeing me, Gusev got up and came around the desk to greet me. As usual, he was wearing corduroy trousers, a Bulgarian jacket made of imitation leather, and a dark blue beret.

"How are you, old man," he said in a burst of enthusiasm, pumping my hand.

Why get upset, I thought. "It's like the Writer says—there's no time squeeze, let's shoot the breeze."

"But I've come to see you on business," said Gusev.

"You're going to do an article on me?"

"How did you know?"

"You can't put anything past me," I said. "Was it Silaev who let you know?"

"It was," said Gusev, taking out a thick note pad with an elastic band around it.

I took this as a bad omen. If they've decided to do an article on me, there'll be no peace from here on in.

"I hear you're going to be chief engineer soon?" asked Gusev. He sat down opposite me and crossed his legs.

"Not so fast," I said. "There's still a chance I might not. Besides, you should be writing about somebody else. Shilov, for example, best brigade leader we've got."

"I already did an article about him," said Gusev and made an entry on his pad, no doubt concerning my modesty. "Come on, let's not waste any time. Tell me a few words about yourself."

"What do you need that for?" I asked. "No matter what I say, you're still going to write: Everyone in Zhilstroi knows Senior Construction Supervisor Samokhin. It is no accident that this tall, broad-shouldered man with the open face and friendly eyes enjoys the respect of the entire collective. 'Our Samokhin' is how the workers fondly refer to him."

Gusev laid his note pad on the table and, laughing politely, said: "Why bother with that kind of talk, old man? I don't deal in clichés. I want to start with the war. Were you at the front?"

"Yes," I said. "I can tell you some good stories."

"That's not necessary right at the moment," said Gusev. "But there'll be a holiday issue for the twenty-third of February; that'll be the right time for your stories. Meanwhile, I just need the war for openers. I'll write something like: 1945, you're summoned to the division commander, who orders you to blow up the railroad station . . ."

"Hold it," I said. "I don't remember being summoned

by any division commander. I spoke with the regimental commander once during the entire war. I was in the rear and he pulled me out of formation because my boots weren't polished."

"That's not important," said Gusev with a wave of his hand.

"You know, I said the same thing to him, it's not important, and he slapped me with five days in the guard-house, strict regime, for talking without permission. Of course, I didn't have to go, the next day we were sent to the front."

"Listen, all that's very interesting," said Gusev. "But what does the guardhouse have to do with anything? I'm doing an article, I've got to get a little creative here and there. Don't I have the right to?"

"You do," I said. "But the point is that I wasn't in the war in '45. I was already studying in the institute, racing from floor to floor on crutches because all our lectures were in different halls."

"What, were you wounded?" asked Gusev in surprise. "I didn't know. That's very interesting." He made a note.

"Very interesting," I said. "Especially when they're taking the anti-tank-grenade shrapnel out of your butt. An excellent feeling."

"I'm sure," said Gusev sympathetically. "It must have been painful. But I was just interested in the war for openers. What I have to do is show you blowing up houses while you dream of building them. The struggle for peace is a very important theme right now. Were you an officer during the war?"

"No," I said. "I was a sergeant, and I didn't blow up any houses, because I was in reconnaissance."

"What's the difference," said Gusev. "It's important for

the story that you blew up houses. Now tell me when you decided to become a construction engineer, was it during the war or when you were a child?"

"How can I put it?" I said, faltering. "You see, after I was wounded I lived across the street from the Construction Institute. You had to take the trolley to the other institutes and just cross the street for that one. And since I was on crutches at the time . . ."

"I see," said Gusev, but without making any notes. "Now tell me, have you invented anything, do you have any ideas for modernizing construction?"

"No," I said. "I don't want to invent anything on principle, to see what people can accomplish without my help."

"Yes, and so?"

"People are doing pretty well, I think. They've already invented a bomb that'll leave cars and buildings intact and turn you and me into a little white cloud. But I can assure you that I had no part in that invention."

"Is that right," said Gusev, though the silence that followed said more.

"Yes, that's right," I said. "But do you know who invented the tea kettle?"

"The tea kettle?" Gusev rubbed his brow in thought. "Lomonosov?"

"Right," I said. "Lomonosov discovered the law of the conservation of energy, wrote poetry, and invented tea kettles in his spare time. But not the kind they sell in our department stores, with the handles that break right off. They were invented by Yurka Golikov, who works as an engineer at the Kitchen Goods Plant."

I was fed up with Gusev and I was purposely babbling all sorts of nonsense to derail him. But it looked as if he was getting fed up, too. He put his note pad back in his pocket, flipped his cigarette at the stove, and stood up.

"I think it's better I write it up and show it to you after, all right?" he said.

"Fine," I said. "You write it up and then we'll work things out."

Gusev left. I sat there a little while longer, then went off to make the rounds of the floors. I found the usual pandemonium when there is an unrealistic deadline to be met. Some of the workers were going full force, rushing about, while others weren't working at all, just sitting on the windowsills, smoking, and swapping dirty jokes. No one paid me the slightest attention, as if I had nothing to do with any of it. I even felt like a fifth wheel there myself, and I continued my inspection without interfering. But then I encountered one shaggy-looking worker hanging doors in section 4. He was attaching the door hinges by banging the screws into the wood with one, maybe two blows of his hammer. His toolbox was on the ground behind him, his tools and screws strewn all over the floor.

"Don't you have a screwdriver?" I asked him.

"No," he said. "What do I need one for?"

"Don't you know you're supposed to put in screws with a screwdriver?"

"This way's good, too," he said with a wave of his hand, and he picked up the next hinge.

"Whose sector are you from?" I asked him.

"Ermoshin's."

I picked up his tools myself and laid them neatly in his toolbox. He stopped hammering the screw and looked curiously at me. I handed him his toolbox.

"Goodbye," I said. "My regards to Ermoshin."

He took his toolbox from me and gave me a long, hard look.

"Son of a bitch!" he said with real feeling, spat, and started down the stairs.

I went back to the office and called Silaev. I intended to tell him that I was not going to turn over the building until it was completely in order. Ermoshin could buy me the bottle of cognac. Let him learn that not everyone was like him, that there were still people who never went against their conscience. I nearly burst with a sense of my own nobility; I felt beautiful and brave. But my ardor was cooled by Lyusya, who told me that Silaev had left for a session of the district soviet and would not be back that day.

What of it. Our talk could wait one day.

16

I returned home that day earlier than usual. Ivan Adamovich met me at the door. There was something odd about his smile and he averted his eyes as if he was feeling guilty about something. I understood immediately that something was up, but there was no way of telling just exactly what. When I looked at Shishkin he seemed to wilt under my gaze. He gave a foolish giggle. I shrugged my shoulders and went into the kitchen for a drink of water. A girl about two years old, wrapped in a not particularly clean towel, was sitting on a chair in the kitchen. There was a dish of kasha in front of her on the kitchen table. The little girl was scooping up the kasha and smearing it across her face; if any fell in her mouth she spat it out onto the towel.

"So you see," giggled Ivan Adamovich in embarrassment, "my niece left her here this afternoon. She says— I'm going to the movies. That was six hours ago and she's not back yet . . . Come on, come on, don't be naughty," he shouted sternly at the little girl, who had decided to speed up the tiresome process of smearing the kasha and had now thrust both hands in the plate. "Don't be naughty," said Ivan Adamovich. "Or else I'll tell the man to put you in a sack."

The little girl pulled her hands from the plate, looked first at Ivan Adamovich, then at me, and burst into tears.

"Don't cry now," Ivan Adamovich began pacifying her. "Go away, man. We won't give Mashenka to you."

The little girl kept crying and Ivan Adamovich grew angry.

"I don't hear you crying, you understand?" he said. "I don't hear it and that's all there is to it." He made a nasty face. "There isn't any crying. There isn't any you and there isn't any me. Just empty space! A total vacuum! That's all!"

The little girl looked closely at him and then began crying even louder than before. I went back to my room.

"I threw a letter for you in there, Zhenya," Ivan Adamovich shouted after me.

The letter was lying on the floor. I picked it up and opened the envelope. There were just a few lines.

Greetings, Zhenya, old buddy,
I decided to drop you a line even though it's been a long time since I heard from you. Obviously, you've become completely arrogant (only kidding) and forgotten your old friends. I'm now the head of a construction project out here and am building quite a little plant. Come see me when you get tired of sitting around the same old place. We'll do a little work together. You can be a senior supervisor to start. Like they say, it's clean work and the pay's good. As far as

an apartment goes, I can't make any promises right now but we'll figure something out after. That's it. Stay well and think it over. Sevka sends his regards. He's working for me as head of the PTO, he's married, has three kids, but he's still painting landscapes like he used to.

Anyway, come. I'll be waiting for an answer. I send you a hug.

Vladik

I read the letter twice. Dammit but it's good to get a letter you didn't expect from an old friend. Sevka and Vladik working together. I wonder what they're like now. They could have at least sent a snapshot, the bums. Sevka has three children. Imagine that. I remember him as just a kid, red hair, scrawny, his face always scratched up, always fighting with his older sister. He was a pretty fair painter; we thought he'd go right into painting. But looks like it didn't turn out that way. Maybe he didn't have enough talent, maybe it was something else.

I read the letter one more time. How about that, it seemed to have come just in the nick of time. An easy way out. Let them turn over the building themselves and I'll go off to Siberia. I won't have to do their sloppy hack work and I won't have to feel ashamed of myself.

It would solve the Klava problem at the same time. Our relationship had dragged on too long anyway. Now that'd be it. It's not worth it to deceive each other, torment each other.

Just then the doorbell rang. We don't have many visitors at our apartment and I listened hard to hear who it was. I heard Ivan Adamovich open the door and begin talking with someone. An unfamiliar woman's voice was asking for me. I went out into the hall. There was a woman on the landing. Ivan Adamovich was talking to her through a crack in the door, holding on to the door, ready to slam it shut if need be. I moved Shishkin aside and invited the woman in. She swished past me in her expensive fur coat speckled with raindrops.

"Of course you don't remember me," she said, looking me over, blinking nearsightedly. "We met last year at Klava's birthday party."

But I remembered her quite well. She was the fattest woman there. I even remembered that her name was Nadya and that she was a gynecologist in the polyclinic where Klava worked.

"What makes you say that, Nadya?" I said. "It'd be strange if I didn't remember you."

I hung up her coat, then invited her into my room, apologizing for the mess.

"That's all right," she said, entering the room and looking around. "Bachelor life. Now if you had a wife . . ."

"If wishes were horses . . ."

I closed the door behind her, but not completely, so that Ivan Adamovich would not work himself up with idle speculations.

Nadya began the conversation by saying that her visit must seem unusual to me. Purposely correct in my tone, I answered that her visit was unexpected, but a pleasure just the same.

"I don't think it will be that much of a pleasure." She took a cigarette from her purse and lit it. "This is something of a delicate subject . . . But I'm a doctor and I can allow myself to be straightforward. You know of course that Klava is pregnant."

"Of course. I'd just about guessed."

"Just about guessed," she mimicked me. "But what's there to guess? You'll excuse me, but it's obvious even to the untrained eye. The point is that Klava wants to, as they say, terminate her pregnancy. In no case must she do this. She would be risking death. I'm not exaggerating in the least."

"Why couldn't you have told her yourself?" I asked.

"I have. More than once. She doesn't want to listen. She values your opinion more. You should try to persuade her."

"All right," I said uncertainly, "I'll try."

"Yes, give it a try," she said, rising. "My advice to you is get married. I've lived alone a long time and I still haven't found anything good about it."

"You and I are different," I observed diffidently.

"Differences are purely relative."

I was not about to argue and accompanied her to the door. So, I thought, returning to my room, now everything's fallen into place.

I sat there a little longer, then took my jacket from the chair. It was eleven-thirty.

Ivan Adamovich was waiting for me in the hall, holding a diaper in the air with two fingers. He looked completely lost.

"Zhenya," he said, "look what that little brat's gone and done. You see that?"

"No, I don't," I said.

"How's that?" said Ivan Adamovich, taken aback.

"It just is." I shrugged my shoulders. "I don't see it, that's all. It's all just your imagination, Ivan Adamovich."

Ivan Adamovich rubbed the back of his head with his free hand.

"But it sure does stink," he said uncertainly.

17

Klava hadn't gone to sleep yet. She was sitting in front of her mirror, in her nightgown, smearing something on her hair. The sight of me threw her into confusion and she shoved some little bottle into the drawer.

"What were you doing?" I asked, knowing I should have kept my mouth shut.

"Nothing."

She looked over at me, still confused and embarrassed. Her hair was wet. I guessed she must have been touching it up with a color restorer. I felt sorry for her, and to hide it, I said: "You silly fool."

Guiltily she pressed her powdered cheek against mine. Then she asked: "Why did you come?"

"No special reason. What's the matter, aren't you glad to see me?"

"Of course I'm glad. It's just that I didn't expect you."

"A pleasant surprise then," I said. "Look . . . Nadya was just at my place . . ."

"She was?" Klava's guard went up. "Well, what did she tell you?"

"She told me everything that needed to be said."

"That idiot!" said Klava angrily. "That idiot! Did I ask her to do it? What's she interfering for?"

"She says it's very dangerous for you."

"A pack of lies. What does she know? Don't believe her. I'm a doctor, too, and my grasp of these things is every bit as good as hers."

"Klava, I want to say that if it's really true . . ."

She looked mockingly at me. "Naturally, I value your noble instincts, but it simply is not true. Don't be upset, everything will turn out fine."

All right then . . . Since she doesn't think there's any danger herself . . . And after all she *is* a doctor.

"You know what," I said. "I got a letter from Vladik. Do you remember me talking about him?"

"What did he have to say?"

"Nothing special. He invited me to work with him. He's building some kind of plant out there in Siberia."

"Do you want to go?" Klava asked quickly.

"I don't know," I said. "Not too much right now."

"Go if you want to," said Klava. "I won't keep you. Nothing important has happened. Nothing has changed."

"No," I said. "It would just be stupid to leave now. I'll be chief engineer soon."

"Really?" said Klava in surprise. "How did that happen all of a sudden?"

"I don't know. It came from upstairs."

"I'm very glad for you." She pulled my head to her and kissed me. "Listen, if it's better for you without me, go, I won't keep you. I don't want you to feel tied down."

"Don't talk nonsense," I said. "I don't ever intend to leave you."

"But do you love me?"

"I do."

She looked at me with disbelief but did not say anything.

In the morning, as I was getting ready to leave for work, Klava said: "We won't see each other before the holiday, will we?"

"Why not?" I said. "We could even see each other today."

"Really?" Klava brightened. "Let's go to the movies tonight."

"Sure," I agreed, even though I didn't feel like going to the movies. But I wanted to make Klava feel good.

18

The day was rather uneventful. Practically no one called me, I wasn't summoned anywhere. I even began to think they'd forgotten about me. At five, after the workers had quit for the day, I called the main office and said I couldn't make the meeting because I wasn't feeling well. Then I left for the polyclinic to pick up Klava.

The film Klava and I wanted to see had already left, but there was another new film playing at the Novator Theater; a lot of new films were being released at the time.

We wanted to see the six o'clock show, but the only tickets left were for the ten. We had a lot of time on our hands and it was raining. Klava said: "You live close by. Let's go to your place for a while. In all this time you've never invited me over. I have no idea what your place is like."

As usual, my place was a mess, which made my invitation a reluctant one.

On the way there, we bought a small donkey on a wooden stand for Mashenka, whose mother had disappeared.

The sight of a strange woman frightened Mashenka and she started crying. I took Klava to my room, having warned her of the state it was in and not to even think of straightening it up. Then I went back to Mashenka and handed her the present. She was indifferent to the toy, but Ivan Adamovich was quite pleased.

"Look at the nice little elephant Uncle Zhenya's brought for you," he said merrily.

"It's not an elephant, it's a donkey," I corrected him.

Ivan Adamovich read the label letter by letter: "D-o-nk-e-y." Setting the toy back in place, he said stubbornly: "Spells elephant."

I wasn't about to argue with him. "The mother's still not back?" I asked.

"No," said Ivan Adamovich sadly. "She sent a telegram from Voronezh. She got married there."

I went back to my room. Klava was standing by my table holding Rosa's picture and examining it closely. "Is this your new sweetheart?" she asked with exaggerated calm.

"Put that back where it belongs and don't touch it again," I said.

Surprisingly, this seemed to disturb her greatly.

"Is that so? And what if I won't?"

"Klava, put it back," I said quietly, restraining myself.

"And if I won't?"

"Put it back!" I raised my voice.

"I won't!" said Klava obstinately.

At that point I started shouting and stamping my feet. I'd never been that angry before. To this day, it makes me ashamed to remember it.

Klava suddenly flung the picture to the floor. The glass broke with a crash. So here we go, domestic scenes already!

I walked silently over to her. She looked up at me and turned pale.

"Don't you dare! Don't you dare!" she cried. "You'll be sorry afterward! You'll feel ashamed of yourself!"

I must have looked terrible at that moment if Klava thought I might strike her.

The door opened partway. Eternally nosy, Ivan Adamovich peeped into the room, but seeing the rage on my face, slammed the door shut at once.

"Do you know who that picture's of?" I asked in a sinister voice.

"I know," said Klava. "Why are you trying to pull the wool over my eyes? If you're sick of me, you can always run to her, your . . ."

Klava dashed out of the room, wailing.

I leaned against the wall. I was out of breath, my heart was hurting me again.

A little calmer, I squatted down and began picking up the broken glass. The picture was unharmed. I carefully pulled it free of the glass and laid it on the table. Rosa's large eyes watched me pensively, sadly. "Ach, you," I thought of Klava, "now you've really found someone to be jealous of."

My anger had passed. What was Klava guilty of? Of being worse than Rosa? But who knew what Klava was like at eighteen and what Rosa might have become if she'd lived and her life had turned out like Klava's.

Catching myself at my thoughts, I was surprised—what did all this mean? Had I begun to feel less for Rosa? And more for Klava? I was even experiencing pangs of conscience and considered running after her and bringing her back to my room. But then, estimating that she must be fairly far away already (maybe even at the bus stop), I realized that I'd have to run too fast and I did not feel like running. "I'll call her tomorrow and apologize," I decided.

I lay down on the couch without taking off my coat.

19

After a while I'd had enough of lying there on the couch and went out. The rain had stopped. The lights were on in the cafeteria across the street. Zoya was the only one there. She was drying the forks and spoons in preparation for leaving. She was surprised to see me.

"This is the first time you've ever come here at night," she said. "Looks like your wife doesn't feel like cooking tonight."

"I don't have a wife," I said.

"Tell me about it," laughed Zoya coquettishly. "All men say they don't and then it turns out they have a wife and children."

"I don't have a wife, Zoya," I said a second time. "And I don't have any children."

There was nothing in the cafeteria except cold cutlets.

While I was paying, the movie tickets came out of my pocket along with the money. I'd forgotten all about them.

"Would you like to go to the movies, Zoya?" I proposed, to my own surprise.

"I'd be glad to," said Zoya. "But you're probably just kidding me."

"Not at all, Zoya, seriously," I said. "Here are the tickets."

She agreed to go and we left the cafeteria together. I helped her lock up. There was still about an hour till the show and we decided to go for a walk.

I didn't quite know what to say to her, and so I asked: "Zoya, what do you do in your spare time?"

"Depends," she said. "Sometimes I go to dances or the movies with my girlfriends. Or else I just sit home and copy down expressions."

"What?"

"Expressions. You know, like the expression 'It's better to die on your feet than to live on your knees.' Dolores Ibarruri, 'La Pasionaria,' said that one. Or here's one from Victor Hugo—'Life is a flower and love is its honey.' I have two whole albums full of expressions like that. When I have enough, I won't have to read any more books."

"Is that so! Interesting," I said. "So your album contains wisdom in its pure state?"

"That's right," she agreed. "You know, I have very beautiful handwriting even though I didn't finish high school. My sister's been to college, she's a teacher, and you wouldn't believe how she writes. She can't even read it herself. Did you go to college?"

"Something like that," I said.

"Is it true you're very strong?"

"Where'd you hear that?"

"A guy told me. He's a friend of our cook. He says he works with you. His name's Sasha."

"Could be," I said. "I've got a lot of Sashas working for me. What's his last name?"

"I don't remember. He's blond with long, long hair."

"Aha, the Writer," I said.

"Is he really a writer?" said Zoya in surprise.

"Uh-huh," I said. "A writer. Listen, it's cold, let's go in the lobby. We can warm up a bit and look at the magazines."

She agreed and we went in. But we didn't have a chance to look at any magazines because the director of the film was giving a talk in the lobby. We listened to it, standing by the wall. The director told how the film was made, how heroically the whole film collective had worked, and what hopes they had for their work. At the end of his talk, he said: "If our film causes you to think or if you become even a little bit better or wiser after seeing it, we'll consider that we've accomplished our job."

Seeing the film did not make us either better or wiser. As we were leaving the theater, Zoya said nothing and kept sighing to herself, deep in thought. Finally she asked: "But anyway, Zhenya, what is love?"

"I don't know," I said.

She sighed again and said pensively: "Love is a stormy sea, love is an evil hurricane."

I agreed with her that it was. We walked to her house, where I quickly said good night to her. I saw that now I'd have to buy breakfast in a different cafeteria.

20

At last the long-awaited day arrived. That morning Silaev summoned me to his office. He informed me that the order concerning my appointment had been confirmed and that I would assume my new duties after the holiday. I still hadn't made up with Klava. I was in a foul mood and the news of my appointment did nothing to cheer me up.

"Well, Evgeny, you're moving up in the world," said Silaev heartily. "Pretty soon you'll be a big shot. Today you'll turn over the building and after the holiday you'll start your new job. So what are you frowning about?"

"You know why," I said. "I don't like sloppy work."

"What can you do?" said Silaev. "We can't always do what we want. If the district committee says turn over the building, you don't go against them. There's something else. Section 1 is probably the best in your unit?"

"Probably."

"And the asphalt's been laid near the entrance but the other units don't have theirs yet, right?"

"Yes, and so?" I didn't see the point.

"What's with you? Is this your first day on a site?" Silaev spread his hands wide in a gesture of quiet exasperation. "It's muddy out, the commission people will be wearing good shoes, they're more the intellectual type, you know."

"So you think they won't want to walk through the mud?"

"That's right, they won't," said Silaev confidentially. "I know them. I'm that way myself."

None of it mattered to me any more. You do what you want and I'll do what you want—things'll be more peaceable that way.

I left his office. The reception room was crowded. Lyusya, the secretary, was tapping away on her typewriter, typing up the act of transfer. Sidorkin was sitting in a chair beside her, declaring his love for her.

"You mean you won't marry me?" he asked, his face dead serious.

"No," answered Lyusya. "You're old and skinny."

"But that's good," said Sidorkin. "When I die you can sell my skeleton to a museum for a lot of money."

"What are you hanging around here for?" I asked him.

"Waiting for Bogdashkin. I want to have a little talk with him, he's a helluva nice guy, you know."

At that moment Drobotun, the representative of the district committee and the permanent chairman of all committees concerned with the transfer of new buildings, appeared in the reception room. I hadn't seen him for about three months. He'd grown even stouter in that time. His shoulders had thickened, and the military uniform which he'd been wearing since he retired several years ago was now coming apart at the seams. Drobotun nodded to me and to Sidorkin, then looked to see what Lyusya was typing.

"Ready yet?" he asked.

"In a minute," answered Lyusya. "Should we type in the rating now or will you write it in after?"

"Let's do it right now," said Drobotun. "So it won't have to be handwritten. Put 'Building accepted with the rating of good.'"

"But what if the building was excellent?" asked Lyusya.

"Impossible," said Drobotun. "Rastrelli or Rossi, they used to build excellent. Now the best they can do is good."

21

Two more members of Drobotun's committee arrived a few minutes later. The sanitation inspector, a tall, thin man with a sunken chest and gold teeth, and a representative of the district Komsomol committee, a student of some sort. A representative of some other political organization was also supposed to come, but Drobotun was not about to wait for him.

"All right," he said. "If he wants a look, he can do it later. The holiday's almost here and my wife wants me to do some shopping for her."

"I'd like to make it quick, too," said the sanitation inspector candidly. "I've got to pick up my suit from the cleaners."

The student obviously had no important errands and said nothing.

We went outside. It wasn't raining but it could start at any moment. The clouds were low in the sky. It was cold. The clay soil between buildings was so soggy that we had to go the long way around to keep on the asphalt. Drobotun in his fluttering rain jacket walked out in front, keeping his eyes on the ground, carefully avoiding the puddles, which were violet from machine oil. I looked at his clean, felt-topped shoes and thought that Silaev had been right—the representative of the committee would not want to soil those shoes.

We walked up to the building and stopped. The carpenters had already taken down the fence and the building was visible from the walkway, its fresh paint and newly washed windows shone.

"Doesn't look bad from the outside," said Drobotun. "Let's take a look inside."

"But what's that?" asked the student, who hadn't said anything so far. He pointed at the wall.

"Where?" asked Drobotun.

"That crack over there. You've just finished the building and it's already cracking."

At first we did not understand, but when we did, Drobotun exchanged glances with the sanitation inspector and they both smiled condescendingly.

"That's not a crack," I growled. "It's a sedimentary seam."

The young man was embarrassed and blushed, but he said very sternly: "We'll check it, and then you can show us your blueprint."

I realized he was going to be trouble.

And so he was. While we were walking through the first section, where everything was in good shape, the student ran off somewhere. The three of us kept walking. Drobotun tapped the walls absentmindedly with his finger; he looked at the windows and doors. In one apartment he pointed out a wet floor to me.

"It should have been wetted down earlier," he said gloomily, "so there'd been time for it to dry a little."

That was the Writer's work. If he had appeared in

front of me at that moment, I'd have shaken the life out of him.

The sanitation inspector was attending to his own affairs; he inspected the kitchens, bathrooms, tugged at the toilet handles. He had no interest in doors and floors.

We'd been on every floor when I proposed to Drobotun and the sanitation inspector that we take a look at the second section. This I did only for the sake of my own conscience, knowing they'd certainly refuse.

"What's to see there?" said Drobotun. "We've got the picture. Where's the paper?"

I pulled the document, which I'd folded in four, from my pocket. I thought now everything was over and done with, and I felt better. If I couldn't do things the right way, then the less fuss the better.

Just then the door opened and in walked the student, drenched from head to foot, his shoes and pants caked with mud.

"Start raining again?" asked Drobotun mockingly, looking over at the student.

"I was over in the second section," said the student, panting for breath.

"And so?"

"Terrible. None of it's any good. The building cannot be accepted."

"You mean it is really unacceptable?" questioned Drobotun.

"It is," said the student confidently. "I won't sign the paper."

"You'll sign," said Drobotun.

"Go take a look at it."

Drobotun looked down at his shoes, then over at the sanitation inspector.

"We've got to go," said the sanitation inspector, though the thought depressed him.

We went back outside. A series of bricks had been laid along the wall from the entrance to section 1 to that of section 2, but they had been spread too far apart. It was immediately obvious that Drobotun's shoes would not be spared. The student, who no longer had anything to lose, plunged ahead with an air of self-assurance.

There was nothing so terrible in the second section, just our usual work. Here and there a door that wouldn't close.

"See," said the student, "the doors don't close."

"It's the dampness," explained Drobotun. "That's why they don't close."

"If at least one of them closed . . ." said the student.

"The dampness affects all the doors equally," remarked the sanitation inspector. Of the three of them he was the least interested in doors. No doubt he was thinking about the fact that he had to get to the cleaners, where in two hours the line would be endless.

"Now let's go further up," said the student, who now spoke with an air of confidence as if he were in charge of us. He started bounding up the stairs and we trudged after him.

"Ambitious," said Dobrotun softly, staring at the student's back. "So young and he's already currying favor."

"If you don't start when you're young, it'll be too late after," observed the sanitation inspector matter-of-factly.

The student led us out onto a balcony on the fourth floor, where he pushed hard on the railing. The railing tore loose from its side fastening and began shaking back and forth. It was the railing Deryushev had been welding.

"So you see," said the student triumphantly, looking at Drobotun, who frowned.

"Now that's serious," he said. "What if someone fell? There'd be a criminal case. Have someone reweld it today."

"And then we'll sign the paper," said the student.

"We'll sign it right now," said Drobotun. "He'll weld the railing, don't you worry."

"And what about the doors and the windows?" asked the student.

"Those are trifles," said Drobotun. "When the weather clears up, they'll dry out fine. You want everything to be perfect. You have to remember this man had a deadline."

"Deadlines, deadlines," said the student. "Everybody's racing to turn over the building and it'll need major repairs almost at once. They used to make buildings to last five hundred years."

"They used to mix egg yolk in with the mortar," remarked Drobotun. "But now we'd rather eat the eggs ourselves."

Their conversation digressed and became abstract. I stood off to the side as if none of it were my concern. I was angry at Drobotun. He didn't care a bit about the building. All he wanted was to be done with it quickly and report to the authorities that everything was in good order. I was growing so incensed that I no longer gave a good god-damn what would happen. If it came to that, I could go to Siberia—even people with families went. So, when Drobotun gave me the paper to sign, I refused.

"What, are you joking?" Drobotun was astonished.

"I'm not joking," I said. "He's right. It's too soon to hand over the building."

"Do you know what you're saying? There'll be an uproar. There've been announcements everywhere that the building is ready to be given to Komsomol families as a present."

"The young man is right," I said. "Nobody needs a present like that."

"But let's not go overboard either," said the student, who was now having his doubts. He must have been feeling sorry for me.

"Leave now," Drobotun said sternly to him, and the student left.

For a while Drobotun stood by the window picking at the putty with his fingernail. "Why are you making a fool of yourself?" he said. "Do you realize what a stink this can make? Sign it quickly, and we'll sign, too. And so will the student."

For a second I began to waver, but then I was carried away again. I thought to myself: No matter what, I won't sign. In the end, for better or worse, this is my work. And if I can't do it the way I want to, to the best of my ability, then why drag all this out?

"Here's what," I said to Drobotun. "I won't turn over the building yet. We'll meet again after the holiday."

He looked over at me and realized it would be pointless to argue any further.

"As you wish," he said. "It's your funeral."

22

I didn't go to the main office immediately. First I peeked in my own. All the workers were sitting there, smoking, talking things over, waiting for me. They all stopped talking when I appeared, and all their heads turned toward me.

"What are you looking at?" I said, stopping in the doorway. "Get to work."

"So they didn't accept the building?" asked Shilov.

"No."

"Why?"

"Because things have to be done right, that's why. Get the carpenters together now, have them go around to all the apartments and adjust the doors. If they don't finish today, we'll work after the holiday and every day thereafter, until we make this place first-rate. Deryushev, you didn't reweld the railing?"

"I did," said Deryushev uncertainly.

"Well, go weld it again. Then I'll come check it myself."

The telephone started ringing. I asked Shilov to get it.

"Hello," said Shilov. "Who? I'll see, hold on. It's Silaev," he whispered, covering the receiver with his hand.

"Tell him I've left and I should be there in a minute," I said.

Drobotun obviously had managed to call the office while I was on my way, and by the time I arrived, the commotion had already started. Lyusya, the secretary, was on the phone requesting that some order or other be canceled. Gusev was standing beside her, asking what he should do with his article, which had already gone to the printers. "Maybe I can speak with Silaev and he can give me someone else?"

"Why not?" said Sidorkin, who was still hanging around waiting for Bogdashkin. "All you have to do is change the name and the rest will fall into place."

"A good journalist makes everything fall into place when he has to," said Gusev, looking past me as if I weren't there at all.

"Silaev in his office?" I asked Lyusya.

"He is. He's waiting for you," she answered dryly.

It wasn't exactly a conversation we had. As soon as I entered his office, Silaev began stamping his feet and shouting at me that I had betrayed not only him but the entire collective, that now we would not win the challenge banner or any other prizes, and the district committee would draw its own conclusions as far as I was concerned.

The more he said, the worse it got. Silaev said that now my character was an open book to him, that he'd sooner give me his own ears than the post of chief engineer, and that he would drive me away like a dog.

All that was bearable, but when he said that it was only his position that kept him from smashing me in the face, that was more than I could bear. I picked up the plastic paperweight from his desk and crushed it like an empty eggshell. I said I'd do the same to him if he dared lay a hand on me. Then I walked out.

I ran into Gusev at the door. Sidorkin was sitting by the wall, smoking in silence. Lyusya was still rapping away at her typewriter.

"So," asked Sidorkin, "did you have your talk?"

"We did," I said. "Still no Bogdashkin?"

Sidorkin was about to answer when Gusev came red-faced out of Silaev's office. He carefully closed the door behind him, shrugged his shoulders, and left the office. Sidorkin and I waited a minute and then we, too, left.

I felt my hands tremble with the match as we lit up. It must have been the excitement. My hands had never trembled before.

"You're getting nervous," said Sidorkin, looking up at me. "You need to take some medicine."

"All right then, let's go get some," I said.

23

We started off straight across the vacant lot. I was wearing rubber boots and so I went ahead. We went halfway across without saying a word. Then Sidorkin said: "So what kind of brainstorm hit you today?"

"It wasn't any brainstorm," I answered. "I just don't want to do sloppy hackwork. I want to be honest."

"Honesty," guffawed Sidorkin from behind me. "Who needs your honesty?"

"I need it," I said.

We bought a bottle of vodka and dropped by the cafeteria. The workday wasn't over yet and the place was practically deserted. Marusia was wiping off the tables. She shook her head in disapproval when she noticed the bulge in Sidorkin's pocket. We sat down at our usual little table in the corner. Sidorkin poured the vodka into our glasses and we drank it down.

"You lunkhead," said Sidorkin, tasting his vinaigrette. "You could've been chief engineer."

"I'll get by."

"You'll get by," said Sidorkin. "That's why you're going to be a senior supervisor the rest of your life. That is, unless they demote you."

"You think happiness comes from the position you occupy?" I asked.

"What do you think?"

"I don't know," I said. "Maybe it does, maybe it doesn't. But at least I know that I'm living the way I want to. I'm not brown-nosing, I'm not playing the game, I'm not shaking in my boots about keeping my job."

"That's right," said Sidorkin. "And that's why you have to keep moving on. They'll eat you up alive here now. Where will you go?"

"I'll go to Siberia," I said. "A friend of mine from the institute wants me to come work there."

"And will they have an apartment ready for you?"

"It isn't the apartment that matters," I objected.

"Who knows, maybe it is. How long can a man kick about without a place of his own, without a family, without . . . Ah, what's the use of talking!" Sidorkin dismissed the subject with a wave of his hand. "Let's drink."

I had never seen him so serious. We drank again and Sidorkin put the bottle under the table. Just in time, too, for our two friends, the policemen, had entered the cafeteria. They stopped by the door, took a quick look around, then headed straight for our table. The tall one lifted the tablecloth and glanced under the table.

"Lift up your feet, please," he asked Sidorkin.

"Of course," said Sidorkin and lifted his feet.

There was nothing under the table. The two policemen exchanged glances and shrugged their shoulders.

"All right, let's go," said the tall one, and they headed for the exit. Sidorkin stopped them, asking: "You want me to show you again, you guys?" He was back at his tricks.

The two policemen looked over at each other. The small one was the first to give in.

"Show us," he asked.

"Same agreement as before, not a word to anyone," Sidorkin reminded them, just to be on the safe side.

"Not a word," growled the tall one.

"What am I going to do with you," sighed Sidorkin. "Look." He lifted up his right pants leg and there was the empty bottle balanced on his shoe.

24

Shilov, Deryushev, and the Writer were sitting in my office when I returned.

"Shilov," I asked, "are the carpenters working?"

"Yes, they're working," said Shilov. "But what's the point of it? They won't make it. There's only half an hour left."

"It's all right," I said. "Whatever they get done is what they get done. Deryushev, did you reweld the railing?"

"No."

"Why not?"

"Simple." Deryushev shrugged his thick shoulders apathetically. "The oxygen cylinder has to be hoisted up to the fourth floor, and none of the cranes are working."

"You mean three lugs like you couldn't lift one cylinder?" I asked, perfectly calmly but feeling I could explode any minute.

"What do you mean, lift it. That thing weighs over two hundred pounds," said Deryushev.

"Did you know that when the Egyptians were building the pyramid to Cheops they used to lift blocks weighing two and a half tons a hundred and forty-seven meters?"

"Without cranes?" asked the writer skeptically.

"Without cranes."

"Without cranes, I doubt it." Shilov shook his head.

Of course I could have stamped my feet and shouted at them, but you couldn't get through to them that way.

"Come on, let's go," I said and walked out of the office first.

The cylinders were lying in the mud near the entrance. I upended the cylinder, then picked up a piece of wood from the ground and used it to scrape off some of the mud. Then I hefted the cylinder up on my shoulder. Shilov, the Writer, and Deryushev played the role of spectators. After the first ten steps I realized that I'd bitten off more than I could chew. Five years ago I could have carried a cylinder like that three times as far, but now it was too much for me. I staggered. On the landing between the second and third floors I stumbled and almost fell, but I leaned the cylinder against the radiator just in time.

Shilov ran over. "Evgeny Ivanich, let us help."

"It's all right," I said. "I can manage."

Had I really grown so weak that I couldn't do anything any more? I started walking again. I still had enough strength to set the cylinder carefully down on the floor.

"Well, now do you see how Cheop's pyramid was built?" I said.

"You're as good as a crane, Evgeny Ivanich," joked the Writer respectfully.

I didn't answer him. I told Deryushev to reweld the railing immediately and Shilov to close up my office and bring the key over to the main office. Then I went home. I wasn't feeling well at all.

Back in my room I undressed, washed up, and made myself some tea. Mashenka came in to visit and we had tea together. I poured hers into a saucer for her. Sitting on my lap, she blew on the tea for a long time to make it cool enough to drink. Then I started to feel sick again. I took Mashenka off my lap and started for my bed. The bed seemed too far away and I dropped to the floor. Mashenka began laughing, thinking I was playing. The floor started swaying beneath me and so did the walls. Suddenly I felt as if I was flying upside down, which is how they say weightlessness feels at first.

25

Ice and snow struck after the holiday. Everything was white—white snow, white sheets, white hospital gowns.

I was in one of the best hospitals in the city. It was warm and cozy, light and airy. At first the smell of medicine bothered me, but gradually I grew used to it.

There were twelve beds in our ward. The patients changed all the time. When someone was about to die, the head nurse, whom we called Auntie Nyura, would set out clean linen beside his bed ahead of time. Hospital beds were at a premium.

Everyone knew that fresh sheets placed by someone's bed meant that he wasn't long for this world. Auntie Nyura claimed that she had not been wrong yet.

On the whole she was a friendly, helpful old woman. She spent all the twelve hours of her shift on her feet, going from bed to bed, straightening one patient's blanket, bringing a bedpan to another, performing one service or another. I always greeted her with the same question: would she be setting out fresh linen by my bed soon? The old woman would laugh softly, glad to have such a jolly patient.

A hospital is a good place to reflect on things. You can look back on your past and evaluate it. You can think about the present and the future.

Mine had not been the happiest life, nor the unhappiest either. Lots of people had it worse than me. Maybe in other circumstances I might have become . . . But just what could I have become? And in what other circumstances? Yes, of course, if I hadn't gone to the front and I'd graduated from the institute on schedule, if I'd taken an active part in meetings, joined the party, never stood up for anyone, didn't care about my work, rushed to obey the orders of any high-ranking idiot, and climbed over people on my way up . . . But then I wouldn't have been myself. Was there anything worth destroying yourself for? I always knew there wasn't. I had wavered only once in my life, but then I had stood my ground, and I have no regrets.

But sometimes the thought crosses my mind that I've somehow messed up, that I've left the most important thing undone, but for the life of me, I can't remember just what that thing is. That terrifies me. I'm only forty-two. That's not all that old. I could still live quite a long time and do that most important thing which I cannot still quite remember.

If I die tomorrow, no trace of me will remain. I'll be buried at my union's expense, and Ermoshin, or someone else just as glib, will spout lies at my graveside, saying that my memory will live forever in the hearts of men. And the other senior supervisors, the only portion of humanity who had any idea of who I was, will soon forget me, and if by chance I did come into their mind, it would be some foolish thing like my bending the crowbar around my neck.

Klava visited me every day between six and seven. Making use of her connections, she even came when the hospital was under quarantine and closed to visitors.

She'd sit beside my bed and we would spend time talking about nothing at all, our life in Pechora, how we'd met. She'd ask me all sorts of questions and I'd answer them, and strange as it may seem, they didn't irritate me at all.

Once she said that as soon as I was better she was going into the hospital herself.

"What for?" I asked.

She blushed suddenly and said: "You know what for."

I was surprised that she blushed. She was no girl, after all, and we'd known each other for years. But still, somehow I liked it that she blushed.

"You're not going anywhere," I said to her. "Especially if I get better. Let everything stay just the way it is. We'll have the child and we'll never argue. I just need to feel a little better, that's all."

"Everything will be fine," said Klava. "I spoke with your doctor and she assured me you'd be on your feet in a week."

"She assured you, how can she assure you of anything when the rupture isn't healing?"

"By the way, I keep meaning to have a talk with her— maybe she'll allow me to take care of you."

"No, no, no," I said, alarmed. "That's all I need is you changing my bedpan."

"It wouldn't be so terrible." She smiled.

Of course I couldn't let her do that, though I knew it would have made her happy. Somehow I couldn't imagine Rosa in that role. Maybe that's what real love is, changing someone's bedpan.

Sidorkin visited me once. He was as skinny as ever, though for some reason I thought everything would have changed in all this time. Sidorkin was wearing a white hospital gown and his usual muddy boots. Amazing, where did he find mud in weather like this. Auntie Nyura gave his boots a look of reproach but said nothing.

Sidorkin sat in a chair by my bed and put a bag of tangerines on my night table. "So they've got you in bed."

"As you see."

"So what happened to you, you collapsed?" said Sidorkin. "Was it nerves or what?"

"No," I said. "I just lifted too much. What's new over our way?"

"I've got scads of news," said Sidorkin. "But look, I brought you a present."

He pulled a ragged newspaper from his pocket, unfolded it, and handed it to me. There was a column called "Heroes of the Seven-Year Plan" and that day's article was headed "Principles." This is how it began:

> *Everyone in Zhilstroi knows Senior Construction Supervisor Samokhin. This tall, broad-shouldered man with the manly face and friendly eyes enjoys the respect of the entire collective. The workers fondly refer to him as "our Samokhin."*

At least I hadn't been wrong about Gusev . . .

1962

A DISTANCE OF HALF A KILOMETER

It's half a kilometer from the village of Klimashovka to the cemetery. To cover such a distance on foot, the average person needs no more than seven minutes.

On Sunday a small event occurred—Ochkin died. Filippovna stood near the house of the deceased and, her arms spread wide in surprise, said: "I saw him just yesterday. I was on my way to Lavrusenkova's to get my sifter back . . . It's such a good sifter, too, except it leaks a little on one side. Lavrusenkova's had it a good long time, too. She keeps saying she'll bring it back the next day, but she never does. And I need my sifter, what can I make without it. So I'm going along the path when I see Ochkin coming toward me. Sober and in a pretty good mood. He asks me where I'm going and I tell him I'm going to Lavrusenkova's to get my sifter back. Then he says, So go. And now just look, he's dead."

2

Afanasy Ochkin had been in perfect health that morning. He'd gotten up, dressed, washed, and while his wife, Katya, was making breakfast, he'd gone off to the village store to buy salt. The village store only had rock salt, and so, after passing the time of day with the salesgirl, Ochkin had walked the length of the village to the other store.

This store, too, was out of table salt, though they did have in stock some vermouth in large dusty bottles. Ochkin gave the salesgirl, Shura, all his money and she in turn poured him a glass of vermouth, not a full glass, however, since he was two kopecks short. Ochkin chatted with her a bit, then he poured two teaspoons of damp rock salt from a beer mug on the counter into a paper cone. He was just on the verge of going back home when he spied two of his friends, Nikolai Merzlikin, the carpenter, and Timofei Konkov, the bookkeeper, who had come to the store for a drink. Ochkin knew his friends wouldn't treat him, but just on the off-chance, he began studying the tin cans displayed on the counter.

He was patiently examining the cans while Nikolai and Timofei were buying wine and a bite to go with it. They selected a bottle of vermouth, sprats in tomato sauce, and a hundred grams of soybean candy. Then they left the store, and having spread out a newspaper on the grass, they sat down in the cool shade of a tree. Afanasy watched them through the window. He waited until they had broken open the vermouth and the sprats and only then did he walk over to them.

"Enjoy yourselves," he said politely, sitting down beside them.

His friends looked over at him with eyes narrowed in hostility and began drinking, smacking their lips silently. Timofei began fishing in the can with his knife for a sprat. Nikolai spat.

"Worse than water," said Ochkin sympathetically. "You won't find any vodka now. The wife went over to Makinka the day before yesterday, nothing there either. Looks like they're clamping down on guys like us."

Ochkin picked up the bottle with what was left of the wine, turning it back and forth in his hands. "Look, there's not enough left there for two," he said, looking hopefully over at Nikolai.

"What's it to you," said Nikolai crudely, grabbing the bottle back. "When are you going to pay me back the thirty kopecks?"

Besides his knowledge of carpentry, Nikolai also knew how to cut hair and from time to time would pick up a little side money at home, since there was no barbershop in the village. Two days before, he had cut Ochkin's hair on credit.

"You see, next week Katya'll bring the sour cream to town, I'll pay you back then," promised Ochkin, sadly observing Nikolai dividing the wine evenly into their two glasses. "All right then," said Ochkin, starting reluctantly to his feet. "I've got to give the wife a hand around the house. Goodbye."

No one made any effort to detain him. On the way home he ran into Filippovna and she was the last person to see him alive.

3

Back at the house, Ochkin quarreled with Katya over the money he'd wasted on wine, which put his nerves on edge. It put her out of sorts as well. She poured him some soup and then went out to her vegetable garden to finish digging up the potatoes.

When Katya came back she saw her husband sitting at the table, his face in his plate, his red hair drenched in pea soup.

After examining the corpse, Nonna, the paramedic, ordered the funeral to be delayed, then left to phone the city for a doctor to come establish the cause of death.

Meanwhile, the crowd around Ochkin's house kept

growing larger. All sorts of assumptions and conjectures were being voiced. Filippovna, for example, said that Ochkin must have been poisoned; otherwise, why would he have died just like that.

"She'll go on and on," Lavrusenkova, who had just walked up, snapped sullenly. "No matter what happens, us women are going to be wagging our tongues. Now me, I came an inch from dying last year, remember?"

"No, I don't," said Filippovna.

"Well, I do. And how'd all that happen? I was in the city selling milk. I'm standing behind my counter and up comes this woman. 'How much's your milk?' 'Same as everybody's,' I say. 'Three roubles.' 'That's awful high,' she says. 'What do you mean, high. Listen, you look after the cow, clean up after her, and lay in hay for the winter, then maybe you'd give away the milk for nothing.' Just then she kind of takes a quick look at me. 'Aren't you Marya Lavrusenkova?' 'That's me,' I say. 'And you don't remember me? Last year I spent a whole month in Klima-shovka. It's been quite a while since we've seen each other.' 'Quite a while,' I say. Meanwhile, I'm thinking to myself, 'And I wouldn't be seeing you now if you hadn't walked up to me.' Then she begins to flatter me: 'Look how full and sleek you are, your cheeks are as pink as milk and blood.' And she keeps on staring at me with those horrid little eyes of hers. Then I says to myself: 'Saints alive, she's putting the evil eye on me!' Just then I feel my heart sink. I grabbed my milk cans. I didn't care that I'd paid for my spot. I just ran to the bus. And I barely made it home. After that I was in bed a whole week. Thank God, some good people brought in my mother from Mostov. She pulled me through it with spells and cold water. That's how it goes sometimes," concluded

Lavrusenkova, looking condescendingly over at Filippovna.

Then she cocked her head and listened intently. From
the Ochkin hut the widow's wailing could now be heard.

"Now she's wailing," said Lavrusenkova sternly but ap-
provingly, "really wailing. Oh, mother, I remember when
her brother, that'd be my uncle, was killed in the crash,
how she grieved and cried. Quiet-like, but with such pain
it broke your heart. All right, then," she said, after a
moment's silence, "I'll go and ask Katya, maybe I can
lend a hand in there."

4

The sun had reached its zenith, all shadows had fled,
Nikolai and Timofei were still sitting under the tree
arguing about how many columns there were on the Bolshoi Theater. It was an old argument of theirs. They'd
both been in Moscow at different times, and ever since,
they'd been unable to resolve this problem. They'd even
bet a bottle of vodka on it. And not because they had
nothing else to do with their time. It's just that they both
loved a good quarrel and there was nobody around who
could give them a definite answer. The rest of the villagers
had either never been to Moscow or, if they had, had not
bothered to count the columns.

At one point Timofei had written a letter to Soviet
Radio in care of the editorial staff of the program "We
Answer Your Questions," but they didn't answer his question. It remained unanswered. Now, sitting near the store,
working on their fourth bottle of vermouth, the two
friends were trying to resolve the matter by means of
indirect proofs.

"So, you say six?" Nikolai asked again.

"Six," answered Timofei confidently.

"You're so dumb, Timosha," sighed Nikolai sympathetically. "Use your head—how can there be six when even our own House of Culture has six. Every district's got its House of Culture, but there's only one Bolshoi Theater in the whole Soviet Union."

It was a convincing argument. While Timofei was thinking up an even more convincing argument, Marya Lavrusenkova walked up, took one look at them, and shook her head in reproach.

"Bums, that's the only word for you. Bums. They probably haven't even dug up their potatoes yet and they're sitting here from morning on, swilling vodka. What you should be doing is making a coffin for the deceased," she said to Nikolai.

"Who died now?" said Nikolai, puzzled, furrowing his thick brows.

"Who? Afanasy Ochkin, God rest his soul."

"Ochkin? Oh, no," said Nikolai in surprise.

"You just found out?" Now it was Lavrusenkova's turn to be surprised.

"But he was sitting right here just a little while ago. He promised to bring me the thirty kopecks he owed me for the haircut. Tell her, Timosha."

"Six," growled Timofei, who had been thinking about the columns all the while and had still not come up with any convincing argument.

5

Just before nightfall, an ambulance arrived from the city. The corpse was placed in the rear of the vehicle, to be taken for an autopsy. The driver took an old battered pail from the cab of the ambulance and went off to the well to get water for his radiator. While waiting for him, the doctor, a young woman, got into the cab and began leafing through a book. The book clearly had her attention, for she kept frowning and smiling as she read. Nikolai was watching her curiously through the half-open door of the cab. Then his attention was caught by the traveling bag she held on her knees. It was a beautiful yellow traveling bag with metal buckles. Nikolai's wife's birthday was coming soon and he thought it wouldn't be a bad idea to give her a beautiful bag like that. But he had no idea where he could get hold of one and decided to ask the young woman.

"I don't know," she answered, without looking up from her book. "I bought it in Moscow."

"In Moscow?" Nikolai asked respectfully. "You're not by any chance from Moscow yourself?"

"I am."

"Go on," said Nikolai in surprise, but then, having examined her critically, decided to put a finer point on the matter. "From Moscow itself or the surrounding area?"

"From Moscow itself," she said and smiled. She was obviously somewhat proud of originating from Moscow.

"Then I've got a question for you," said Nikolai decisively. "A friend of mine from the village and me are having an argument. About the columns on the Bolshoi Theater. I tell him there's eight, he tells me six. Like they say, you can spit in his face, he'll call it God's dew. And there's nobody around here who can tell us. The people around here, they don't know anything. I'm not going to waste any time bragging, I'm not so bright myself, but at least I can count. I'm the carpenter here. Everybody knows me. Ask any kid, Where does Nikolai the carpenter live?, and he'll show you, no problem. That's my house over there with the iron roof. Put it on myself last year. There wasn't any iron to be found. Had to buy some oil drums . . . I rolled 'em out flat, and just look how nice it came out. No worse than anybody else's, I guess. Next time you're here, drop by for some tea, we can chat. My wife's from the city, used to be a waitress in a restaurant. I brought her here from the city. There's no restaurants here, of course, so her specialty's going to waste. But I don't make her work all that much anyway. I make a good living. Someone needs a new floor, someone needs a door hung, they come right to me. The director just told me to put new window frames on in the office. Sure, always glad to oblige. That's why we're doing so well. My daughter Verunka's started the fourth grade. But that one," said Nikolai, pointing at the rear of the vehicle where Ochkin lay, "didn't have any kids. After all, you've got to feed your children. How could he? He didn't like working. He was always trying to get to heaven on somebody else's back . . ."

Having started talking, Nikolai could not stop. Listening closely to his own voice, he noticed with pleasure how well it was all coming out. He could have gone on talking like that for the remainder of the evening, but he was interrupted by the driver, who, after pouring water in the radiator, hopped in the cab next to the doctor and switched on the ignition.

"Leaving already?" said Nikolai, coming to a sudden stop. "Have a good trip. So it's eight?"

"Eight what?"

"Columns on the Bolshoi Theater," Nikolai patiently reminded her.

"I think it's eight," she said. "But maybe it's six. You know what, I'll try to clear it up for you when I get back home, and the next time through, I'll give you a definite answer. All right?"

"All right," Nikolai agreed dolefully, not believing her. After watching the ambulance drive off, Nikolai turned to Filippovna and said: "And she says she's from Moscow."

6

A better carpenter than Nikolai was not to be found in Klimashovka, not in Mosty, or even in Dolgov. Perhaps there was not a better carpenter in the entire province, though such a statement could not be made with total certainty.

In any case, it was no accident that last year, when the District House of Culture needed its trimmings done, it was Nikolai and no one else who was called upon. He laid the patterned parquet floor and inlaid the walls in the dance hall with small pieces of oak and beech—to make a long story short, the things he made were beyond the capacity of most cabinetmakers.

The architect who oversaw the construction said that, were Nikolai given some mahogany to work with, he could create something truly extraordinary.

But mahogany did not grow in Klimashovka or the surrounding area, and for that reason, when Nikolai returned home from the district center, he kept on doing what he'd done before—he chopped up old huts, laid floors, and made cradles for newborn babies. And, when necessary, he made coffins as well—who else was there to do it?

On the second day after Ochkin's death, Nikolai rose at dawn and went outside into a dense, white fog. The fog was so thick that only the unwhitewashed half of the hut next door was visible. And of that part only the window could be seen, not so much a window as a yellow blur of electric light dissolving in fog. Minute drops had congealed on the shed's iron bolt and rusty lock. "The A-bomb's causing these fogs," thought Nikolai, removing the lock, which he never used and which he hung there just for show. He went into the shed and, lighting his way with matches, dragged four flooring boards from the corner out to the middle of the shed, measured them with a collapsible wooden yardstick, and, using a square and a red pencil, drew lines sharp enough to be seen in that dim light. Then he had a smoke and before it was still quite light he began honing his tools on an oil stone, thick side first, then thin. When it was light, he trimmed off the ends of the planks with his ax and set to work.

As he worked Nikolai thought how strange life was. Only yesterday Ochkin had been sitting beside him near the store, hoping Nikolai would treat him to a glass, and today Nikolai was making Ochkin's coffin. Three days ago Nikolai had cut Ochkin's hair, cutting the sides short and leaving the top long as he'd requested. And although Ochkin had died without paying him the thirty kopecks for the haircut, and though Nikolai had always treated him with scorn, he now felt an indefinable sense of guilt toward him, of the sort the living often feel toward the dead. He felt guilty both because he had not given the man wine before his death and because he had demanded those thirty kopecks from him. Not the kind of money to hound a man about.

Nikolai also felt guilty toward the dead man because he had once made a laughingstock of him; for a quarter liter of vodka he had made Ochkin give him a ride through the whole village in a wheelbarrow. Everybody came out of his house and laughed till he fell down, as

Nikolai sat calmly in the wheelbarrow and looked back at everyone without the slightest expression on his face.

Recalling all this, Nikolai decided to redeem his guilt toward Afanasy by making him a coffin unlike anything he had made anyone before.

Securing the boards on his workbench, he planed their edges, first with a regular plane and then again with a double-bladed plane. He did this so well that the boards fitted together with no gaps between them at all.

Nikolai stopped for breakfast, made a quick trip to the office, where he got leave for that Sunday for having worked the one two weeks before, then worked until two o'clock without even stopping for a smoke.

At two o'clock his wife, Natasha, walked into the barn and called him for lunch.

"There's time," said Nikolai, pulling a crumpled pack of Surf cigarettes from his pocket. "You'd be better off taking a look at what I made." He nodded casually at the finished coffin.

"What's there to look at?" objected Natasha. "A coffin's a coffin. A box."

"That's nice, a box." Nikolai was offended. "I'll never understand you, Natashka. You've been living with a carpenter, how long, fifteen years, and you don't show any interest in his work. Just maybe this box ('Quite a thing to call it,' he thought to himself.) has dovetailed corners. But none of that means anything to you. Dovetailed or regular, glue or paste, it's all the same to you."

Nikolai had one peculiarity. He gave his favorite creations human names and conversed with them. For example, he called the kitchen table Tanya, and the fretted shelf by the washstand Shura, and he started calling the coffin Boris, because it sounded close to "box."

"Don't let it bother you, Boris," he said after his wife had left. "Everybody knows women are fools. She's got no idea that you might just be like the Bolshoi Theater, one of a kind in the whole Soviet Union. All right, doesn't matter. We'll just give you a coat of varnish, even if you are made of pine. You'll be something to look at. That is, if people got eyes to see with."

Then Nikolai set to work on the cross, but without any particular gusto. He cut the two crosspieces, measuring by eye, notched them, then glued them with the glue, which was halfway to turning cold. Just to be on the safe side, he named the cross Kostya, but didn't start any conversations with it.

7

The morning of that same day, Nonna, the paramedic, came to town to find out what Ochkin had died of. She told Katya Ochkin what she'd found out, but Katya could not remember the name of the illness. Nonna wrote it down for her on a piece of paper. The illness was called "Myocardial infarction." This surprised many people. After reading what was written on the paper, Lavrusenkova said straight out: "I never heard anything like it in all my born days. Used to be the old men would say people died of cholera or plague. Last year Vaska, the accordion player, died from angina. But this"—she looked down at the piece of paper—"we never had anything like this before. He didn't live like a regular person and he didn't get a regular person's disease."

The ambulance arrived for a second time in the early afternoon. Two men carried the corpse into the Ochkins' unheated hut and laid it on a table covered with an old oilcloth. The young woman doctor gave Katya some sort of paper to sign and waited impatiently while Katya, sobbing and wiping her eyes, slowly traced out her wriggly signature. Then the doctor took the paper and went back to the ambulance. She had just opened the door and had one foot on the running board when she was stopped by Nikolai, who had just delivered the new, red-lacquered coffin.

"Doctor, the thing I asked you about," he inquired timidly. "You didn't forget?"

"I didn't forget." She began rummaging in her beautiful traveling bag and then pulled out a crinkled postcard, which she handed to Nikolai. "I found it in my album."

Nikolai had no chance to thank her. By the time Nikolai had finished counting the columns, the driver had shifted into gear and the ambulance pulled away, leaving a trail of yellow dust in the air.

Nikolai had been right. There were eight columns. He began to walk, paying no attention to the road, imagining how he would stun Timofei when they met face to face.

"I'll go and see him right now," thought Nikolai. "First, I'll tell him: Go and get half a liter, Timosha. And he'll say: And to what do I owe the honor of running out for half a liter? And I'll say: How many columns on the Bolshoi Theater? And like always he'll say: Six! Then I'll say: Looks like you're no good at counting. Maybe you don't have enough fingers. Then Timofei'll get offended and fly off the handle: Don't you be counting my fingers, he'll say, they were lost at the front. We weren't like some people, we shed our blood. And then I'll say to him: And we didn't defend Tashkent? . . ."

Lost in such musings, Nikolai suddenly collided with Marya Ivanovna, his daughter's teacher. As usual, Marya

Ivanovna began telling him that his daughter Verunka had begun the school year badly again. Verunka does not listen in class, Verunka does not complete her homework.

Nikolai patiently heard the teacher out and then blurted out, apropos of nothing: "Listen, Marya Ivanna, I've just won half a liter from Timofei on a bet."

"A half liter of what?" said the teacher, somewhat taken aback.

"Of what? The usual stuff . . ."

Nikolai wanted to tell her the whole saga of the columns and to show her the postcard, which had unexpectedly decided the argument in his favor, but suddenly noticing the beautiful, white, stitched leather shoes on the teacher's feet, he remembered the present he still hadn't bought his wife.

"Where'd you get them?" Nikolai asked point-blank.

"Get what?" said the teacher, quite startled.

"The shoes, the shoes," said Nikolai impatiently.

"Oh, the shoes." The teacher sighed with relief. "My brother sent them to me from Moscow."

"That does it!" said Nikolai in anger. "Bags from Moscow, shoes from Moscow, brothers from Moscow . . ."

"What's the matter?"

"Nothing's the matter."

Nikolai waved his hand in dismissal and went on his way. However, after the meeting with the teacher his thoughts took an entirely different direction. He was now thinking that he ought to invite all his neighbors to his wife's birthday, his work brigade too, and it wouldn't be a bad idea to have one of the bosses. Andriolli, the director, would probably refuse, but he had to be invited anyway. Work super Pozdniakov, too. And, so it wouldn't be boring, he could invite Timofei; at least there'd be somebody to talk to and argue about things with.

Nikolai came to a halt. What would they argue about if he showed Timofei the postcard today? He gazed in confusion at the postcard and mechanically counted the columns once again.

"Of course, half a liter wouldn't be all that bad either," reflected Nikolai, "especially with a little something nice to eat. And Timofei has some great cucumbers down in his cellar. Must be some bacon fat, too; he slaughtered a suckling pig last week. Except I can buy myself a half liter any time I want to. I'm not poor. Now there'll be nothing to talk about at the party . . ."

Nikolai himself did not notice how he ripped first one corner then another from the postcard . . . And when he did notice, he ripped the card to pieces and threw them all down the toilet as soon as he returned home.

8

Late in the day the sky clouded over. A damp wind sprang up. Katya Ochkin quickly straightened up the house and, as soon as it was dark, climbed up onto her tall bed and got under her quilt. She hadn't made a fire. Now she lay listening to the windowpanes rattling as the wind blew against the side of the house. She heard the first drops of rain spattering against the glass.

"I've got to putty up those windows," thought Katya with some reluctance. "And trim down the door. It's swelled up and won't close."

This was really men's work, but Katya was long used to doing men's work. Her father had built that house in 1939 and left it to his daughter when he was dying. He died in the district hospital after being run over by a tractor while sleeping in a field. Katya became the mistress of the house, where she lived alone. Just before the war started, she brought her husband, Afanasy, to the house to live. She was eighteen at the time, he was nineteen. They were planning a long and happy life together when the war broke out. Afanasy was called up a few days later.

He was working at the cattle yard at the time. That day Afanasy went to work with the idea of lifting the kolkhoz bull and getting a hernia. He lifted the bull but he didn't get the hernia. So Afanasy sharpened his ax and with one carefully calculated blow hacked off his right index finger, making it impossible for him to pull a trigger. At his trial the prosecutor demanded Afanasy be shot as a deserter, but the judges took a milder view and sentenced him to ten years. Ochkin never served those ten years—he was released in 1945 in the general amnesty honoring the Soviet victory. He returned home and that first night as they lay together on the bed he spent hours questioning Katya about the people from their village and she spent hours answering those questions. She told him how rough it had been for everyone during the war, especially for people with children. She told him about the evacuees who came to the village from the Ukraine and Belorussia. There wasn't enough space for them all and they were quartered in people's homes. Two families had stayed with Katya. They were forever quarreling, but Katya grew used to them, and when they were leaving for home, she found it very hard to part with them. Practically all the men had been taken off to the front; many had not returned. Timofei Konkov had lost three fingers in the fighting.

"Sort of like me," grinned Ochkin and then asked Katya about his friend Fyodor Korkin, who'd been called up at the same time he had.

"Probably all covered with medals, huh?" asked Ochkin.

"He didn't come back," said Katya softly.

"Killed at the front?"

"No, he didn't make it to the front. Their train was bombed on the way."

For a long while Afanasy said nothing. Then he recalled: "When they arrested me, Fyodor called me a fool. He was the smart one—now he's six feet under and I'm walking around on top."

Ochkin was in no hurry to start working after the camp and he took a good careful look at everything. Including the ration cards in the state farm's cashbox. He was caught with the ration cards by the night watchman and was taken away on a prison train to rebuild Dneproges. He never did rebuild Dneproges. Returning home after the amnesty of 1953, he told Katya that a smart guy could make out all right even in a labor camp. In the summertime he'd take refuge from the heat in the cool spot at the bottom of a stack of boards and in the winter he'd take an iron barrel, pierce it with lots and lots of holes, and then fill the barrel with firewood and pieces of roofing felt (there was always plenty of both on any construction site) and make himself a "little tropical Tashkent." This Tashkent had one drawback—it didn't throw heat evenly and you had to keep turning your front to it, then your back, but still it was better than chopping wood in the wind or pushing a wheelbarrow that'd ice over in half a minute.

They weren't fed all that well in the camp, but still it was free food and it would have taken some little work to earn that much food on the outside. On top of that, they had their own bathhouse and club, where there were movies or concerts three times a week.

On the whole, to judge by his stories, life in the camps suited him fine. Perhaps it was because it suited him so well that Ochkin smashed the window in the village store and once again departed on a prison train, this time for the great Siberian construction sites.

This spring marked his final return; he had intended to go back to Siberia, but death intervened.

Perhaps Katya was remembering all this as she lay alone in the dark, unheated room. Or perhaps she was not remembering anything at all and was simply lying there listening to the autumn wind begin to howl.

The wind had shifted. Now it was blowing straight at the windows; the room was growing colder and colder. Katya got out of bed, took her old sheepskin work coat down from the nail in the wall, and, unaware of what she was doing, covered her dead husband with her coat.

9

It kept raining off and on. Only toward morning did it stop and clear up. The director of the state farm, Matvei Matveevich Andriolli, was sitting at his desk in his tarpaulin raincoat, busying himself with the sort of things people usually do on rainy days.

Work superintendent Pozdniakov was the first to arrive that day. He brought in for Andriolli's signature the work papers of the temporary construction workers, who now, at the close of the season, were preparing to return home. The director glanced quickly at the papers and remarked that Pozdniakov was paying these migrant workers too generously, but he affixed his signature anyway, since the papers had already been drawn up in strict accordance with current pay scales.

Then Filippovna arrived to report that she was leaving for her native village and asked if the state farm would buy her hut. The director looked over at Pozdniakov, who said he knew the hut and that there was no sense in buying it, since it was already falling apart.

"For firewood maybe," said Pozdniakov.

"For firewood we won't buy it," said Matvei Matveevich. "We've got enough firewood of our own. We couldn't pay much anyway, a hundred roubles at the most."

"Well, as you wish," said Filippovna. "I'll sell it to Nikolai the carpenter, he'll give me a hundred and fifty."

"Where is that carpenter?" Andriolli asked Pozdniakov. "He was supposed to put in the window frames today."

"I gave him the day off," said Pozdniakov. "He's making a coffin for Ochkin."

Somehow Ochkin's death had slipped the director's mind, and he now recalled that he wanted to stop by and see the widow and console her however best he could. He'd known Katya since she was a girl. When she was very young she worked in the vegetable garden and then later as a milkmaid on the farm. She was a very good worker, perhaps the best of the lot. Her photograph had been up on the board of honor for many years. Andriolli knew how to value his best workers and considered it his duty to give them his attention. All the more so since, as a rule, they didn't pester him with useless requests.

Of course he would have dropped by the widow's yesterday, but he didn't know how to offer his consolations. Usually in such cases people say of the deceased that he did such and such and that his memory will last for ages on end.

Andriolli tried to remember what Ochkin had done but he couldn't remember anything good. But just then something came to mind. This year they needed a banner made to help celebrate Milkmaids' Day, and as bad luck would have it, the Komsomol organizer, who usually took care of such things, was out sick. To everyone's surprise, Ochkin volunteered. He spread out a length of linen in the office and worked on it all night, crawling back and forth on his hands and knees. By morning he'd completed the whole slogan and he may even have made a cleaner job of it than the Komsomol organizer would have. He might even have had some talent in that line. But, after that, he started doing nothing again, although they did offer him all kinds of jobs. While the director was trying to remember what else Ochkin had done, the driver, Lekha Prokhorov, popped his head in the door. Seeing Andriolli there, he slowly removed his crumpled cap and walked over to the desk, leaving a trail of damp footprints behind him.

"Here, I've brought my application," he said, taking a sheet of paper folded in quarters from his pocket. "It's for leave without pay."

"What do you need leave for?" asked Andriolli.

"I've got to go to my mother's and mend the roof. She wrote and told me it's leaking. Just for a week, Matvei Matveevich. I'll be back on the job next Monday. On the dot," he assured the director without much hope.

But, to Lekha's surprise, the director agreed readily. "All right then, go," he said. "But first drop in on Katya Ochkin and take Ochkin's body over to the cemetery."

"In two shakes! Quick as the wind!" In high spirits, Lekha started running for the door.

"Hold it." Andriolli stopped him. "Don't make a fool of yourself. Maybe that's the way you drive a load of wheat, and that'd be overdoing it, too. This is a dead person," he said significantly.

"There's corpses and there's corpses," objected Lekha.

"The dead are all the same," insisted Andriolli, although he wasn't sure he was right.

10

The rain had started again. It didn't let up but it grew no worse either and just kept rustling monotonously against windowpanes, roofs of straw, and balding tree-tops. Having covered themselves with whatever was closest at hand, a crowd of women, each holding a purse, had formed near the village store: there had just been a delivery of dishes.

Lekha Prokhorov climbed in behind the wheel of his jeep and shifted into gear. The jeep started skidding. He would have to use front-wheel drive.

One way or the other, the jeep made it to the Ochkin house. Lekha came to a stop directly in front of the porch and went in. Quite a few people were already there. The widow, touching a clean handkerchief to her dry eye, was standing at the head of the coffin.

Lekha called her aside. "Auntie Katya," he said in a respectful whisper, "let's get moving. It's time to take him. The road'll be so bad even four-wheel drive won't be enough."

"You'll manage," the widow answered darkly and went back to her place.

Upset by this delay, Lekha went back outside and stood against the shed near the porch. The road didn't have anything to do with it. His jeep had taken worse than that. It was just that Lekha had to drive three kilometers to the station to catch the five o'clock train and it was already around four. Glancing impatiently at his watch, he stood against the shed, smoking and growing angrier by the minute at the people who kept arriving at the house of the deceased.

"So many people in such a ridiculous little village, no

end to them," he thought with increasing irritation. "What's drawing them all here, is the corpse smeared with honey or something?"

"Where're you going?" he said to a fat old woman mounting the porch. "Never seen a dead man before? Just you wait, they'll be coming to look at you soon enough."

The old woman did not reply. Her lips pursed, her feelings hurt, she went inside. Lekha went in after her.

In the main room, people were saying that the late Ochkin had never done anyone any harm. And if he had, it hadn't been much. True, he'd done even less good. That said, they began speaking of their own affairs in a half whisper.

Filippovna was telling Lavrusenkova that her daughter, who lived in the Ukraine, had had a baby and now she had to go take care of her grandson. Lekha apologized to the fat old woman, explaining that he hadn't meant to offend her and had only spoken that way because he was in a hurry. Timofei, who had a reputation in the village as a bookman, was telling Chekhov's story "Kashtanka" to Nikolai, who liked the story and said: "So, Chekhov was a good writer, right?"

"It's a matter of taste," said Timofei. "Lev Nikolaevich Tolstoy didn't like him."

"How come he had that opinion of him?"

"Who knows with that one. 'You write poorly,' he says. 'Shakespeare wrote badly,' he says. 'And you write even worse than him.' Shakespeare was an English writer."

"Yeah, and so, was he a bad writer?"

"Not so much bad as illiterate. They fixed him up in Russian, but in his own language he was definitely on the weak side . . ."

Everyone stood and went to accompany the coffin.

The rain had stopped. The sky was no longer entirely clouded over; the light could now be seen shining through.

Lekha flung open the tailgate and the men pushed the open coffin into the back of the jeep. Someone had placed a painted stool by the head of the coffin. Katya made herself comfortable on the stool and began wailing, but this time without any anguish, just for decency's sake.

Lekha got behind the wheel and looked at his watch. Five o'clock. He'd be on the train now. And in three hours he'd have been home sitting at the table and his mother would be fussing over him, serving him good little things to eat. He'd better go see the director and tell him not to count today as a day off. Lavrusenkova tapped on the window. Lekha understood the signal and let the jeep start moving forward slowly.

Nikolai and Timofei walked ahead of the jeep. They were carrying the top of the coffin. Nikolai was holding the back end and kept swinging the coffin top to the left or the right, depending on where the people were walking closest. He did this so they could see some real handiwork; some of them might even want to study with him. His sole regret was that his work, which should really have been placed on public view in a museum, was instead going to be buried in the ground; worms and fungus would eat through it and in a year all that'd be left of his work would be some moldering boards, and in a few more years, even that would be gone.

It began to drizzle again as they drove up to the cemetery and took the coffin from the jeep. And so Nikolai hurried putting the top on and nailed it shut. The coffin was lowered on two ropes into the grave and was soon covered by the soaking wet clay, which kept sticking to the shovels. Up above, Nikolai drove the cross into the ground.

Andriolli, who had just walked up to the graveside, noticed streaks of glue on the cross and thought he better tell Nikolai to use casein glue on the exterior window frames, since it resisted dampness better.

Andriolli was also thinking that the cross made Ochkin the equal of everyone who lay there beside him. But then he realized that wasn't right. After all, the memory of a person was not determined by where he lay but by what he'd done in life. Those there with Ochkin had all had different lives, had all worked differently, and the distance between the day of their birth and the day they were buried was different in every case. Ochkin, born half a kilometer from his own grave, had traveled and seen a lot, but all the distance he had covered was this half kilometer, which an average person could walk in seven minutes.

1961

FROM AN EXCHANGE OF LETTERS

One day a letter was delivered to our regiment. Beneath the name of the town and our unit number the envelope had been marked: "First Recipient." This turned out to be Kazik Ivanov, the clerk and postmaster, but he had no use for the letter and passed it on to the airfield quartermaster, Junior Sergeant Ivan Altinnik, who had a reputation for liking pen pals.

The letter was brief. A certain Ludmilla Sirova, a medic from Kirzavod Station, proposed to her unknown addressee that they begin a "correspondence with the aim of a subsequent personal acquaintance." Besides the letter, the envelope also contained a three-by-four photograph of Ludmilla, with a place for postage on the reverse side. The photograph was old, hard to make out, but Altinnik's experienced eye discerned a girl of twenty or twenty-two with braids wound neatly around her head.

Altinnik placed the letter in the trunk under his bed, where he safeguarded innumerable letters from all his other pen pals (around one hundred), and hid the photo in his album, having first written in tiny letters on the reverse side: Sirova, Ludmilla. Kirzavod Station. Medic.

Year of birth—? Then, from that same album, he took out a nine-by-twelve photograph of himself wearing a diagonally cut tunic and a first-class specialist's badge (someone else's); the pose he had struck made it seem that the camera had caught him composing poetry or reflecting on the mysteries of the universe.

He laid the photograph of himself on his night table and set to work on a reply. It must be said that Altinnik was not overly generous with his portraits. At times, for a joke, he would send a photo torn from the bulletin board, where pictures of the top students in political and military science were posted. But he did not feel like playing any tricks on Ludmilla Sirova—she had made a good impression on him. Besides, he still had a good supply of photos on hand.

2

Letter writing was Altinnik's number-two or perhaps even his number-one profession. In any case, he gave more time to writing letters than to his basic military duties. No matter where he found himself—in the quartermaster's, in the barracks, or on detail—as soon as there was a free moment he'd settle himself by a table or a barrel of hydromix or on the wing of a plane, whatever was handiest, and begin joining letter to letter, word to word, in his intricate, ornate handwriting, of which he was quite proud. He was also certain that, to a considerable degree, his handwriting was responsible for his many successes (by mail) with women.

He wrote easily, rapidly. One word brought forth another and Altinnik was barely able to get them all down on paper. While writing, he would swing his free hand in the air, utter little cries, sob, shake his head; he would stop rarely, just long enough to rub his numbed hand, catch his breath, or once more to marvel that one man should possess so much talent. His only problem lay in never knowing where and what kind of punctuation he should use. This, however, caused him little confusion; he would scatter punctuation marks haphazardly, trying to use an equal amount of each.

Having begun his letter to Ludmilla Sirova with his usual "Sincere and ardent greetings and heaps of the very best wishes for your young and blossoming life," Altinnik got right down to business, wasting neither time nor ink:

I received your letter, Luda, from our postmaster, Ivanov, Kazimir, who gave it to me and said: Ivan, you've been wanting to correspond with a nice girl for quite some time now and so here I'm giving you a letter and an address, and the reason I'm giving it to you and not to somebody else is because you're our best-educated non-com, even though you didn't finish high school. Then I opened your letter and I really liked you and your photo both as far as the general outlines and the separate parts of your outward appearance go, for example, eyes, nose, cheeks, lips, etc. Unfortunately you sent a small photo which made it hard to inspect your face closely, so, if you have the time and opportunity, send a larger one, I am sending you one of me. If you don't want to send a full-length picture then send one at least half, as far as good figures go, Luda, that's not what I'm looking for, because beauty and figure are qualities of a person

*that can be lost later in life, what I'm looking for is
intelligence and character ...*

Altinnik went on to describe his life in detail and from
his description it emerged that the author of the letter
was an orphan, had been raised in a Children's Home
among strangers, and from his youth on had grown ac-
customed to deprivations, humiliation, and hard physical
labor.

All this flowed freely and easily from his pen, although
it did not bear the slightest resemblance to the actual
facts of his life, which had been no worse than most.
Altinnik had been raised in an average worker's family.
During the war his father had not even been at the front,
because he suffered from bronchial asthma. His father had
died the previous year, but his mother was alive and well;
she worked at a factory, casting from molds, but she intended to retire that autumn at age forty-five because of
the unhealthy nature of her work.

But it would not have been quite fair to say that Altinnik was lying. He was simply giving his hand free rein,
knowing that his hand would not let him down. The
author of the letter was so shaken by the full range of
his unhappy, joyless childhood spread across the page
before him that his pity for himself reached the point of
tears and he sincerely wished "that, after so much suffer-
ing, Luda, and enduring all possible sorts of wrong from
bad people who are still to be met, Luda, even in our
country, to find an independent, industrious girl with a
cheerful character, not with the intention of playing
tricks on her or laughing at her but with quite another
aim in mind: either marriage or matrimony after an acquaintance of short duration."

It is difficult to say what Ludmilla Sirova made of this

letter but she wasted no time; her answer arrived in the time it takes for a letter to travel from where Altinnik's unit was billeted to Kirzavod Station and back.

Their correspondence had begun.

Whenever Altinnik would receive a letter from his new acquaintance he would read it closely and would under-line various phrases in red pencil—for example, that Luda had her own home, garden, and cow and that she (Lud-milla, not the cow) loved to sing and dance, enjoyed pleasant company, and was herself capable of laughing and joking when others were, too. Altinnik made use of his red pencil in his correspondence with other women as well. He copied out the information on separate cards and then would spread them all out before him and com-pare them—not out of any self-interest, but because he liked order in everything. He did not seriously count on ever meeting any of his pen pals and carried on these correspondences just to while away the time, without any particular aim in mind.

He probably would never have met Ludmilla Sirova if suddenly, late in autumn, he had not been summoned by the squadron commander, Major Zadachin. We will be-come better acquainted with Major Zadachin later on. For the time being, I shall say only that the major ordered Altinnik to depart at once on an assignment concerning the acquisition of certain equipment for the airfield.

Strange as it may seem, Kirzavod Station was on the very route Altinnik had to travel. But it really wasn't all that strange either, because without exception our hero's pen pals lived near railway lines, highways, or country roads, and who could tell what any of these other roads might have held in store for him.

But it was this one that came his way.

Another of his pen pals, Natashka, lived along the

same route, two stations down from Kirzavod. Just to play it safe, Altinnik sent both women telegrams.

3

He had to change trains in Moscow. Altinnik had never been to the capital before, though he had long hoped to go, and now he definitely planned to visit Lenin's tomb, and the Tretyakov Gallery, time permitting. He did not make it to the gallery but instead made a quick trip to the Agricultural Exhibition and even had his picture taken with the Golden Sheaf fountain in the background.

The weather was terrible—wind and drizzle. Altinnik bustled from one end of the city to the other, taking trolley buses and the metro. By the end of the day he had grown completely used to escalators and he no longer jumped off with bulging eyes, afraid of being drawn into the slit, but instead he stepped off it with ease, quite casually, like a regular Muscovite.

4

Altinnik settled in an upper berth because, according to his travel warrant, a soldier on assignment, even if he was traveling all the way to Vladivostok, is not allowed a reserved seat. At least the conductor turned out to be a decent person and allowed him to take one of the extra mattresses, which had neither sheet nor pillow. Altinnik had no need of a pillow, for he had a soft suitcase of Polish manufacture. In a good trade Altinnik had swapped a pair of old topless box calf boots to Sergeant Efremovsky for the suitcase. (Incidentally, this sergeant was nicknamed de Gaulle because of his height and a certain resemblance to the general.)

Although the conductor had promised to wake him, Altinnik could not rely on him and kept tossing and turning in his upper berth, afraid to oversleep; he kept lighting matches to check his watch and the fat old woman with the child sleeping in the berth beneath his thought he was smoking and kept sighing dramatically, "Och!"

Altinnik mimicked her, himself saying: "Och!"

He wasn't smoking. He was thinking. Considering his forthcoming meeting. It would be good if Ludmilla came to meet him and he recognized her right away. But what if there were lots of people there and he couldn't find her in the crowd, or what if she didn't come at all and he'd gotten off the train and had to wait until the next one came along? But suppose she did come and they recognized each other right off, how should he greet her? Shake her hand or take her in his arms? Altinnik did not know.

After taps in the barracks, when the conversation turned to women, Altinnik would always hold forth like the finest connoisseur on the subject. None of his listeners had the slightest doubt that, no matter what anyone else said, it was Altinnik who knew all there was to know about women. What they had and where it was and what you should do with them. But, if the truth be told, thus far Altinnik's relations with women had been confined to the mail.

Before joining the army he had known one girl, who lived in the neighboring courtyard. She was studying gymnastics and wore glasses, both of which endeared her to Altinnik. He went to the movies with her twice and had stood four times with her in her doorway. They talked about all sorts of trivial things while he kept thinking how to approach her. Finally one day he plucked up his courage and said: "You know, Galka, there's something I want to ask you."

"What?"

"You won't get sore?"

"What at?"

"No, tell me you won't get sore."

"But I don't know what you're going to ask," she parried.

"Well, anyhow, I want to ask you, well, this . . . uh." He inhaled a chestful of air and blurted out: "Is it all right if I kiss you?"

She moved away into the corner and asked, frightened: "But what for?"

He didn't know what for. He thought that was what you were supposed to do.

Sometime later Galka married an ex-sailor and he apparently explained everything to her, for, precisely nine months later, Altinnik's mother wrote him (he was already in the army) that Galka had given birth to a daughter.

Recalling Galka and pondering his forthcoming meeting with Ludmilla was all too much for Altinnik and he fell asleep. The conductor did not fail him, but woke him up, as promised, at quarter past one. Altinnik climbed down, shook his head to wake up fully, dragged down his suitcase, and walked out to the corridor.

The conductor was sitting on a bench opposite the train crew's sleeping compartment. There was an unlit electric lantern in front of him.

"Well, Pop, will we be getting to that Kirzavod Station soon?" asked Altinnik.

"Another ten minutes or so," said the conductor, yawning.

Altinnik sat down across from the conductor and casually tossed a pack of Kazbek cigarettes he'd bought in Moscow onto the little table.

"Have a smoke, Pop, you'll be kicking off soon enough."

"I'm not a smoker," the conductor refused.

Altinnik pulled out a cigarette and rolled it between his fingers; he didn't feel right smoking in the car but he didn't feel like going out to the platform. He looked out of the window at the flickering whiteness, which surprised him.

"Snow, huh?"

"Snow," confirmed the conductor.

"You see that, it's raining in Moscow but you go three hundred kilometers and it's already snowing. My sergeant says to me, Take your fur cap, but me, like a fool, I take my forage cap. But it's a good thing I took my overcoat, you could die out there, don't you think?"

"And how," agreed the conductor, who'd gotten into the habit of agreeing with the passengers.

Altinnik fell silent for a while, sighing from time to time. He decided to share his doubts with the old man.

"So here I am on my way to that there Kirzavod Station, and whether I'll be met there or not, I don't know. If I was going to see my mother, she'd meet me of course. Any time, day or night. But it's a woman I'm going to, old man. I got to know her through the mail. From the photo she sent me she's not bad-looking, kind of pretty even, but I haven't set eyes on her yet, so there's nothing I can really say. She kept writing—come see me. That's not what I had in mind, of course, but then all of a sudden there's this assignment, some important supplies.

So who gets sent? Me. And here I am. I fired her off a telegram telling her to meet me. But I don't know whether she got it or not. I didn't get any answer. Now there's another question, too—even if she meets me, it'll be the first time she's laying eyes on me and maybe she won't want to sleep with me. Maybe she'll say let's get married, then you can dip your spoon, but I've got no reason for marrying right now. I'm still young. I'm going to go to a technical school when I get out of the army and then maybe even to an institute. I want to get my diploma, so I can frame it and hang it on the wall so everyone can see that Altinnik, that's my last name, Altinnik, is an educated man. I've got another woman living two stations farther down, Natashka. Another pen pal. But that one, to tell you the truth, is a little on the lame side. She wrote me herself: 'Vanya, I ought to warn you right from the start that I have a handicap. As a result of an injury my left leg is two centimeters shorter than my right, but if I wear one slightly higher heel, you can't practically notice.' Anyhow, notice or not, I don't think she'll be finicky, because no matter what kind of heel you put on, a cripple's still a cripple, no getting around that. Of course I don't blame her for it and I don't laugh at it either, because it's the kind of thing that can happen at any minute. Let's say you're standing on the platform, the train starts up, you go for the step and whish! you slip and off go both legs. On the other hand, she should understand her handicap, even though I sympathize. I'm no cripple. Look"—Altinnik got up and took three steps toward the platform and back—"see, no limp. So she should be a little more modest and take what comes or she might not even get that. The problem is that I don't know if I ought to get off here, who knows what kind of trouble this one might make, or should I keep going on down to Natashka's, even though she's lame. What's your opinion, old man?"

"You know better than me," said the conductor. "That kind of stuff hasn't been on my mind for quite a while. I've got a grandson who started school this fall."

"Yes," sympathized Altinnik, "but you still look young. Here's what I've decided—live and have a good time till I'm forty. Then, no waiting around, I'll put a rope around my neck and it's hello, Sergei Esenin."

"Live to forty first." The conductor smiled ironically. "Nobody ever wants to die."

"That I can understand," said Altinnik, afraid he'd hurt the old man's feelings. "This is just how I worked it out for myself. I figure I'll live to forty, forty-five tops, and that's it. After that, just walking around can be hell. Either your back's killing you or the weather's making your rheumatism ache. Ech . . ."

Altinnik waved his hand in annoyance, looked out the window, and grew lost in thought, trying to picture himself as a pitiful, sick old man, but this proved nearly impossible and his thoughts took a different turn; he was again wondering whether Ludmilla would meet him or not. It was late Saturday night going on Sunday.

5

The train arrived at Kirzavod Station right on schedule. The conductor opened the door, and standing on the platform with his suitcase, Altinnik felt the cold, raw air. The wind was howling; raggedy snow was piling up and turning reddish in the station's one and only light. Beneath that light stood the stationmaster in his red service cap and a small snow-spattered figure. "Her" flashed through Altinnik's mind. And indeed the small figure began running alongside the train, her eyes darting from car to car in search of the one she had been waiting for. Altinnik stepped back from the platform, following her with one eye. He was still vacillating.

"What's your advice, old man, get off here or not?" he asked, pinning his last hopes on the conductor.

"Get off!" The conductor waved his hand and stepped aside, clearing the way.

"Whatever happens happens," decided Altinnik. "Stay well, old man, take care of yourself."

He jumped down onto the wet platform.

When they met, Altinnik realized that he had been cruelly deceived: the photograph, which he had so carefully placed in his album, was at least ten years old.

"Hello, Vanya," said Ludmilla, offering him her hand.

"Hello." Setting his suitcase down, Altinnik shifted from foot to foot, in a state of doubt. "Ludmilla?" he asked, just to be on the safe side, hoping it wasn't her but, say, her older sister.

"Uh-huh," she confirmed lightheartedly. "Our clock stopped. And it was too late to go ask anyone the time. So I came an hour early. All right then, let's go." She bent down toward his suitcase as if she were going to carry it for him.

"One second," said Altinnik, taking a firm grip on his suitcase. His mind was racing—should he get back on the train before it was too late?

The stationmaster in the red service cap rang the bell. The train's brakes hissed and it began to move slowly forward without even a single hoot from its whistle. Altinnik was still vacillating. Stay, or take a running leap onto the step?

The last car slid slowly by and the conductor let the

collapsible platform fall shut with a crash. Now there was nothing left to decide.

"All right, let's go," sighed Altinnik and reached down for his suitcase.

6

The wind was blowing; damp snow flew into Altinnik's eyes as he walked off to one side. He held his suitcase in his right hand and with his left pressed the collar of his overcoat over one ear to keep the wind out. Houses and fences loomed darkly on either side. There were no lights, no sounds anywhere, not even a dog barking.

Ludmilla walked silently out in front, her snow-encrusted form disappearing, then bobbing back into Altinnik's sight. They kept turning to the right, to the left, then to the right again. At times it seemed to him that they were going around in circles. At one point he grew terrified; hadn't he heard plenty of stories about a woman leading some trusting dunce to a dark place and there . . . After all, nobody knew there was nothing of value in his suitcase besides a change of underwear and his puttees. If worst came to worst, he could always hurl the suitcase away and take to his heels. But where could you run when you were in unknown territory and it was wet and slippery to boot. And, as bad luck would have it, there wasn't a stick or a stone underfoot.

"Still far to go?" he asked suspiciously.

"No, not far," answered Ludmilla without turning around.

"Boy, you got some weather here," said Altinnik loudly. Things never seem as scary if you talk. "I left your address with my friend, he's supposed to pop by in the morning, I hope you don't mind."

He had just invented the friend on the spot so that she'd realize that if anything happened her address was known.

"Of course not," said Ludmilla.

Her agreement afforded Altinnik some comfort and he did not launch into his second story that, in case anything happened, he, Ivan Altinnik, as a serviceman indispensible to his country, would be the object of a massive search which would turn this lousy town inside out. Then, realizing that they'd been seen by the stationmaster, he regained his calm completely.

They turned to the right one more time and stopped in front of a plank fence.

Ludmilla stuck her hand through the fence and jiggled the latch. The gate squealed open.

"Go on in," said Ludmilla.

"No dog?" asked Altinnik cautiously.

"No," said Ludmilla. "Last year we had one called Little Ace, but my brother shot him with his rifle."

"For what?" asked Altinnik in surprise.

"He bought a new rifle and he wanted to test it out."

"And didn't he feel any pity?"

"Pity for who?" asked Ludmilla.

"For Little Ace."

"But he was just a dog."

Ludmilla spent a good while banging her small fist in its woolen mitten on the door. Then, tramping through a fresh snowdrift, she pushed her way to the window. A curtain fluttered to the side, revealing a face blurred in the darkness.

"Open up, Mama," said Ludmilla softly.

An electric light flashed on inside. Quiet but heavy steps could be heard. The door opened and the large figure of an old woman wearing felt boots and a linen undershirt appeared in the doorway. She was holding an illuminated Chinese lantern in one hand.

"Come in," said Ludmilla and went in first herself, showing him the way. Standing off to one side, the old woman lit the way for them. A yoke and a bucket on the wall glittered dully in the light. Altinnik's nose was struck by the odor of sauerkraut.

Leaving the passageway, Altinnik found himself in a well-heated room lit by a shadeless lamp. He deposited his suitcase by the door, stamped his feet irresolutely, and took a look around.

"Take off your things," suggested Ludmilla, herself setting the example. She unwound her downy kerchief and took off her coat, which had a gray, artificial astrakhan collar. She was wearing a low-cut, dark wool dress. Altinnik looked at her and sighed. Perhaps he had been mistaken back there on the platform. The picture hadn't been ten years old, but even older than that.

He hung his overcoat on a nail by the door and pulled his field shirt down flat behind his belt.

The old woman came back and set the lantern on a stool.

"Mama, introduce yourself," said Ludmilla.

The old woman smiled politely and offered Altinnik her dark and crooked hand.

"Ivan Altinnik," said Altinnik loudly.

"A strange last name," said the old woman, shaking her head and failing to introduce herself.

"What's so strange about it?" said Altinnik, offended. "It's a completely normal last name. It comes from the word 'altin.' You ever heard that word?"

"No, never heard it," said the old woman.

"How's that possible?" Altinnik was amazed. "In the old days an altin was a kind of money."

"Ech, my boy," sighed the old woman. "We didn't have any money in the old days and we don't have any now either."

"That's enough of your poor-mouthing," objected Ludmilla. "We're no worse off than most. Vanya's probably a *malanets*, right, Vanya?" She turned to Altinnik and smiled.

"Who, what?" said Altinnik, confused.

"A *malanets*."

"Aha, a *malanets*," agreed Altinnik, to save an argument, even though he had no idea what the word meant.

"Oh-ho-ho," sighed the old woman and, kicking off her felt boots, climbed up on the stove.

Altinnik walked up and down the room, his hands in his pockets, giving the place the once-over. It was a completely ordinary room in a country house. There were buckets of water on a bench by the door, a washbasin to their right, a portrait of Kaganovich on the wall, and beneath it a picture frame filled with photographs one on top of the other. A soldier in pre-war uniform with a triangle in his lapel; an old man wearing glasses; a naked child on a table; people in groups, people alone, and, in among them, Ludmilla. There was that photograph of Ludmilla which Altinnik knew, as well as others taken more recently. Had Ludmilla sent him one of the more recent ones, Altinnik would already be embracing Natashka the cripple two stations down.

Continuing his inspection, Altinnik came across a towel hung askew on which a flat-chested, one-eyed girl in shorts and halter had been embroidered. The girl was lying on her stomach with her legs up and holding something in her hand that looked like an open book. The inscription beneath the picture read: At the Health Resort.

Altinnik took a step back and squinted first with one eye, then with the other.

"You did the embroidery?" he asked with respect.

"I did," answered Ludmilla modestly.

"Not bad. In general this . . ." He thought for a moment but, finding nothing definite to say, waved his hand in annoyance.

Altinnik's eye slid without curiosity across the dark icon in the corner (he held religious prejudices in low esteem), and then, through a half-opened door, he glanced into a room, which was, however, too dark to see. Just at that moment he heard someone snuffling behind the embroidered calico curtain which separated the space between the stove on which the old woman had climbed and the door.

Altinnik moved abruptly toward the curtain and jerked it open. He saw a tow-haired boy of about fourteen sleeping with his face to the wall in an iron four-poster.

"Who's that?" Altinnik looked sternly at Ludmilla.

"My son," said Ludmilla, lowering her eyes in shame.

"No grandchildren, then?"

"Stop that," she said, taking offense. "I'm still young."

"Youthful's more like it," corrected Altinnik, walking over to the table by the window. He sat down and leaned his elbows on the tablecloth embroidered with pale flowers in a satin stitch. The girl "at the health resort" was on the wall opposite him and her one eye looked not at her book but at him. He got out his Kazbeks and lit up without requesting permission.

"When's the next train?" he inquired.

"We only have one train, the one you came on," said Ludmilla. "The others don't stop."

"Aha, so that's how it is." He drummed his fingers on

the table. "So what are we going to do then?" He raised his eyes and glared insolently at Ludmilla. Embarrassed, she blushed.

How about that, she still blushes, Altinnik marveled to himself.

"So, I'm asking you, what are we going to do?" He repeated his question, now feeling he could say whatever he wanted.

"Would you like to eat?" asked Ludmilla softly, not raising her head.

"Eat?" repeated Altinnik knowingly and looked at his watch (it was five of three). "What's the choice, let's eat."

In one minute Ludmilla had whisked the tablecloth from the table, replacing it with an oilcloth, and before Altinnik knew quite what was happening, there was a half liter of vodka, fried potatoes (still warm), and bacon fat and mushroom piroshkis on the table.

"To our meeting," said Altinnik, raising his glass.

"To our meeting." Ludmilla nodded.

7

Altinnik hoped to get drunk quickly, but even though he downed the entire bottle, it had little effect on him, despite the fact that he'd had nothing to eat since the morning except the two meat piroshkis he'd bought at the Kursk station. Warmth spread through his chest; his mood improved. He took off his boots and belt, and unbuttoned his shirt. He felt light and free. The appetizers seemed especially tasty, and he began looking at Ludmilla with increasing benevolence.

The vodka had enlivened Ludmilla as well. Her cheeks were flushed; her eyes sparkled. She no longer seemed so old to Altinnik as she had at first glance, but even rather attractive. He no longer had any doubt that the day spent waiting for the train would be a day well spent, and he had no desire for any more than that. The fact that Ludmilla was no longer in her first youth now assumed positive value for Altinnik. What use did he have anyway for silly little fools like that Galka, who fancy themselves the devil knows what. This was a real woman sitting in front of him, not some adolescent. She knew why people kiss and what you do after. Her lips and eyes held much promise and he was sure that this time he would stand his ground and not act like a dunce, as he had that time with Galka. He grew even more cheerful because of his confidence that everything would go the way he planned. He polished off the potatoes and set to work on the piroshki, which seemed especially tasty to him.

"These piroshki are simply wonderful," he said, to please his hostess and because he felt funny about his excessive appetite. "You know what they give us to eat in the army—horse rice, and lousy kasha. They could give a soldier a piece of butter now and then, but no, it's not allowed. And why? We feed all our friends, don't we. After all, a soldier's a human being, too. You can ride him like a horse, but at least give him a little butter, I say. The kasha just gives you gas and it's got practically no calories or vitamins. Now for mushrooms I have a lot of respect. Dried or fresh doesn't matter. Because, number one, they've got a high taste level"—Altinnik bent down one finger—"and, number two, for caloric value, they can hold their own with meat."

"Perfectly true," agreed Ludmilla. "During the war when there was nothing to eat we kept alive on mushrooms. From time to time you go to the woods with your basket . . ."

And having begun with mushrooms, she kept right on going, skipping from topic to topic, non-stop, telling Altinnik the story of her life, from the autumn of 1944, when she married a fellow who worked as an electrician at the station. They lived together until December, when he was taken into the army, where he managed to get as far as Berlin alive and well, but on the way back he caught cold in the train and died and she was left to live for the child, allowing no one to approach her, although quite a few did try, because they knew she was a pure and independent woman and everyone respected her, not only her neighbors but her colleagues at work too, there were even some physicians from the institute who came to her for advice, after all, no matter how much you study, theory is one thing and practice is another, and none of the doctors from the institute had as much practice as she did, they just couldn't, because the station wasn't like a polyclinic in a big city where surgery is separate and therapy or neuropathology is separate, here a toothache, a baby being born, they all come running to her, yesterday, for instance, they came running to her from the other end of the station in the middle of the night, an old woman had fallen off the stove, that old woman'll live to be a hundred, but for me it's get up in the middle of the night and run there because people, they don't realize, if you're a medic they think they can get you up at any hour though they work their eight hours then they're free but no one gives you a second's thought, even a factory worker's got it better or a bookkeeper like her brother Boris, who lives in the district capital twenty kilometers away, he's got his own house there too where he lives with his wife Nina and his daughter Verushka, who turned two last week, they're not doing all that well even though Nina graduated from a technical school, what a sloppy woman she is, wherever you go in her house there's always dirt up to your ears, dirty dishes, she can't even look after herself let alone the child, of course, she, Ludmilla, never says a word to Boris, he married her, he's got to live with it, but still it hurts, your own brother, three years younger, they grew up together and then when she was done studying she helped him through school, sent him fifty roubles every month, money stolen from herself and her own child, now Boris has forgotten all that (people have no gratitude), he comes home every Sunday and if he'd just give his old mother some calico for a dress or a pound of candy for her birthday or for the eighth of March, it's not a question of money though of course he knows they don't pay a medic much even after all your long years of service, but still every time he comes he demands she set out a half liter, everybody knows a man would sell his own mother for a half liter, like for instance her neighbor, a teacher, his drinking got so bad that his wife left him and his children renounced him, a man in name only that one, and really he's nothing but grief, better to live out your life alone than to join it with someone like that . . .

At first Altinnik had listened patiently and even agreed and gasped in the appropriate places, but then his face began to crinkle up and his mind started wandering. He had long since lost interest both in her past and in her future. He hadn't come to hear the story of her life; he had something quite different in mind and he wanted somehow to hint at it, but it had been impossible to interrupt her. One story after another came pouring from her like grain from a sack and in such a complaining tone that now he no longer felt like doing anything but going to sleep. But he had to keep his eyes politely on her and pretend that he found it all terribly interesting. When she started in on the teacher, he couldn't hold himself back any longer and said: "Excuse me for interrupting you, Ludmilla, but won't we wake up your mother?"

"Don't worry, you could shoot a cannon off right beside her head," Ludmilla assured him, about to begin again. "So where was I?"

Altinnik, too, had lost the thread, did not remember and did not want to remember what she'd been talking about. He stared sullenly off into space, twirling the empty bottle by the neck.

"Perhaps you'd like some more to drink?" guessed Ludmilla.

"Is there any?"

And though of course Altinnik wanted to go to sleep, he remembered his purpose in coming. He had only one day at his disposal, and if not now, then when?

"Of course," she answered and went off to a side room, immediately to reappear with a flat bottle whose wide neck was stuffed with a piece of newspaper.

"Home-brew?" asked Altinnik.

"Pure alcohol."

"Pure alcohol?"

"I'm a medic, after all." Ludmilla smiled.

"I love pure alcohol," said Altinnik, brightening, though he had never once in his life tried it. "Back at the base we drink chassis liquor."

"What?"

"It's a hydromix," explained Altinnik. "You pour it into the uprights on a plane's chassis. Seventy percent glycerine, twenty percent alcohol, ten percent water."

"And it's all right to drink?"

"Yes, it's all right," said Altinnik. "Of course it gives you the runs, but all in all it's pretty drinkable."

They diluted the alcohol with water, drank it down, and took a little food as a chaser.

"But I didn't finish telling you about the teacher," recalled Ludmilla.

Altinnik looked over at her. "No need to talk about the teacher."

"So what about, then?" said Ludmilla, surprised.

"Not about anything," he said and moved his chair over to her. Altinnik laid his hand on her shoulder. She made no move. He pulled her head a little closer to him. Then, without any resistance at all, she suddenly turned and sank her lips onto his.

This was so stunning that Altinnik was totally at a loss for a moment, but then he rushed forward to meet what awaited him, giving his hand free rein, regretting that he had only two and that they were short and could not grab everything at once. Without tearing herself from his lips, Ludmilla pressed her breasts and knees up against Altinnik, shuddering and breathing heavily as if she were about to die from insane passion. Then suddenly she shoved him away so abruptly that his elbow struck the table. Clutching his elbow, Altinnik stared at Ludmilla in amazement.

"For what?" he asked, stuttering from shortness of breath.

"No reason." Ludmilla smiled enigmatically.

It was obvious that at last the alcohol was taking effect. Altinnik looked at Ludmilla and could not comprehend what it was she wanted.

"Big man, huh." She broke out laughing and tapped him lightly on the head. "You think a woman's all by herself, you can get everything you want from her right away?"

"You mean I can't?"

"That's the only thing any of you ever want," she said. "I swear all men are like dogs. You don't even want to have a little talk, there's only one thing on your mind."

Altinnik was confused. "But we had a little talk," he objected hesitantly, and then promised: "And afterward we'll have another one."

"Idiot," she said and laid her head down on the table.

Altinnik began thinking. Obviously he had done something wrong, since at first Ludmilla seemed to be yielding to him and now she had turned ornery. It was probably just her way of playing.

Altinnik tried to put his arms around her again but again she pushed him away and put her head back on the table.

"Ludmilla," Altinnik said after a moment's silence. "Why are you acting like that? You're not a young girl, you ought to know why you invited me here and why I came, not to laugh at you or play tricks on you, but for us to give each other pleasure in a friendly sort of way. If you're going to start acting like a young girl about it, you should've said so right off or at least hinted, because my time's limited, you know how it is for a soldier."

She said nothing. The old woman was snoring softly on the stove, smacking her lips in her sleep. Altinnik looked at his watch but was too drunk to tell the time—it was either three-thirty or twenty past five. Ludmilla was still sitting with her head resting on her arms. Altinnik, too, did not move from his chair, sighing and scratching his head. He felt badly that he had wasted so much time and still had not gotten any sleep.

He bent over and got one boot from under the table, took out his puttees, and began winding them around his leg. This turned out to be no simple task, because as soon as he pulled up one leg he would lose his balance and have to grab the edge of the table to keep from falling off the stool. Finally he somehow coped with the boot and went for the other.

Ludmilla raised her head and looked over at Altinnik in surprise. "Where are you off to?"

He shrugged his shoulders. "To the station."

"Why?"

"What's for me to do here? I'm leaving."

"Where are you going? It's still twenty-four hours till the train comes."

"I don't care. I'll wait," he said, starting on the second boot.

"Your feelings hurt?"

Altinnik did not reply, concentrating on the attempt to sink his foot into his boot.

"Oh, you silly fool!" Ludmilla tore the boot from his hand and tossed it back under the table. He was on the verge of anger when she grabbed him and began kissing him. Once again he forgot everything and once again he did not have enough hands and there wasn't air enough to breathe.

"Wait a minute," she whispered. "I'll put out the light and we'll go in the side room."

It took considerable effort for Altinnik to unglue himself from her. He could not wait very long. After one last kiss, she walked on tiptoe to the door and clicked the switch. The light went out.

Altinnik waited impatiently, feeling his heart beating wildly just as if it were being tugged by a cord. Ludmilla had not returned.

"Ludmilla!" he called out in a whisper.

"One minute, Vanya," she whispered in the dark.

Altinnik rose, and feeling that his legs were not able

to support him, he grabbed the edge of the table and peered, squinting, into the dark, trying to make out something, anything. But not catching sight of anything at all, he carefully let go of the table, and just as he was, one boot on, set off toward where he thought Ludmilla should be.

After walking for what seemed forever, he ran into a stool, overturning it, almost falling himself and badly bruising his knee. The stool fell with such a crash he thought he must have woken the whole house. And, in fact, the old woman on the stove uttered a brief cry, but it must have been in her sleep, for a second later she was snoring and smacking her lips again. He realized that he'd gone too far to the right and continued walking, trying to keep to the left, and ran up against a rag of some sort, which he guessed was the curtain behind which Ludmilla's son was sleeping. He started back, but the curtain was now behind him. And to his right, and to his left. To free himself he began waving his hands over his head as if trying to fend off a swarm of bees. Now totally entangled and seeing no other means of escape, he jerked himself to the side with what little strength he had left. Somewhere something started to rip. Altinnik tumbled to the floor, this time striking his head. "Oh, Lord!" he thought melancholically. "I'm going to kill myself like this." He tried to get up but lacked the strength. He began fumbling until he found some sort of twig broom, which he placed under his head, and fell asleep.

8

He awoke because his eyes had begun to ache. The sun was shining right on his face through the half-frosted window. Turning his head slightly, he could see that he was lying in a totally unfamiliar room on a wide bed with a soft feather quilt and a huge feather pillow. A boy of about fourteen in an old school uniform was sitting at a round table in the middle of the room between the window and the mirrored dresser. It looked as if the boy was preparing his lessons, but in fact he was lighting one match after the other and sticking them, still lighted, into his mouth and then breathing out the smoke in front of the mirrored dresser, making horrible faces. Altinnik began watching him in the mirror. The boy struck the next match, opened his mouth, and at that moment met Altinnik's reflection in the mirror. He jumped, shut his mouth, and closed his hand around the match, probably burning himself. Then he turned around and for an interminably long moment they took each other in.

The boy was first to break the silence. "Mama ran to the store," he said.

"Aha," murmured Altinnik, signaling that everything was clear, though nothing was the least bit clear to him. "What grade are you in?" he asked the boy.

"Eighth."

"Pretty good," said Altinnik, impressed. He'd only gotten as far as the seventh himself. "And what's your name."

"Vadik."

"Good boy," praised Altinnik, half closing his eyes. His head was aching. Either because he'd done so much drinking the night before or because he'd hit it on something. He had the feeling that some vitally important link had slipped from his memory, but he could not recall what it might be. Vaguely he remembered looking for something in the dark and not finding it. Then lying down on the floor. But how had he ended up in a bed? A memory glimmered faintly in his brain—Ludmilla lifting him from the floor and taking him into her bed, something had gone on between them and then she'd asked: "Why did you say you were a *malanets?*"

And he had asked: "What's a *malanets?*"

"A Jew."

"So why say *malanets?*"

"Well, it feels funny to say Jew to a person," explained Ludmilla.

Now he was totally unable to remember whether all this had been a dream or whether it had really happened. But he didn't feel like thinking and soon fell back to sleep.

9

When Altinnik opened his eyes again, Vadik was no longer in the room. Deciding it was late, Altinnik got up, pulled on his pants (which, along with his field shirt, were hanging on the back of the chair in front of the bed), put on his boots without the puttees, and walked into the next room.

The old woman, wearing a calico dress torn under the arms (through which her undershirt could be seen), was standing by the stove, her back to Altinnik; hunched over, she was blowing on the coals. Altinnik came up behind her and shouted right in her ear: "Hey, old woman, where's your bathroom?"

"Oi, saints preserve us!" shrieked the old woman, raising her frightened eyes to Altinnik. "Oi, you scared me. Why did you shout?"

"I thought you were deaf," said Altinnik, frowning and waving his hand in a gesture of irritation. "Ech, I feel sick. I swear my head feels like it's made of cast iron."

"You need a hair of the dog." The old woman smiled sympathetically.

"What are you talking about, a hair of the dog. I couldn't even look at it. I tell you I feel like I've swallowed a rat. Do you have anything cold to drink?"

"There's some kvass."

"Is it cold?" asked Altinnik, livening up.

"Sure it is, ice-cold."

Altinnik beamed. "Give me some quick before I keel over," he urged. The old woman ran out to the passageway and returned with a three-liter bottle of red, beetroot kvass. Altinnik took a mugful.

"Oooo," he hummed with satisfaction. "That's kvass. Takes your breath away. Hold on, don't take it away. I'll go run and take a leak and then I'll have some more. There isn't room for another drop in me right now."

It was sunny and frosty outside. Squinting because of the blinding snow, Altinnik ran through the garden to the outhouse; bursting back into the hut refreshed, he drank more kvass and then tried to light a cigarette. It wouldn't light and he threw it away. Altinnik asked the old woman if Ludmilla had returned.

"Not yet," she said, still fussing with the samovar.

"And where's Vadik?"

"Out for a walk."

"All right, move aside, I'll blow on it," said Altinnik, nudging her with his elbow.

He was better at blowing on the coals than she, and soon the samovar was humming.

"That's how you have to blow," said Altinnik, unable to resist a little boasting. "I blew three times and it caught. You can see what kind of lungs I've got. Watch my chest expand." He took a chestful of air and his chest bulged out improbably large. "See what I mean. Doesn't make any difference that I'm average height. I was a jazzman in civilian life. Played in a brass band, trumpet. The trumpet's small, but you can get more out of it than a bass horn. The bass is easy if you're healthy. You just have to know how to puff out your cheeks, no brains required. But on the trumpet you have to press your lips together harder and go like this—poo, poo, poo. The sound you get, let me tell you, is pure and fine. I don't care what they say, a bass horn bellows like a ram— be-eh, be-eh—but a trumpet . . ." Altinnik took an imaginary trumpet in hand and began fingering it just as if he were pressing actual keys. He was about to imitate the sound of a trumpet when someone began playing an accordion outside in the yard. The music stopped as it approached the house. Heavy footsteps resounded in the passageway. The door was flung open and an enormous muzhik appeared in the doorway, dressed in a dark blue winter coat and felt boots up to his knees. An accordion, small compared to the man, was dangling on his chest. Altinnik was still holding his imaginary trumpet, ready to play.

Paying no attention to either of them, not even saying hello, the new arrival took off his accordion and set it down on the bench by the buckets, then began leisurely brushing off his boots.

"Beautiful weather," he said, clearly addressing the old woman.

"You came alone?" she asked.

"Yes. Verushka's got a cold. She's running a temperature, so Ninka stayed home with her." Tossing the twig broom back into its place, he walked past Altinnik and sat down at the table.

"Why didn't you come last Sunday?"

"It was what's his name, Vaska Morozov's funeral," he said in the same impassive manner he said everything.

"Oh, he died?" the old woman said in surprise.

"What else. Him and his supervisor from work were slugging down wood alcohol. The super went blind in both eyes, and Vaska . . . It was Wednesday they did the drinking, so Thursday morning, the way his wife Raika tells it, Vaska gets up for work. Everything's normal, he gets out of bed, washes up, she makes him his breakfast. He sits down at the table, everything's regular. We should turn on the radio, he says, and check the time. He reaches for the radio, it's about three feet away, no, even less than that, say, a foot or so . . . So he's reaching out, then all of a sudden he starts wheezing and he falls back from the table. Raika says, Vasya, Vasya, but Vasya's gone."

"Oh, Lord," sighed the old woman. "Raika must be dying of grief?"

"Ah, that bitch." He waved his hand in disgust. "She got involved with that Grishka the policeman . . . The whole street knows about it. And Vaska knew, too. He used to beat her for it, tie her to the bed—didn't matter. And now of course she's dying of grief. So she won't lose face."

Altinnik sat down. He and the muzhik gradually began to look each other over. Altinnik noticed that he looked a lot like Ludmilla and guessed he must be the brother who killed the dog. The silence was becoming awkward. The old woman was now bustling around the stove.

"And who's this guy?" the muzhik asked the old woman, his voice startlingly loud. He nodded his head at Altinnik as if Altinnik were no more than a cupboard or a tree.

"Him, he's come to see Ludka," the old woman explained indifferently.

"And where'd she find him?"

"They're pen pals."

"Aha."

The muzhik issued a surprisingly loud sigh, rose, walked over to Altinnik, and offered him his enormous paw.

Shuddering, Altinnik looked him up and down. "What do you want?" he asked, smiling ingratiatingly.

"Let's introduce ourselves."

"Aha." Altinnik hopped to his feet, and shook the hand offered him. "Ivan."

"Pleased to meet you, Ivan. Boris is my name." They sat back down and began groping for something to talk about.

"You on leave?" asked Boris.

"No, on assignment."

"You an a-vee-a-tor?" It was not so much a question respectfully put as an observation Boris made to himself. "I don't like a-vee-a-tion. The noise hurts your ears. I served in the signal corps, as a cook. It was all right, except the sergeant was impossible."

For any soldier the subject of sergeants is inexhaustible. Ludmilla returned just as Altinnik was crawling on all fours across the floor to demonstrate de Gaulle's method of teaching a raw recruit the proper way to wash floors.

10

Ludmilla had brought back a bottle of vodka. They all sat down to breakfast. No matter how disgusting the sight of the vodka was to Altinnik, he had to drink. The old woman put fried potatoes, thickly sliced pickles, and yesterday's mushroom piroshkis on the table. Ludmilla was sitting beside Altinnik, acting as if nothing at all had happened. He kept glancing over at her out of the corner of his eye, trying without success to decide whether they had actually done something or whether he had just dreamed it all.

Boris poured the vodka, a full glass for himself and Altinnik, a half glass for his sister, and just a drop for his mother so she could be sociable.

Altinnik almost choked on the vodka. Though he had drunk it down in one gulp, he was seized by a long and shameful series of coughs and grimaces.

"Went down the wrong way," said Boris understandingly.

"Take a bite of piroshki, Vanya," said Ludmilla, handing him one. "He liked your piroshkis," she said to her mother.

"Who wouldn't," said Boris. "Specialty of the house. All in all, it's a good life we have here, Vanya. The place is loaded with mushrooms like those. Come in the summertime, we'll take a couple of rifles, go off in the woods, pick mushrooms, shoot rabbits."

"You and your shooting," said Ludmilla. "You never hit anything in your whole life except Little Ace and that was because he was tied up."

"Don't listen to her, Vanya," countered Boris. "We've got a good life here. Our own vegetables, meat, we'll be slaughtering the hog soon. Our own milk. You saw the cow?"

"No," said Altinnik, "I didn't."

"Come on, I'll show you." Boris rose from the table.

"Now where are you dragging the man?" said Ludmilla in exasperation. "What do you think, he's never seen a cow?"

"He's never seen yours." Boris stuck by his guns. "Come on, Vanya."

Altinnik did not want to go but it would have been awkward to refuse. He, too, rose to his feet.

"Boris!" Ludmilla raised her voice.

"So let him have a look," said Boris, unyielding. "Maybe he's interested. He's from the city. Maybe he never saw a cow in his whole life, maybe he grew up on powdered milk."

"Why pester a person?" The old woman took Ludmilla's side. "Sit down, you hear."

"Well, all right," yielded Boris. "Come on, Vanya, we'll finish off the bottle and we won't give them any more."

He poured what was left into their glasses and they drank it right down.

"Mama, you said he's a *malanets* but he's no *malanets*," Ludmilla said suddenly, winking at Altinnik.

The blood rushed to Altinnik's head. This meant that everything he so vaguely remembered had actually happened and had not been a dream at all.

"Did he tell you that himself?" said the old woman in disbelief.

"No, he showed me his passport," said Ludmilla and burst out laughing shamelessly.

Boris did not understand the allusion and said: "Soldiers don't have passports. They have military ID's. You have a military ID, Vanya?"

"Sure," said Altinnik. "Here it is." He unbuttoned his right front shirt pocket and handed the document to Boris.

Boris took the ID booklet and began leafing through it. Ludmilla could not restrain herself and she, too, began looking over her mother's shoulder.

"What's that they've got written there?" she asked.

"Shoe size, hat size," explained Boris, turning the page. "No identifying marks," he read and then turned to Altinnik. "Says here you're not married. If you want, we can go over to the village soviet right now, Katya's working over there, and get yourself stamped right up as married."

"That's all I need," objected Altinnik. "Give it here." He took back his ID and placed it in his pocket. "I'm doing fine without that. I'm still young to have that stamped on my ID."

"Just how old are you?" asked the old woman curiously.

"Twenty-three."

"Young," said the old woman mistrustfully. "But young or not, you should settle down and get married, have children. What a joy they are, little children."

"Ludmilla," said Boris, "do you have any alcohol?"

"No," said Ludmilla. "There was a little left but we drank it yesterday."

"Come with me," said Boris, taking her aside into the next room. He began discussing something with her—it sounded as if he was asking for money and she was refusing him. A moment later they came back in together.

"Come on, Vanya, let's go for a walk," suggested Boris. "You can have a look at our village, you probably couldn't see anything last night."

"Sure, let's go," agreed Altinnik.

11

In a small store across from the train station they each had another half a glass of vodka and a mug of warmed beer straight from the keg. They stopped by the station to check the train schedule and had a glass of red wine each while they were there. On the way home they popped back in the store for another beer. Boris shoved a bottle of vodka into the left inside pocket of his coat.

"Hey, Nastyonka," said Boris to the girl at the counter, slapping himself where the bottle bulged, "mine are bigger than yours. If I put another bottle in there, I could play a woman on amateur night."

"You're not going to take another one?" asked Nas- tyonka.

"No time," joked Boris, rubbing his fingers together as if counting money.

Then they went back along a path that cut through people's gardens. The path was narrow. Altinnik's left leg gave him no problems, but for some reason his right kept sinking in the snowdrifts. "Must be the shortcut," he thought.

Once back, they sat down at the table again. Altinnik drank yet another half a glass, after which he started losing track of himself. For some reason the conversation returned to age.

"And here I am, going to be thirty-five soon," said Ludmilla. "But no one can ever guess my age. They say twenty-six, twenty-eight at the most."

"You'll marry ten more times," said Boris.

"Vitka Poludenov came here after the army"—the old woman broke into the conversation—"and got hitched up with Nyurka Krinina; she's twenty years older than him, and with three children, too. They get along as fine as can be."

Altinnik was suspicious. He knew what the old woman was driving at. But he was in a good mood now and he said: "Go on, you sly old woman. You think I don't understand why you're always hammering away at that. What, do you want me to marry you?" He whacked his hand down on the table. "Hey, Boris, then you'll be calling me Papa and you'll have to pay her and me money for our old age."

This idea seemed so funny to Altinnik that he could

not quiet down for quite some time, his body shaking with small waves of laughter, probably from nervousness. No one, however, joined in with Altinnik. On the contrary; the three of them started frowning and exchanging bewildered glances. Realizing that something he'd said had hurt the old woman's feelings, Altinnik stopped laughing. The old woman's thin lips were pressed tightly together.

"What, your feelings hurt?" asked Altinnik in surprise.

"Sure, what do you think," said Boris suddenly. "What kind of a thing is that to talk nonsense to an old person?"

"Come on, come on," said Altinnik, annoyed. "What a bunch this is. Petty, big-bellied, and touchy as hell. You spit in their face and they're ready to fight. I was only kidding. It's just my fun-loving nature. I love to kid around and have a couple of laughs, that's all. You were saying that this . . . what's his name . . . married a woman twenty years older than him and I said, All right, come on, old woman, let's get married. Of course you're not twenty years older than me, because you've got a daughter old enough to be my mother. Anyway, I still got no reason to get married. I'm still young. Twenty-three. You could say I've got my whole life in front of me. When I finish with the army, I'm going to go to a tech school and from there to an institute. I'm going to be an engineer, that's right, I am."

Altinnik suddenly felt so sad that he wanted to cry. Everything he had just said sounded as if he had been sentenced to the hard, thorny path of the engineer, a sentence not subject to appeal.

Ludmilla, who was sitting beside Altinnik, reacted in a most unexpected fashion. She suddenly rose, blushed, and slammed her fork against the table with all her might.

The fork went flying and hit the window, without, however, breaking it, and then fell to the floor between the table and the windowsill.

"What's with you, Ludka?" asked Boris, jumping up.

"Nothing," she said and rushed out of the room.

Boris went after her. The old woman sighed and started clearing the dishes. Altinnik, at a total loss, remained at the table. Everything had gotten mixed up in his brain and he could not for the life of him understand what had just happened, whom he'd offended, and how. Having cleared the dishes, the old woman began washing them in a basin of warm water by the stove. The rumble of Boris's voice could be heard from behind the door of the next room, measured and monotonous; it was impossible to make out a single word he was saying, though Altinnik in fact wasn't making much of a try. Then a strange, thin, broken sound could be heard, as if the radio were broadcasting a signal by which musical instruments could be tuned.

"These people!" Altinnik made a gesture of irritation and disgust and let his head fall to the table. But, in the second it took for him to close his eyes, Altinnik along with the table and chair began to capsize; he grabbed the edge of the table, jerked his head up, and everything went back into place.

The door from the next room opened and Boris walked in. He took his former place at the table, helped himself to a piece of pickle from the plate, and gobbled it down.

"What's going on in there?" asked Altinnik, not because he was genuinely interested but simply because it seemed the right thing to do.

"What do you mean what?" Boris spread his hands in a gesture signifying the hopelessness of the situation. "You hurt Ludka's feelings."

"From what, all of a sudden?" said Altinnik, surprised.

"I don't know." Boris shrugged his shoulders. "You should know. Yesterday you promised to marry her and now you turn your nose up at her."

"Who, me? I promised?" Altinnik's surprise grew even greater. "That's a fine kettle of fish!" Altinnik propped his head on his hand and lost himself in thought. Could he really have been drunk enough to blurt out something like that? It couldn't possibly be, he never had anything of the sort in mind.

"Marry her," he mumbled. "That's all I need. What can you do. Even if I wanted to . . . any girl . . . Before the service, I had a girl, eighteen years old. She studied gymnastics. She wore eyeglasses . . ."

Boris gobbled his pickle in silence, paying no attention to what Altinnik was saying, his fingers beating out a drumroll on the table.

Altinnik looked over at him, rose from his chair, and went to the next room. Ludmilla was lying face down across the bed, whimpering. It was that whimpering which had seemed to Altinnik to resemble a signal for tuning up instruments.

"Hey!" Altinnik pushed her legs to the side and shook her by the shoulder. She went on whimpering the same note.

"Listen, Ludmilla, stop." Altinnik tugged at her shoulder. "I didn't . . . I mean . . ." He was tongue-tied. "I hate it when they cry."

"E-e-e-e-eeee," wailed Ludmilla.

"There she goes with that music of hers again!" Altinnik slapped his knee in a fit of annoyance. "Listen, will you, Ludmilla, why cry? We can talk this over like two adults. You say I promised to marry you?"

Ludmilla stopped wailing and started listening.

"I have no memory of it. I don't even remember if we did anything or not, I swear it. You know yourself the things you can say or do when you've had too much to drink. After all, Ludmilla, you're a grown woman. You're older than me, quite a bit older. To tell you the truth, Ludmilla, I mean, you really seem more like a mother to me."

Upon hearing these words, Ludmilla issued such a high note that Altinnik clutched his head.

"Oi, what is this!" cried Altinnik. "Ludmilla, stop it, I beg you, Ludmilla. All right, if I promised you, I'm ready, Ludmilla, but please, just even for a minute, put yourself in my position, take pity on me. You know I'm still young, Ludmilla, I want to study and broaden my horizons. What do you need to ruin a young life for? Find yourself somebody your own age, I'm not ready for family life yet, I haven't any idea what it's about . . ."

Without altering one note of her song, Ludmilla sat up on the bed, letting her feet fall to the floor, and continued to wail, her mouth wide open, her bulging eyes staring senselessly off into space.

Altinnik ran from the bed and pressed himself against the wall. Not ceasing to wail for even a second, Ludmilla began plucking pieces of lace from her blouse as if they were the petals of a daisy and she were saying: "He loves me, he loves me not."

Altinnik went cold and dashed out of the room. Just as before, Boris was sitting at the table. Now, however, he was gobbling a piroshki.

"Boris!" cried Altinnik.

"What?" asked Boris indifferently.

"Ludmilla's feeling bad. Water!"

"Over there, pour it yourself." Boris coolly indicated a bottle of water with a glance of his eyes.

Altinnik's hands were shaking and half the water missed the glass. He ran back in to Ludmilla with the glass. By this time Ludmilla's silk blouse had already significantly decreased in size.

"Ludmilla," Altinnik said tenderly, "here, take it, have a nice drink of water and it'll all pass."

He took hold of her head with one hand, and with the other tried to pour the water into her mouth, but because his hands were shaking, all he did was knock the glass against her teeth, spilling the water onto her breasts.

With one abrupt movement she knocked the glass out of his hand. The glass struck the back of the bed and smashed to smithereens.

"E-e-e-e-e-e-eee!"

Altinnik's patience came to an end. He ran out the door. "That's it!" he shouted to Boris. "I'm leaving! The hell with it! Where's my suitcase?"

"Where's his suitcase?" Boris asked his mother, who was sweeping with the same twig broom that Altinnik had used as a pillow the night before.

"Over there," said the old woman, flicking her hand in the direction of the door.

"Over there," repeated Boris.

Altinnik walked to the door, but stopped at the threshold. The sound reaching him from Ludmilla's room caused his knees to start shaking.

"Boris!" implored Altinnik. "Tell her I agree. That I'll marry her, even right now, today. Like the saying goes, I offer her my heart and my hand. My heart and my hand," he repeated and broke out laughing, the phrase seemed so funny to him.

Suddenly everything began swimming in front of his eyes, whirling about at a furious speed. He barely made

it to the table, where he laid down his head and immediately fell asleep.

12

"Hey, c'mon, get up!"

Someone was shaking Altinnik by the shoulder.

Ungluing his eyelids with great effort, he saw Boris
in front of him.

"Get up, Vanya, let's go," said Boris fondly.

"Where?" Altinnik had not understood.

"To the village soviet, of course."

"What for?"

"Forget, did you?" Boris smiled sympathetically.

Rubbing his temples, Altinnik caught sight of Ludmilla.
She was putting on lipstick in front of a mirror held by
the old woman. Ludmilla's face was heavily powdered,
especially under the eyes, but a trace of her recent
hysteria still remained. While Altinnik had been sleeping,
she'd changed her clothes again. Now she was wearing
a blue suit and a new white blouse; if you met her on
the street, you'd think she was from the district committee.

Racking his brains, Altinnik tried without the least
success to remember where he was intending to go with
these people and what relation their village soviet had
to him, a military man.

"C'mon, let's go," said Boris impatiently.

"All right."

Still a blank, Altinnik got up (since they were saying,
"Let's go"). He staggered from one side to the other until
he reached the doorway.

"Hold it." Boris stopped him. "Put on your overcoat.
You don't know what you're doing. It isn't summer out
there, you know."

Boris handed him the coat, and Altinnik spent a long time trying to stick his arms where the sleeves were supposed to be, without any luck at all. Finally he succeeded.

"That's the way," said Boris, buttoning up Altinnik's topcoat. "We'll just fasten all these little hooks, then we'll put on your belt and straighten your cap—two fingers from the left ear. Ludmilla, hold him for a second so he doesn't fall over." And while Ludmilla held him up, Boris took two steps back, looked Altinnik over with a critical eye until he was completely satisfied. "All right, everything's perfect. You could even parade through Red Square. Did you ever parade through Red Square?"

"No," said Altinnik.

"You will," promised Boris.

They went outside. Boris walked in front, playing his accordion. Two steps behind him, Altinnik fixed his gaze on Boris's back and kept craning his neck because it seemed to him that Boris was floating off somewhere and Altinnik was afraid to lose his way. Behind Altinnik came Ludmilla, her face flushed from wine, tears, and her excitement at what was soon to occur.

People kept coming out to the road. Old women black as beetles dragged themselves out to see. Altinnik had never seen so many old women all at once. They watched the procession with amazement, as if it were not Altinnik who was being led down the road, but a bear.

"Excuse me, dear," an old woman asked Boris. "Where're you taking the sick man?"

"Where he's going," answered Boris, stretching out his accordion.

They came to some sort of a hut. Boris gave Ludmilla his accordion to hold while he went inside. A few moments later he returned with some girl who was wearing a new quilt jacket and a checked shawl which looked like a blanket.

"And he's willing?" she asked, throwing a quick glance at Altinnik.

"Sure he is, Katya," Boris answered her. "You know yourself, we're not a bunch of swindlers. We've lived our whole life in the same neighborhood. He came here himself and offered her his heart and his hand, that's his own words . . . Tell her, Vanya."

"Heart?" repeated Altinnik. "What about the heart?" Then suddenly he broke into song. "The heart, it does not wish for peace . . ."

"All right, let's go," said Katya.

They walked to yet another hut. This one had a sign on it. While Katya was stamping her feet from the cold and rattling her keys in the lock, Altinnik attempted to read the sign. The letters hopped around in front of his eyes, absolutely refusing to form into words. Then he attempted it from the end and managed to read: ". . . puties of workers."

"What's that mean, 'puties'?" he asked Ludmilla loudly.

"Go on in," said Boris, letting Altinnik enter first. Then, having let Ludmilla in, he entered himself and closed the door behind him.

The small, cold room was jammed with two desks, an iron safe which blocked half the window, and a tangled row of chairs along the side wall.

"What is this, the police station?" asked Altinnik.

"The police station," said Boris and, pressing lightly on Altinnik's shoulders, seated him on the chair closest to the door.

Ludmilla stood beside the table, either the cold or her excitement making her teeth chatter.

The girl opened the safe, withdrew a large book of the sort bookkeepers use and some sort of forms, and laid them on the table. She dipped her pen in the inkwell but the ink had frozen.

"Here, Katya," said Boris, offering her his fountain pen.

"Where's his service book?" asked Katya.

"Vanya, where's your ID book?" asked Ludmilla tenderly.

Altinnik opened one eye. "My what book?"

"Your ID book. You were showing it to us. Boris, do you remember where he put it?"

"It should be in his right-hand shirt pocket," reasoned Boris, after a moment's thought. "The left-hand pocket is for your party or Komsomol card, and the right-hand one for your service ID."

He walked over to Altinnik, unbuttoned his right-hand pocket, and a second later the service book was on the table in front of Katya.

Katya spent a long time blowing on the frozen, rectangular stamp, then affixed it to his book, pressing it down with the force of both her hands.

At that moment Altinnik sobered up for an instant and realized that some terrible, irreparable fraud was being perpetrated.

"Eh-eh! Eh!" he shouted and tried to get up, but as soon as he left his chair he felt the floor beneath his feet start rising toward the ceiling, flipping over at the same time.

Altinnik quickly grabbed hold of the back of his chair, sat down, and waved his hand in a gesture of surrender. He had no recollection of their setting the paper in front of him, placing his fingers around the pen, and guiding his hand . . .

13

Then they celebrated the wedding, not that it was all that much of a celebration. There was a table pulled out to the middle of the room; there were some guests. They drank vodka, red wine, and diluted home-brew. Altinnik sat at the head of the table with Ludmilla, and the guests kept crying, "Bitter." Each time he would rise obediently and place his lips on those of his bride, though he found it all disgusting.

Boris played the accordion. A fat peasant woman around forty-five danced, tugging at a stick on a rope hidden under her skirt while calling out obscene ditties. A friend of Boris's, wearing a scarf and an apron, pretended to be the bride. The guests all laughed.

Ludmilla's mother bustled around the stove, making sure that everyone had enough of everything and that no one took any more than that.

Then Ludmilla danced with Boris, and a young man wearing a three-cornered scarf took over on the accordion.

An elderly man wearing an old army tunic without any shoulder straps was sitting beside Altinnik in Ludmilla's place. This was the local schoolteacher, Orfei Stepanovich.

"I served in the army, too, Vanya." He drew closer to Altinnik's ear. "I served before the war, too. That's right. People were getting shot. Though I"—he sighed—"didn't have to do any shooting."

"How come?" asked Altinnik in surprise.

"Health reasons." Orfei Stepanovich spread his arms in a gesture of futility. "Vanya, I have a daughter; she married a major, too. Serves over in Germany. He gave me this tunic as a present. But I'm divorced from my wife. She left me because I'm a drunk. There was a court case," he said with a tone of great respect.

"Is it hard, getting divorced?" asked Altinnik curiously.

"Nothing to it," said Orfei Stepanovich, letting his head fall into a plate of salad.

Then, somehow or other, Altinnik found himself in the garden behind the bathhouse vomiting onto snow white as sugar. A shabby black dog kept slinking up to him and Altinnik had no idea where the dog had come from.

Ludmilla appeared out of nowhere. Slinging Altinnik's arm over her shoulder, she tried to move him, speaking tenderly to him as to a child.

"You're not feeling so good, Vanya. Let's go home, we'll make up the bed and you can have a nice sleep. You have to get up early tomorrow."

"Go away!" Altinnik shook his head and clutched his stomach. Once again his body was contorted by spasms, but there was nothing left to vomit. Unaware of this, the dog, who had run two steps away, continued wagging his tail and staring with hungry, hopeful eyes at Altinnik's mouth.

"Get out of here!" Ludmilla stamped her foot.

The dog ran back another step and again began wagging his tail, now at a safe distance.

At that point Ludmilla started to lug Altinnik across the length of the garden while his feet weakly pawed at the ground. He lingered on the porch for a moment. On the street along the fence, old women dark as the dog near the bathhouse were standing and staring. They were smiling ingratiatingly in the hopes that, even if they weren't invited in, at least some refreshments might be brought out to them. Not because they were hungry, but just for the holiday feeling of it.

On the porch, Altinnik pushed Ludmilla away.

"Hey, you women," he started shouting, making some sort of meaningless circular gestures with his hands.

"C'mon, all of you, over here! We'll have a good time! Altinnik is getting married!"

He tried to perform something like an Indian ritual dance but lost his balance and would have fallen off the porch if it weren't for Ludmilla, who grabbed him in the nick of time.

The old women cackled in pleasure and began immediately flocking through the gate; it was as if a dam had broken.

"Goddam you, where do you think you're going!" cried Ludmilla, supporting Altinnik with her shoulder and nudging him toward the door. "You've got no shame!"

"The host invited us!" persisted the little old woman leading the procession, setting one foot on the porch, her chin thrust forward.

"The host, the host," mocked Ludmilla. "The host can't even stand on his own two feet and all you want is to eat and drink at someone else's expense. Shameless!"

She shoved Altinnik into the passageway and slammed the door right in the face of the little old woman. A muffled hubbub of displeasure arose from behind the door.

Altinnik crawled into the room, now almost on all fours. Out of the blurred and spinning multitude of faces, Orfei Stepanovich emerged, glass in hand.

"Drink some wine, Vanya, it'll help," he said, sticking a glass under Altinnik's nose.

The sight of it alone was enough to contort Altinnik's face and he began roaring like an animal, shaking his head desperately back and forth.

"Get out of here, you lunatic, get out of here!" Ludmilla shouted to the teacher, poking him in the face with her little fist. Blood spurted from Orfei Stepanovich's nose and dripped onto his tunic. Throwing his head unnaturally high in the air, Orfei Stepanovich walked like a blind man to the table, holding his glass in his hand at arm's length before him.

Boris and Vadik appeared. Together they took Altinnik under the arms and dragged him into the side room. Ludmilla ran in ahead and pulled back the covers; Altinnik sank into the downy featherbed as if into the netherworld. The last thing he remembered was someone pulling off his boots.

14

He had barely managed to fall asleep when they were waking him up.

"Vanya, get up." Ludmilla was standing over him.

A bare bulb suspended from the ceiling was on. It was pitch-black outside.

"Is it morning or night?" asked Altinnik.

"One-thirty in the morning," said Ludmilla. "The train'll be here soon."

Altinnik obediently lowered his feet to the floor. Getting dressed proved difficult. His head ached, his chest was on fire, and his hands were shaking. When he bent over to put on his puttees, he felt so sick he almost fell down. Somehow he managed to get his clothes on and he went out to the main room. The old woman, barefoot and in her undershirt, was fussing around the table.

"Have some breakfast, Vanya," she said.

There was a frying pan with an omelette, some piroshki, and a half bottle of vodka on the table. The sight made Altinnik's stomach turn.

"What kind of breakfast is that?"

He knelt under the washbasin and pushed up the metal drain plug with the back of his head. The water trickled over his ears and down his collar. Then he shook himself like a dog and wiped his face with a towel the old woman had handed him. He drank a ladleful of water from the bucket. The water was warm and tasted of iron. He hung the ladle on the bucket and stood for a long time, staring senselessly at the wall in front of him.

"Let's go, Vanya," said Ludmilla, touching his sleeve.

He put on his overcoat, pulled his cap down over his eyes, then touched it with one hand. The little red star was at the back, but he had no desire to turn his cap around; every movement cost him too much effort. He picked up his suitcase. The old woman thrust him a bundle tied up in an old but clean scarf.

"What's that?" he asked.

"Piroshki with mushrooms." The old woman smiled fawningly.

"Oh, what the hell do I need your piroshki for," said Altinnik, making a face.

"It's all right, all right, a bite to eat for the road," said Ludmilla. She took the bundle from her mother and opened the door.

Altinnik shook his head and offered the old woman his hand. "Goodbye," he said and went out the door first.

It had warmed up a bit outside and there was a thick, sticky fog. Altinnik walked in front, his feet slipping and sliding in the clay under the melted snow. He took each step carefully, thinking only of keeping from falling; there'd be no getting back up. Ludmilla was behind him, trying to follow in his footsteps.

At the station Ludmilla barely had time to run to the cashier to have Altinnik's ticket punched before the train arrived. Altinnik climbed up on the platform and stood there with the woman conductor beside the open door.

"Take the piroshki." Ludmilla handed him the bundle.

He sighed but took them anyway.

Small, pitiful, holding the handrail, Ludmilla stood down below and gazed up at Altinnik with devoted eyes. He said nothing and kept shifting from foot to foot, waiting for the departure signal.

The stationmaster struck the bell. The brakes began hissing, the train started moving. Still carefully holding the handrail, afraid to slip and fall, Ludmilla walked alongside the train.

"Now, don't forget, Vanya, write a little more often," she said, "or else me and Mama will worry. And if you need any food or clothing, just write."

Altinnik vacillated—should he say something or not? Then he made up his mind: whatever happens happens.

He bent forward and shouted: "Don't you wait for me, Ludmilla. I'm crossing out everything you did with me and I'm never coming back to you again!"

"Ach!" Ludmilla had time enough to open her mouth, but now she had to let go of the handrail, the train was picking up speed.

15

Perhaps three months or so had passed since Altinnik, his head heavy, had left Kirzavod Station, completed his assignment, and returned to his unit. Altinnik did not say a word to anyone about what had happened while he was away, and no one saw any change in him, except perhaps for Kazik Ivanov, who noticed that Altinnik ceased writing letters, though Kazik himself attached no significance to his discovery.

Letters continued coming from Altinnik's pen pals. He'd glance through some of them; others he'd just throw away without reading them. Naturally, he did not write to Ludmilla, and there was no word from her either.

During the October holidays the last of the soldiers whose terms were up that year were demobilized. Now Altinnik had seniority and had entered the home stretch, as they say. But it had all started to get to him. He was fed up and he started counting the days, but there was no telling precisely how many days were left. They could release him early; they could also delay his release. Lately he had been avoiding work on the airfield, trying always to get on duty in the flight mess, headquarters, or, if worst came to worst, the air squadron. So he kept himself busy, at least from morning till evening, twenty-four hours on duty, twenty-four off, then back on duty again.

Amid the cares of army life he almost forgot about his marriage; sometimes it seemed no more than a nightmare. But it was not at all difficult to convince himself that it had not been a dream: he could just take his ID book from his pocket and open it to the page marked "personal data."

Of course it was possible to protest his illegally conducted marriage, but Altinnik did not believe anything could be accomplished by complaints. That might make things even worse, since he had three times (and in the most flagrant manner) broken army law. First, he had in fact been absent without leave, and any absence without leave greater than two hours was considered desertion. Second, he had drunk to the point of intoxication, which was also forbidden. Third, he had married without the permission of his unit commander.

He tried to remove the seal with egg white, but without any luck. He thought of spilling ink on the page but was afraid he'd be jailed for tampering with documents.

All he could do was wait until, sooner or later, he was found out, or else somehow he would get through till his time was up and then exchange his service book for

a fresh passport and then it'd be goodbye forever, Ludmilla Ivanovna.

16

Once, shortly after New Year's, Altinnik was chosen
squadron duty officer. It was Monday, a vegetarian day
(the soldiers called it Italian Day), as well as Political-
Theory Day. After breakfast the squadron was assembled
and marched to the club to see an institutional film,
Defense against Nuclear Attack. After cleanup, Sergeant
de Gaulle took two of the duty officers to the storehouse
to get the fresh linen. Altinnik went through all the rooms
in the barracks a second time, checking that all beds were
well made, straightening the towels folded into the shape
of triangles, and then went out into the corridor. Near
the entrance to the barracks the duty officer, Pidonenko,
was sitting astride a night table and pecking at it with
his dagger.

"Pidonenko," Altinnik said to him, "watch out, the
major is supposed to drop by; he'll go crazy if he sees
you sitting there like that. He'll slap forty-eight hours of
silence on you."

"Don't worry, he won't," said Pidonenko. "The division
commander's orders are 'No brig for tech staff.'"

"That's for the summer," objected Altinnik. "When
there's a lot of flights. But now there's none and nobody
needs you."

He did not, however, insist on it, and besides, Pidonenko was not about to obey him. The aviation boys
weren't afraid of officers, not to mention a junior sergeant.

Altinnik went back to his room and, unfastening the
top snap on his overcoat, lay down on his lower bunk,
pulled his cap over his forehead, and set his feet, without

removing his boots, onto a small stool. The barracks were so warmly heated it made him feel like dozing right off. No sooner had he closed his eyes than Pidonenko's stentorian voice rang out in the corridor: "Squadron, attention! Duty officer to the exit door!"

Slamming his head against the bunk above him, Altinnik jumped up and quickly arranged his bed and his cap, fastened his coat, and, knocking over the stool, dashed out to the corridor.

As before, Pidonenko was sitting astride the night table, his feet dangling, his face expressing total satisfaction that he had managed so cleverly to trick Altinnik.

"There's no cure for idiocy," said Altinnik, twirling one finger by the side of his head. He was about to return to his room when Pidonenko called him: "Altinnik!"

"What?" Altinnik looked suspiciously at him, expecting another dirty trick.

"Kazik brought a letter for you."

"Sure, tell me about it."

"You don't believe me, you don't have to." Pidonenko pulled a rumpled envelope out from beneath him and began reading the return address out loud: "Station . . . I don't get it, is it Pivzavod, or what?"

"Give me that!" Altinnik rushed at him.

If he had just asked for it, without emotion, Pidonenko would have handed it over. But now he felt like teasing the duty officer; he jumped off the night table and ran to one side. "No, no, first you dance for me. Who's this? L. I. Altinnik," he read. "Your wife?"

"Give me that, I tell you!" His hands in fighting position, Altinnik went after Pidonenko. The chase was on. The night table was knocked over. Finally they agreed that Pidonenko would hand over the envelope in exchange for being able to punch Altinnik four times (one for each corner of the envelope) in the nose. His nose reddened, his eyes beginning to tear, the letter in his hands, Altinnik returned to his room, where, by the window, he opened the letter, his hands shaking in agitation.

Greetings from Kirzavod Station!!!
Hello, my dear and beloved spouse. Vanya, greetings to you from your spouse Ludmilla, good day or evening!

First, I will report that we are alive and well and we wish you the same in your young and flowering life and also in the difficulties and privations of military service.

Everything's fine here, Vanya. Orfei Stepanovich, the schoolteacher who you saw at our wedding, fell under a train while in an intoxicated state, due to which his daughter Valentina came back from the German Democratic Republic for the funeral. She wept and grieved terrible. We slaughtered the hog for the October holidays so now we've got bacon fat and meat, there's only one problem, you don't live close by and haven't written us for three whole months. Mama keeps asking when your term of duty is up, and Vadik says—Mama, will I be able to call Uncle Vanya Papa? What do you think, huh???!

Enough about myself.

The weather's been cold, lots of snow. The old men say it means a bumper crop. Boris joined the KPSS party because he was promoted to the position of head bookkeeper which is very serious work.

I remain your loving wife Ludmilla.

P.S. Vanya, come see us soon, Mama has baked some piroshkis with mushrooms, they're waiting for you.

Having no desire to postpone answering, Altinnik at once made room on his night table and started writing:

*Ludmilla, in the first lines of my short letter allow me
to communicate to you that I consider our lawful
marriage null and void because you and your Boris
(now he's a Communist!) deceived me when drunk,
in view of which I consider the marriage null and
void, and ask you not to bother me any more.*

Sincerely not yours, Ivan.

P.S. As for the piroshki, eat them yourselves.

He did not address the letter to Ludmilla Altinnik but
to Ludmilla Sirova.

He gave the letter to Kazik Ivanov and requested that
it be mailed by regular civilian post.

He waited with bated breath for whatever troubles
would come. Two weeks later he received another letter.
Ludmilla wrote as if nothing had happened:

*Vanya, I received your letter, thanks a lot. Everything's
the same here. Mama was a little ill with catarrh
of the upper respiratory passages but it is all better
now. Our neighbor Yurka Krinin got a shock while
fixing a television. The men here buried him in the
ground, but they should have given him artificial
respiration, mouth-to-mouth was necessary, as a result
of which the fatal outcome was inevitable.*

*Vanya, I want to let you know of the enormous
joy which is overflowing from my heart and soul.
We're going to have . . . a baby!!! How does this
look to you, eh???*

It looked to Altinnik like he was going to pass out.
In his answer he wrote:

*Ludmilla, cut out the jokes, because you and I were
only together once and that one's still not clear. You
should have protected yourself against this if you had*

*no confidence in yourself. All the more so since it
was with a man you didn't know, who you were not
personally acquainted with before, but knew only
on the basis of a correspondence to which you added
a photo of yourself taken before the Revolution. And
if you're having a baby, it won't be mine, which a
legal examination will show; you're a medic working
in public health and ought to know this yourself,
so put that in your pipe and smoke it. And I got sick
of your piroshki a long time back, sincerely not
yours, Ivan."*

This letter, too, he sent by civilian mail. In spite of this,
Ludmilla continued to write regularly, communicating
the latest news from the station, what happened and to
whom. And even when Altinnik stopped answering her
letters and ceased even to read them, returning them un-
read and postage due, Ludmilla did not despair or lose
heart but continued to write with enviable persistence.
On February 23, Altinnik received a happy-holiday telegram, and on May 1 a package arrived which he refused
to accept, showing no interest in its contents, which he
took to be piroshki with mushrooms.

17

In the summer the regiment moved camp to the village
of Grakovo.

The season began with several flight incidents. One
pilot lost his way in the air, used up all his fuel, and
landed in an open field forty kilometers from the airfield
with a mangled chassis. They wrote off the plane.

Another pilot broke the front strut on his chassis while
landing; his cannons came unscrewed and one even

pierced the gas tank. When they broke through the cabin with a wedge-shaped lantern, the pilot was up to his throat in gasoline, and was lucky that he hadn't caught on fire.

A high commission headed by a general arrived to investigate the two incidents. For days at a time the general in his long blue shorts waded in the local stream, the Grakovka, with his dragnet, while at night he would play preference with the senior officers. It was said he lost four roubles.

As far as the incidents themselves were concerned, it was the conclusion of the commission that poor military discipline was entirely to blame.

Naturally, it was the non-coms who caught hell because the pilots didn't know how to fly their planes. The rank-and-file soldiers and sergeants were deprived of leave for one month. But there was no place to go anyway. There were only old women in the village, and the few young girls who were still there all worked in the unit as cooks and waitresses in the flight mess. The waitresses snubbed the common soldiers and sergeants. There were plenty of officers in the summertime.

About three kilometers from the village there was the Grakovo train station, and the Grakovo Sovkhoz. Altinnik knew a girl there by the name of Nina. She was seventeen and in the tenth grade at school. Altinnik had serious intentions concerning Nina and he was waiting impatiently for the damned month to be over so that at last he would be a free man again.

And then, finally, that day arrived. On Saturday, after the flights, seven men formed a line in front of their tents. Master Sergeant de Gaulle, his hands behind his back, walked in front of the line, checking the cleanliness of their undercollars, the shine on their buttons and shoes. He stopped in front of Altinnik and examined him thoroughly. Altinnik went totally tense, afraid any second the sergeant would find fault with something.

"Altinnik," said the sergeant, "you've been summoned to the squadron commander's."

"What for?" asked Altinnik in surprise.

"If they want you, there's a reason."

He found the major in the building across from headquarters, where the pilots did their flight critiques and the mechanics received their political training. The major was sitting at an eight-sided table on which lay a flight helmet, a pair of eyeglasses, a map case, and a thick logbook in which the major, his tongue protruding, was entering information about the last day's flight.

Had Altinnik met the major on the street in civilian clothes, he would never have believed that this fat, flabby man with his womanish face flew a jet fighter and was considered one of the best pilots in the entire division. Nevertheless, many people considered the major a fool, because he rode a bicycle while the other pilots all had cars.

Having marked off his last three steps in parade form in proper fashion, Altinnik stood at attention before the major and tossed off a brisk salute. "Comrade major, Junior Sergeant Altinnik reporting as ordered."

Taking a second to tear himself away from his log, the major brought his eyes up to Altinnik and shook his head back and forth. "Look at you, you're all shined up like a samovar. All set to be discharged, then?"

"Yes sir, comrade major!" roared out Altinnik.

"Thinking of going on a binge?" The major bent over his logbook.

"No sir!"

"Or maybe you've got a date with a girl?"

"Yes sir!" Altinnik smiled confidentially, as if to say, We men understand each other. But the major did not see the smile because he was writing again.

"Yes, yes." The major turned the page and started scribbling again. "And do you have your service ID book with you?"

"Yes sir!" shouted Altinnik automatically, feeling his heart sink. He realized that what he had feared for so long was now about to happen.

"Lay it right here." With his free hand, the major whacked his desk, indicating precisely where Altinnik was to place his service book, and continuing to write without raising his head.

Altinnik unbuttoned his right breast pocket, felt the document's stiff cover, but delayed withdrawing it, as if hoping that the major might just forget all about it.

"Let's have it, let's have it," said the major, extending his hand without looking up at Altinnik. Sinking with terror and the premonition of disaster, Altinnik laid the document at the edge of the table. The major raked it in. Continuing to write in his logbook, he leafed through the pages of Altinnik's service book, his gaze moving from the one to the other, so that Altinnik, no matter how frightened he was of what lay in store for him, could still marvel how well he did both things at once. Thus, leafing through Altinnik's service book, the major reached the page containing the ill-fated stamp. The major glanced at the stamp, finished off whatever he was writing, put a period at the end of the sentence, then pushed aside the logbook, map case, and helmet. He drew the service book up closer.

"Look at this," said the major in surprise, seeming to be examining the book out of the corner of his eye. "Marriage registered with Sirova, Ludmilla Ivanovna. What is the meaning of this?" He drew back from the service book and poked the stamp with as much disgust as if it had been some sort of bedbug or cockroach.

Not knowing what to say, Altinnik said nothing.

"I'm asking you what's the meaning of this?" The major slammed his fist against his desk with such force that the map case and helmet jumped into the air.

Altinnik did not respond.

"Altinnik!" The major was growing incensed, "I'm asking you in plain Russian who this Ludmilla Sirova is? Who gave you the right to get married without the permission of the regimental commander?"

At that point Altinnik felt everything that had been building up in him form into a lump in his throat and then suddenly come rushing out of him as one wild strange sound resembling the bleating of a sheep.

"What, are you laughing?" said the major, astonished. However, he immediately realized that Altinnik was not laughing at all but, having seized hold of a column, was thrashing about hysterically.

Frightened, the major ran over to Altinnik, grabbed him by the shoulders, and looked at his face. Altinnik was ashamed to be howling and wanted to regain control of himself but could not.

"Altinnik," said the major softly, almost whispering. "Come now, please stop, I beg you. I didn't mean to hurt your feelings. So, you met some woman there, you fell in love, you decided to get married, fine, fine, no one's going to make trouble for you. But you could at least have told me before, so I'd have known. When I got this letter out of the blue." The major took a sheet of graph paper from his map case. Continuing to sob, but much calmer now, Altinnik saw the all too familiar handwriting:

In view of the unsteady moral character of my husband, Altinnik, Ivan, I ask you not to discharge him, so that he can avoid chance meetings with women of easy morals. This will guard against the breakup of a family, a very undesirable thing . . . Yours . . .

This was followed by some sort of flourish and, printed out, in parentheses, Mrs. Altinnik.

Altinnik read the document through, then fixed his eyes on the signature and felt his lips going out of control again. Once more he broke into tears, weeping inconsolably as he had not done since he was a child.

18

In September another group came up for discharge, eight men out of the entire air squadron, Altinnik among them. On the previous evening the major had delivered a solemn speech in front of the formation and handed discharge papers to each of the eight.

The next morning after breakfast the major appeared again while the new civilians were lining up with their suitcases. He wore his full-dress uniform, which his twenty years in the service had still not taught him to wear properly; his belt was askew, his forage cap was on his ears. Altinnik, as the highest-ranking non-com, gave the command: "Attention!"

"At ease," said the major. He walked past the formation.

"Well, well, well, you're all ready. And glad of it, too, I suppose. Fed up, I bet." Looking around conspiratorially, he whispered: "And to tell you the truth, I'm fed up, too. Right to here!" He drew a line across his throat with the edge of his hand.

All eight of them started laughing, and Altinnik joined in, realizing perhaps for the first time that the major wasn't a bad guy at heart. You could see it was no bed of roses for him either, in spite of his being a top-ranking pilot and pulling down good money.

The major shook hands with each of them, wishing them all the things people wish others in such circumstances. Altinnik commanded: "Left, quick march," and they set off toward the gate, no longer in formation, but in a sort of traveling lump.

Naturally, no transportation had been provided for them—there was talk that the major had argued with the regimental commander about this—so they had a three-kilometer walk to the station ahead of them, luggage and all.

Upon reaching the checkpoint, they ran into Kazik Ivanov with his mail pouch. One last time they ran up to him and asked if there was any mail.

"Something for you," Kazik said to Altinnik.

"Where from?"

"Zhitomir."

"Keep it." Altinnik dismissed the letter with a wave of his hand.

"It's a deal," laughed Kazik, beckoning Altinnik off to one side. "Listen, there's some woman waiting for you over by the checkpoint."

"Who is she?" said Altinnik, instantly on his guard.

"I don't know. She's got a kid with her. Says she's your wife."

"Of all the . . ." said Altinnik with a sinking heart. "You guys go on ahead," he shouted to the others. "I'll catch up."

He decided to leave through the gate at the far end of camp. But when he was passing through that gate, the first person he saw was Boris. Wearing a new blue suit, white shirt and tie, Boris was chatting with the sentry. Catching sight of Altinnik, Boris broke into a friendly smile and advanced toward him as he set his suitcase down on the ground.

"What are you doing here?" Altinnik asked sullenly.

"Aw, it's Ludka, she got all panicked," said Boris, laughing. 'Go over there,' she says. 'Stand watch; otherwise he might not know we're waiting.'" Boris turned toward the main gate and, cupping his hand to his mouth, shouted: "Ludka! Over here!"

Altinnik was at a total loss. What should he do, run? But how could he, with a suitcase? They'd catch up to him. And Ludmilla, carrying a white bundle tied with a blue ribbon, was already near.

"Don't cry, don't cry," she muttered as she ran, shaking the bundle. "Here's your dear daddy, here's your dear daddy now waiting for us, so don't you cry." She switched the bundle to her left arm, and before Altinnik realized what was happening, she had wound her right arm around his neck and pressed her lips to his. He pushed Ludmilla away, not abruptly but firmly, stepped off to the side, and wiped his lips.

"What's that?" he said, nodding at the bundle.

"What," mimicked Boris unhappily. "Not what, who. It's a person."

"That's your little son, Vanya," corroborated Ludmilla. "Piotr Ivanovich Altinnik."

A squeal could be heard from the bundle, issued, no doubt, by Piotr Ivanovich. Once again Ludmilla began dandling the infant and speaking softly to him. "No, no, don't cry, Petenka, my little golden baby bird. Your papa's here, he won't leave you."

Altinnik circled his suitcase. "Look here, Ludmilla," he said softly. "Don't overdo it with your kid, because I don't know how you got him and I'm no relation to it. And as for all the rest of it, I don't consider our marriage anything, because you tricked me into it when I was not in what you could call a sober state."

He picked up his suitcase and set off resolutely toward the road leading to the station.

"Oi, God! Oi, this is terrible!" Ludmilla began wailing and mincing at the same time. "Now we've tricked him!" she shouted, her voice surprisingly throaty and repulsive. "Now we've tricked him!"

Altinnik quickened his pace.

"Petenka!" Ludmilla shouted to the little bundle. "My little son! Your papa's tricked you! He's leaving you, your own papa! Oh, my poor dear little orphan boy!"

Altinnik could not bear it and he stopped. He looked back at the gate to the camp. A crowd of off-duty soldiers had come pouring out of the sentry room and were eagerly watching.

"Ludmilla," he said with real feeling, "I beg you, leave me alone. You know it has nothing to do with me."

"What do you mean, nothing?" said Boris, walking up to them. "The child's just the image of you. No matter who we show him to in the village, they all say it's like two peas in a pod. Take a look yourself. Ludka, stop screaming and hand me the baby."

Boris took the bundle from his sister and unwrapped

the top of the blanket. Altinnik squinted up his eyes involuntarily. There was something red and wrinkled in there, which looked more like an unripe tomato than like him, Ivan Altinnik. But some higher force whispered in Altinnik's ear: "It's yours." A nameless sadness came over him and his heart began to ache. But to give in now for the child's sake meant resigning himself to putting aside all his ambitions.

"It's not mine," said Altinnik, licking his lips.

"Ach, it's not yours?" screeched Ludmilla. "Here, you take him!" Before Altinnik could bat an eye, the bundle was in the dust at his feet. "Keep him, you rotten skunk!" cried Ludmilla and started running toward the station. "Boris!" she called, already some distance off. "Let's get out of here. Why are you standing there?"

"Coming," said Boris guiltily. Indecisively at first and then at a run, he went after Ludmilla. He stopped her when he caught up with her, and the two of them had a brief quarrel and then continued on their way, without looking back.

Suitcase in hand, his mouth agape, Altinnik stood a long while watching them go.

"Waaaa!" A faint squeal rose from his feet. "Waaa!"

Altinnik set down his suitcase and knelt beside the bundle. He turned down one corner of the blanket. The little red creature who was nothing but one wide-open mouth was wailing from unbearable grief. Where he got the strength to cry so loudly was more than Altinnik could understand.

"Hey, come on, Piotr Ivanovich!" Altinnik shook his head. "What are you yelling about? No one's leaving you. Here, I'll take you and bring you to your mother. To your grandmother. She's got nothing to do, let her look after you."

19

The sun was approaching its zenith. The train which Altinnik had been rushing to catch had long since departed and he was still no more than halfway to the station. It was so scorchingly hot it seemed more like the middle of July than September. Having removed his belt and unbuttoned all the buttons on his field shirt, Altinnik walked on, staggering in the dust, blinded by the dazzling sun and the sweat pouring down into his eyes. He kept making frequent stops to catch his breath. His mouth was dry, his chest on fire. The suitcase pulled on his right hand, the bundle on his left. The baby had worked its crooked little legs free and was now twisting them around in the air and, howling relentlessly, was trying to wriggle all the way out. Altinnik dandled the baby, adjusted the blanket, and continued on.

At a certain moment he noticed that the baby had stopped crying, and taking a closer look, he saw that he was holding it by the head. "He got smothered," thought Altinnik in horror. He threw down his suitcase and began to shake the baby with both hands, repeating: "A-a-a-a-a-a."

The baby came around and started crying. Suddenly he began growing wetter and wetter as if some huge bubble had burst inside the blanket. Now Altinnik lost his head completely. Grimacing, he laid the baby down by the side of the road and walked off to one side and sat down on his suitcase.

"Cry, go on, cry," he said angrily. "Cry till you burst, I'm not going over."

He turned away. There was nothing but bare steppeland all around him. In the far distance, the dark shapes of the airfield buildings shimmered in the haze. There was no one in sight. If only a car would appear on the empty road. Altinnik lit up a cigarette, though his throat was already scratchy. Now it felt positively horrible. He flung the cigarette away with fury. Remembering the baby, he looked reluctantly over at it and froze in terror. A large filthy crow was circling the baby with quick little steps, its head cocked to one side.

"Get out of there, damn you!" Altinnik rushed at the bird.

"Karrrr!" cried the crow with a screech of displeasure. Flapping its wings wearily, it rose in the air and flew toward a lone, distant tree.

The baby, which had grown quiet, now started crying again. Altinnik walked over reluctantly, folded back the blanket, then the swaddling clothes with two fingers. He saw that the problem was even worse than he had expected.

Overcoming his squeamishness, he began wiping the baby with the dry end of the swaddling clothes, which he then threw on the ground a few steps away. He got his new, still uncut cotton puttees from his suitcase and began wrapping Piotr Ivanovich up in them.

"Altinnik!" he heard from behind him, and shuddering, he turned around. There on the road was the major with his bicycle. Without realizing what he was doing, Altinnik rose to his feet and stood so as to block the baby from view.

"Yours, I suppose?" the major asked sympathetically. Setting his bicycle down on the ground, he walked over and peeked in the bundle. "What a resemblance–" he said, touched by the sight. "He's the image of you."

These words both gladdened and grieved Altinnik. Meanwhile, the major was fussing over the baby like a regular nanny.

"Who wrapped him up like that?" said the major, distressed. "Even though those are puttees, that's a baby you're wrapping up, not your legs. Look, here's how it's done. First this arm by itself, then the other. And now the legs."

And indeed the major, who was unable to dress himself properly, packed up the baby as neatly and snugly as if this was all he'd been doing his entire life.

"So, take him!" He held out the bundle to Altinnik, who took it in his arms and stood awkwardly in front of the major.

"And where's your wife?" asked the major after a moment's silence.

"My wife!" The very words jarred Altinnik. He wanted to explain to the major that she was no wife to him, to tell him how they'd taken him drunk to the village soviet and there perpetrated an outrageous fraud on him. But, not finding any such words in himself, he only indicated the station with his head, saying: "Over there."

"All right, let me give you a hand."

The major picked up the suitcase and hung it on his handlebars. They set off, walking side by side.

Then for the first time that luckless afternoon some luck came Altinnik's way. They heard the sound of a vehicle approaching from behind. Altinnik and the major looked around. A sixteen-ton oil truck was approaching them raising clouds of dust. The major stood in the middle of the road, his hand raised. The truck came to a stop. A soldier (fortunately, no one Altinnik knew) leaned curiously out of the cab.

"Hey, brother!" said the major, running over. "Be a buddy and give your comrade a lift."

"Glad to, comrade major." The driver flung the cab door open.

"So you see, Altinnik, things are turning out all right," said the major in good spirits. "Give the baby here, I'll hold him while you climb in."

When Altinnik was seated, the major handed him the baby. The driver stepped on the clutch and shifted into gear.

"Hold it!" The major waved him down and clambered up on the running board. "Altinnik, the thing is . . ." He broke off suddenly, hunting for the right words. "If it's rough going in the beginning, drop me a line, maybe I can give you a hand, send you a little money. As a loan, of course. Don't be bashful. I earn good money. It's no trouble for me to help you out. So write. You know the address and my last name. The rest is Fyodor Ilich."

Altinnik wanted to thank him, but his tongue would not obey him and his lips began to twitch, just as they had earlier in their conversation.

The major hopped off the running board and waved goodbye. The driver stepped on the gas and they were off.

"Fyodor Ilich," the driver said and started laughing. "Your commanding officer, huh?" He squinted at Altinnik.

"Uh-huh," said Altinnik.

"What a queer duck." The driver turned his head and laughed again. "You could tell right off he was cracked."

Altinnik did not reply and leaned out the window. The major was earnestly pedaling his bicycle, which was too fragile for his corpulent bulk. He did not look up at Altinnik.

20

The driver took Altinnik right to the station.

"Thanks, buddy," said Altinnik sincerely as he was getting out of the cab with the baby.

"It's all right, no trouble." The driver handed him the suitcase, looked over at him, and burst out laughing again. "Take it easy, papa."

Altinnik had no trouble finding Ludmilla and Boris. They were sitting on the grass in the little square by the train station, munching on the piroshkis they'd spread out on a piece of newspaper and taking turns sipping at a bottle of soda. Altinnik sat down beside them without saying a word and laid the baby across his knees. The brother and sister greeted him as if nothing had happened.

"Have a bite of piroshki," offered Boris.

"I don't want any," refused Altinnik.

"Go on, you love them with mushrooms," said Ludmilla sweetly.

The mere memory of those mushrooms caused him a mild nausea. He swallowed his saliva and said quite calmly: "Here's the thing, Ludmilla, I've made up my mind. You don't want to take the baby, I'll keep him with me. I'll give him to my mother, she's on pension now. It'll be a treat for her."

Ludmilla gobbled down a piroshki and did not reply and only looked over at Boris.

"Now it's his mother." Boris took a sip from the bottle, wiped his lips with the back of his hand, and shook some crumbs off his jacket. "How old is your mother?"

"What do you care how old she is?" asked Altinnik hostilely.

"Just curious," said Boris. "Can she breast-feed the baby?"

Altinnik grew thoughtful. Somehow or other he had not given any thought to the question of breast-feeding. Unable to control herself, Ludmilla spat out a mouthful into her fist; apparently a crumb had gotten caught in her windpipe. Her eyes bulging, she turned red and began choking and coughing. Boris pounded her back with the flat of his hand.

"Maybe she'll choke to death," thought Altinnik hopefully, but unfortunately, her fit passed.

Roused by the commotion, the baby woke up and started crying.

"Give him here." Ludmilla took her son, laid him on her knees, and pulled out her breast, white and covered with dark blue veins. The sight of her breast had the same effect on Altinnik as the mention of piroshki had, and he turned away.

He sat for a while without saying a word, then rose to his feet and picked up his suitcase.

"All right then," he said, without looking at them. "You don't want me to have the baby, fine with me. I'm going." And he started walking slowly toward the station.

He had not gone ten steps when he heard a terrible, inhuman cry from behind him. He looked around. One breast dangling, a bestial expression on her face, Ludmilla was charging him, screaming something of which he could make out only two words: "bastard" and "worm." Altinnik took off at a run.

A policeman sprang from the side door of the station. There wasn't time for Altinnik to dodge him. The policeman tripped him and they both went sprawling in the dust. Altinnik's suitcase was knocked open and his winter hat, toothbrush, and a bar of soap went flying out onto the road. The policeman was the first to get hold of himself. He sat on Altinnik and twisted his right arm behind his back.

"Let go!" Altinnik struggled and felt an immediate pain in his elbow.

"Don't try to twist around," said the policeman. "It'll be worse for you if you do. Now up on your feet."

Altinnik got up and began wiping the dust from his cheek with his free hand.

"Aha, so you got caught!" cried Ludmilla with malicious joy. "Arrest him, comrade policeman!"

"What has he done?" asked the policeman sternly.

"Abandoned me!" Ludmilla covered her breast and began wailing. "With a little child . . . still at my breast . . ."

"Uh-huh," drawled the policeman, disappointed, clearly regretting that he'd gotten involved in this spat. "That's what I thought. Straighten it out yourselves!"

Letting Altinnik go, he brushed off his knees and started back to his post.

Altinnik bent down to gather up the items that had fallen from his suitcase. Boris walked over, holding the baby, bent down, and picked up the toothbrush.

"You'll have to wash it," said Boris.

"Give me that!" Altinnik grabbed the toothbrush, threw it in the suitcase, and then began a long struggle with the lock.

Ludmilla was standing beside him, wailing softly, just as she had on their wedding day.

"Stop wailing," said Altinnik in disgust. "I'm not going to live with you, no matter what, so forget it."

"And you'd be doing the right thing, too," said Boris, offering unexpected support.

Altinnik was taken aback and looked over at him. Ludmilla began wailing even louder.

"You were told to stop wailing, and that means stop wailing," Boris shouted at her. "Take the baby and go back where you were."

Shocked, Ludmilla quieted down at once, took the baby, and went back to where she had been sitting.

"Bitch!" said Boris, spitting with gusto as he watched her go. "Now let's talk man to man."

"All right, shoot," said Altinnik gloomily.

"Vanya, I'm begging you," said Boris, putting his hand on his heart, "come with us."

"Not that again!" Exasperated, Altinnik grabbed his suitcase. "I thought you had something different to say."

"No, hold it," said Boris. "First listen to me."

"I don't want to listen," said Altinnik, starting for the station.

"I beg you, listen." Boris ran out ahead of Altinnik. "What I have to say won't cost you anything. And if you still don't agree, that's your business. I'm just giving you some friendly advice. Come with us. You can see Ludka's not herself today. She won't let go, no matter what. She'll scratch your eyes out."

"That's right, she will." Altinnik grinned. "You see this?" He brought his fist up to Boris's nose. "One punch and you're out cold."

"What kind of talk is that!" Boris began waving his arms. "Don't even think about it! You start in like that and the police'll be here in a minute, and then you'll spend the rest of your life in one jail or another. Vanya, I'm giving you this advice from the heart—come with us. Live with her a couple of days for the sake of appearances. Then you can slip away on a night train. I'll carry your bag myself. Just so that people see you there, that's all."

"Quit it, will you," said Altinnik. "Where do you want me to go and for what? My travel voucher is for the other direction. My mother's waiting for me. I haven't got the money to spend traveling all over the place."

"Don't worry about the ticket," Boris assured him. "Your ticket's already been paid for, and I'll buy you your ticket back. I give you my party word of honor. As for your mother, that's no problem. Send her a telegram, she can wait a couple more days. She's waited longer than that already. I'm telling you, Ludka's a very good woman. Educated, clean. Knows how to behave in public. But she's crazy, she fell head over heels in love with you. No matter what you say to her, she always comes back with the same thing: 'I want to live with Ivan, and that's that.' Sometimes both me and my mother tell her: 'What are you throwing yourself at him for? You know he doesn't want to live with you. Is that any way to start a life together, if there's no love from the start?' 'No,' she says, 'I'll force him, he'll love me.' So, let's go, Vanya. You can have a good time for a couple of days with us, rest up, and then, just as soon as she calms down a bit, you can hop on the train and hightail it home."

Altinnik gave it some thought. He had no desire for a scene on the spot, where soldiers from his unit could appear at any moment. Of course, it was risky business going to Ludmilla's, but the truth was he could always run off. In a pinch he could leave the suitcase behind; there wasn't anything all that valuable in it anyhow.

"Well, all right." He was still sorting out the possibilities. All things considered, it would be easier to make his escape later on than right then and there. "So you'll really give me the fare for the trip back?"

"How many times do I have to swear it?" Now even Boris's feelings were a little hurt. "I said it and I will."

"But now listen"—Altinnik decided to throw in a threat for good measure—"any tricks and I'll cut all of you to ribbons. I'll take a firing squad over living with Ludmilla."

21

Four years ago, while on assignment, I happened to travel to Kirzavod Station. While waiting for the car I'd been promised to take me to the district center, I was sitting on the porch of a wooden hut with supports like chicken legs, the local train station. Smoking my cigarettes, I kept thinking where I'd heard the name Kirzavod Station before.

The small square in front of the train station was paved with asphalt, but all the roads leading into it were nothing but dust. In the center of the square was a concrete pedestal, part of a monument to someone either recently deposed or soon to be installed. A red hen and her chicks, fluffy as dandelions, were puttering about in the shade of the pedestal while two boys around twelve, and a young policeman, whose pants were tucked into his brown socks, kept circling the pedestal on their bicycles. The street intersecting the square was deserted. Once a small Belarus steamshovel went by, its shovel in the air; later a calf with a rake tied to its tail ran past, pursued by a pack of children of all ages raising a cloud of dust. The boys bicycling on the square immediately joined in the pursuit; the policeman started after them but then changed his mind and returned to the square, where he continued industriously tracing circles and figure eights with his bicycle.

A man sat down on the step beside me. At first I did not even look over at him. Obviously wishing to strike up a conversation, he sighed, coughed, and said: "Oooo, the heat."

"And how," I agreed, thinking that next he'd ask for a cigarette. Which he did.

"Could you spare a smoke?" he asked, figuring we were

already well enough acquainted to make such a request.

"Sure." I held out the pack, still observing the policeman.

"Look at that, filters!" he marveled. "Take two, all right?"

"All right."

"I left my matches home, too," he said, aware he was getting close to his limit. He bent toward me to get a light off mine. It was then that I really looked at him for the first time and saw who he was. "Altinnik!"

And naturally I also immediately remembered where I'd heard of Kirzavod Station before.

"You don't recognize me?" I asked.

"I don't seem to," he muttered, looking me in the face. I told him my name.

"Aha." He did not display any particular pleasure. "I'll take another cigarette from you. For tonight."

"Go ahead," I said. "Take the rest. I've got more."

"You don't happen to have a fresh pack?"

I gave him an unopened pack from my suitcase.

Then we went to a little store across from the train station. A fat salesgirl in a dirty dress poured us each a hundred and fifty grams of vodka and a mug of beer. I drank my vodka straight, but Altinnik mixed the two. We stood by the window so that the square was in my view and I didn't have to worry about missing my ride.

We talked about one thing and another. We recalled our days in the service, the major, Sergeant de Gaulle, the others. I didn't quiz Altinnik about his life, but I discovered a few things anyway. Altinnik had returned to Kirzavod with Ludmilla and Boris, with no intention of lingering there; he still planned to trick Ludmilla and slip away, but Ludmilla was forever on the lookout. By day she would cause such scenes that it wasn't even worth trying to escape, and at night the slightest sound would wake her up. He kept waiting, waiting for the right moment, and by then she was pregnant again. He tried to force her to have an abortion—she wouldn't hear of it. Now there was nowhere for him to go. Who'd want a man who had to pay a third of his earnings out for child support? And in the meantime he'd grown sort of used to the first child.

"How many do you have altogether?" I couldn't keep from asking.

"Three," said Altinnik sheepishly. "Not counting Vadik, of course."

"Vadik's living with you?"

"No. In Leningrad. He's finishing up at the Railway Institute," he said, not without a certain pride.

"What kind of work are you doing?"

"What kind am I doing?" He hesitated, not wishing to answer. Then he blurted it out defiantly. "I'm a watchman. I work at the crossing. When a train comes, I lift the gate, and then I lower it after it's gone. Can you afford another round of beer?"

We had just placed our mugs on the windowsill when the door to the store flew open, revealing a woman in a red sarafan. Her belly bulged like a soccer ball under her dress, there were telltale spots on her cheeks, her eyes sparkled.

"Aha, so here you are!" she shouted at Altinnik. "I just knew you'd be here, you worm. His children haven't got shoes on their feet, and here he is, drinking away his last kopeck!"

Altinnik shriveled, his whole body seeming to diminish.

"What are you talking about, Ludmilla," he attempted to object. "I just ran into my old friend here. We were in the army together. Introduce yourself."

"Sure, that's all I need, to introduce myself to every drunkard you run into."

"Stop disgracing yourself, Ludmilla," Altinnik beseeched her. "It's him that's treating me."

"I'm supposed to believe that," said Ludmilla, unyielding. "There's only one fool in the whole Soviet Union fool enough to buy strangers drinks, and that's you."

"Ludmilla, it's true the other guy paid," said the fat salesgirl impassively.

"Keep your nose out of this, you lousy bitch." Ludmilla turned to her. "The only thing you know about is making cow eyes at other women's husbands."

Before either the salesgirl could respond or I could regain my bearings, Ludmilla had dragged her husband outside, where all Kirzavod could hear her wild, repulsive screeching.

They were quite a ways off by the time I went outside. Altinnik was walking out in front, his head bowed; Ludmilla was holding him by the collar with her left hand and using her small right fist to pound his head with all her might. On the other side of the street, the policeman with the pants tucked into his brown socks was bicycling slowly, taking in the whole scene.

1968

A CIRCLE OF FRIENDS

(A NOT PARTICULARLY RELIABLE TALE CONCERNING A CERTAIN HISTORIC GET-TOGETHER)

The building stands behind the high red-brick wall known to the entire world. There are many windows in that building, but one was distinguished from all the others because it was lit twenty-four hours a day. Those who gathered in the evening on the broad square in front of the red-brick wall would crane their necks, strain their eyes to the point of tears, and say excitedly to one another: "Look, over there, the window's lit. He's not sleeping. He's working. He's thinking about us."

If someone came from the provinces to this city or had to stop over while in transit, he'd be informed that it was obligatory to visit that famous square and to look and see whether that window was lit. Upon returning home, the fortunate provincial would deliver authoritative reports, both at closed meetings and at those open to the public, that yes, the window was lit, and judging by all appearances, he truly never slept and was continually thinking about them.

Naturally, even back then, there were certain people who abused the trust of their collectives. Instead of going to look at that window, they'd race around to all the stores, wherever there was anything for sale. But, upon their return, they, too, would report that the window was lit, and just try and tell them otherwise.

The window, of course, was lit. But the person who was said never to sleep was never at that window. A dummy made of gutta-percha, built by the finest craftsmen, stood in for him. That dummy had been so skillfully constructed that unless you actually touched it there was nothing to indicate that it wasn't alive. The dummy duplicated all the basic features of the original. Its hand held a curved pipe of English manufacture, which had a special mechanism that puffed out tobacco smoke at pre-determined intervals. As far as the original himself was concerned, he only smoked his pipe when there were people around, and his moustache was of the paste-on variety. He lived in another room, in which there were not only no windows but not even any doors. That room could only be reached through a crawl-hole in his safe, which had doors both in the front and in the rear and which stood in the room that was officially his.

He loved this secret room where he could be himself and not smoke a pipe or wear that moustache; where he could live simply and modestly, in keeping with the room's furnishings—an iron bed, a striped mattress stuffed with straw, a washbasin containing warm water, and an old gramophone, together with a collection of records which he personally had marked—good, average, remarkable, trash.

There in that room he spent the finest hours of his life in peace and quiet; there, hidden from everyone, he would sometimes sleep with the old cleaning woman who crawled in every morning through the safe with her bucket and broom. He would call her over to him, she would set her broom in the corner in business-like fashion, give herself to him, and then return to her cleaning. In all the years, he had not exchanged a single word with her and was not even absolutely certain whether it was the same old woman or a different one every time.

One time a strange incident occurred. The old woman began rolling her eyes and moving her lips soundlessly.

"What's the matter with you?"

"I was just thinking," the old woman said with a serene smile. "My niece is coming to visit, my brother's daughter. I've got to fix some eats for her, but all I've got is three roubles. So it's either spend two roubles on millet and one on butter, or two on butter and one on millet."

This peasant sagacity touched him deeply. He wrote a note to the storehouse ordering that the old woman be issued as much millet and butter as she needed. The old woman, no fool, did not take the note to the storehouse but to the Museum of the Revolution, where she sold it for enough money to buy herself a little house near Moscow and a cow; she quit her job, and rumor has it that to this day she's still bringing in milk to sell at Tishinsky market.

Recalling this incident, he would often tell his comrades that genuine dialectical thinking had to be learned directly from the people.

One day, having parted with the cleaning woman and finding himself alone, he wound up the gramophone and began thinking great thoughts to the music. It recalled for him the far-off days of his childhood in a small town in the Caucasus: his mother, a simple woman with a wrinkled, sorrowful face; his father, a stubborn man who, through daily toil, had achieved considerable success in the art of shoemaking.

"Soso, you'll never make a real shoemaker. You're too crafty, you try to save on nails," his father would say, hitting him over the head with a last.

All this did not pass without its effect, and now, in later life, he suffered from fierce and frequent headaches. If only he could resurrect his father and ask him how was it possible to beat a child over the head with a last. How much, how passionately he wanted to resurrect his father and ask him . . .

But at that moment something else had him excited. Ominous rumors had reached his ears: Dolph, with whom he had recently become fast friends, was planning to betray their friendship and march across the border. He considered himself the most treacherous man in the world and could not bring himself to believe that there existed someone even more treacherous than he. When the others urged him to prepare to defend himself against Dolph, he treated their words as provocation and did nothing, so as not to offend Dolph with their groundless suspicions. The most suspicious man in the world was as gullible as a child in his relations with Dolph.

The closer the shortest night of the year drew, the more his soul was filled with foreboding. It would be frightening to spend that night alone.

On the eve of the shortest night of the year, he put on his faded, semi-military suit, pasted on his moustache, lit up his pipe, and became the person known to all, Comrade Koba. But before going out among people he turned to the large mirror which hung on the wall across from his bed. Pipe in hand, he ambled past the mirror a few times, gazing at his reflection out of the corner of his eye. He found his reflection satisfactory; it returned some of the grandeur the original possessed, if you didn't examine it too closely. (And who would ever allow himself the luxury of examining Comrade Koba that closely.) He grinned, nodded to his reflection, and then crawled into his office by the usual route, through his safe. He sat down at his desk and struck a pose which indicated that he'd been working days on end without a moment's rest. Without changing his position, he pressed the button on his bell. His private secretary Pokhlebyshev entered.

"Listen, my good man," said Comrade Koba to him. "Why are you always walking around with an armful of papers like some kind of bureaucrat. My word. Better you get the boys together, they can come by after work, a person has to relax somehow, get away from it all, talk, have some fun in the company of close friends."

Pokhlebyshev left and returned a short while later.

"They're all here and waiting for you, Comrade Koba."

"Very good. Let them wait a little."

For in the meantime Koba had found himself a most interesting diversion—cutting the pictures of various industrial leaders from the latest issue of *Ogonyok* and pasting the men's heads on the women's bodies and vice versa. It made for the most curious combinations, though it did use up quite a bit of his precious time.

Finally he appeared in the room where they were waiting for him. There were three rows of bottles on the table: Moskovskaya vodka, and Borzhomi, and Tsinandali dry wine. There were appetizers galore. To avoid confusion, the boys had seated themselves in alphabetical order: Leonty Aria, Nikola Borshchev, Efim Vershilov,

Lazar Kazanovich, Zhorzh Merenkov, Opanas Mirzoyan, and Mocheslav Molokov. They all rose from their chairs when Koba appeared, and greeted his entrance with stormy applause and cries: "Long live Comrade Koba!" "Glory to Comrade Koba!" "Hurrah for Comrade Koba!"

Comrade Koba ran his eyes down the boys' faces, noting with no little surprise the empty chair between Vershilov and Kazanovich.

"And where is our trusty Comrade Zhbanov tonight?" he asked.

Pokhlebyshev stepped out from behind Koba and reported: "Comrade Zhbanov requested permission to be late. His wife is in the hospital dying and she wanted him there in her final moments."

Comrade Koba frowned. A faint shadow flashed across his face.

"Interesting situation we have here," he said, making no attempt to conceal his bitter irony. "We're all here waiting, and as you see, some woman's whim means more to him than being with his friends. It's all right, though. We'll wait a little longer."

Shaking his head in distress, Koba left the room and returned to his office. There wasn't much he could do there. He'd already cut out all the pictures from *Ogonyok;* only the crossword puzzle was left. He pushed it over to Pokhlebyshev.

"You read them off to me, I'll try and figure them out. What's 1 across?"

"The first illegal newspaper in Georgia," read Pokhlebyshev, and shouted out the answer himself: *"Brdzola! Brdzola!"*

"What are you giving me the answer for?" said Koba angrily. "I could have guessed it myself if I'd had time to think. All right, what's 1 down?"

"The largest prehistoric animal," read Pokhlebyshev.

"That's too easy," said Comrade Koba. "The largest animal was the elephant. Why aren't you writing 'elephant'?"

"Doesn't fit, Comrade Koba," said the secretary timidly.

"Doesn't fit? Of course, prehistoric. So write—'mammoth.'"

Pokhlebyshev bent over the crossword puzzle with his pencil, tapping the squares with the point, and then raised desperate eyes to Koba.

"Doesn't fit either?" asked Koba, amazed. "What's going on here? Was there really some animal bigger than a mammoth? Give it here." Sucking on his pipe, he examined the puzzle, counting the squares and thinking out loud: "Twelve letters. First letter—B. Could it be 'badger'? No. 'Beaver,' 'bulldog,' but they're all pretty small animals if I'm not mistaken. Why don't we call up one of our eminent biologists? Why should we rack our brains when they can give us a scientific answer if there was an animal beginning with B bigger than a mammoth. And if there wasn't, I don't envy the author of that crossword puzzle."

The telephone rang shrilly in the apartment of Academician Pleshivenko. A hoarse, imperious voice demanded that Pleshivenko come immediately to the phone. His sleepy wife answered angrily that Comrade Pleshivenko could not come to the phone, he was ill and sleeping.

"Wake him up!" An abrupt order was her reply.

"How dare you!" she said indignantly. "Do you know who you're speaking to?"

"I know," the voice answered impatiently. "Wake him up!"

"This is outrageous! I'll lodge a complaint! I'll phone the police!"

"Wake him up!" the voice insisted.

But by that time the academician was already awake.

"Trosha," said his wife, running to him, "Trosha, here, you take it."

Trosha took the phone irritably.

"Comrade Pleshivenko? Comrade Koba will speak personally with you in one moment."

"Comrade Koba?" Pleshivenko leaped out of bed as if lifted by the wind. Barefoot and naked except for his underpants, he stood on the cold floor, his wife beside him, immobile, her expression a mixture of joy and terror.

"Comrade Pleshivenko," a familiar voice with a Georgian accent boomed through the receiver. "Forgive me for calling so late . . ."

"Don't mention it, Comrade Koba," sputtered Pleshivenko. "It's my pleasure . . . mine and my wife's . . ."

"Comrade Pleshivenko," interrupted Koba, "to get right to the point, I'm calling on business. Certain of our comrades here have come up with a rather odd and unusual idea—with the aim of increasing the production of meat and milk, what if we were to somehow reintroduce to our fauna the largest prehistoric animal, what the hell is the name of it again, it's a twelve-letter word, I remember, beginning with B."

"Brontosaurus?" asked Pleshivenko uncertainly after a moment's thought.

Koba made quick use of his fingers: "B, r, o, n . . ." He covered the phone with the palm of his hand and, winking slyly, whispered to Pokhlebyshev: "Fill in 'brontosaurus.'" And then he said loudly into the phone: "Yes, exactly right, brontosaurus. And what's your reaction to this idea?"

"Comrade Koba," said Pleshivenko, all composure lost, "it's a very bold and original idea . . . That is, I mean to say that it's simply an idea of . . ."

"Genius!" said the academician's wife with a little punch in his side as she awoke from her stupor. She did not know exactly what they were talking about, but she did know that the word "genius" was never out of place in such situations.

"Simply an idea of genius!" said the academician decisively, squinting off into space.

"For me it's only a working hypothesis," said Comrade Koba modestly. "We sit around, we work, we think."

"But it's a hypothesis of genius," objected the academician boldly. "It's a magnificent plan for the transformation of the animal world. If only you would permit our institute to get to work on elaborating some of the individual aspects of the problem . . ."

"I think some more hard thinking is still required. Once again I apologize for calling so late."

Pleshivenko stood for a long time with the receiver pressed to his ear and, listening intently to the distant, rapid, whistling sounds, whispered reverently but loud enough to be heard: "A genius! A genius! How fortunate I am to have the chance to live in the same era with him!"

The academician was not sure that anyone had heard him but still hoped that his words had not gone amiss.

Everything was in order when Comrade Koba returned. Anton Zhbanov had been found and installed in his usual seat. Leonty Aria had filled their tall glasses with vodka. Comrade Koba proposed the first toast.

"Dear friends," he said, "I invited you here to celebrate, among friends, the shortest night of the year, which is

now beginning and which shall be followed by the longest day of the year . . ."

"Hurrah!" cried Vershilov.

"Not so fast," said Comrade Koba, knitting his brows.
"You're always jumping the gun. I want to propose a
toast—that all our nights be short, and that all our days
be long . . ."

"Hurrah!" cried Vershilov.

"You son of a bitch!" Enraged, Comrade Koba spat in
his face.

Vershilov wiped the spit off with his sleeve and
grinned.

"I also want to propose a toast to our wisest statesman,
the staunchest revolutionary, the most brilliant . . ." began Koba.

Vershilov was about to shout "Hurrah!" just to be on
the safe side, realizing that butter never spoils the por-
ridge, but this time Comrade Koba managed to spit directly into Vershilov's open mouth.

". . . to a man great in both theory and practice, to
Comrade . . ." Koba prolonged his significant pause,
which he then terminated sharply: "Molokov."

The room fell silent. Merenkov and Mirzoyan exchanged glances. Borshchev unbuttoned the collar of his
Ukrainian shirt. Aria clapped, then grabbed at his back
pocket, which some angular object was bulging out of
shape.

Two silent figures appeared in the doorway and froze.

Turning pale, Molokov set his glass aside and rose to
his feet, holding on to the back of his chair so as not to
fall.

"Comrade Koba," Molokov said in tongue-tied reproach, "what's this about? You're hurting my feelings
without any reason to. You know I'm unworthy of all

that praise, that nothing of the sort ever enters my mind. All my modest achievements are only a reflection of your great ideas. I am, if I may so express myself, merely a rank-and-file advocate of Kobaism, the greatest doctrine of our age. At your command, I am ready to give my all for you, even my life. It is you who are the staunchest revolutionary, you who are the greatest practitioner and theoretician . . ."

"A genius!" proclaimed Aria, raising his glass with his left hand since his right hand was still on his pocket.

"A marvelous architect!" acclaimed Merenkov.

"Best friend of the Armenian people!" interjected Mirzoyan.

"And the Ukrainian!" added Borshchev.

"Antosha, why aren't you saying anything?" Koba turned to Zhbanov, who had a sorrowful look about him.

"What is there left for me to say, Comrade Koba?" objected Zhbanov. "The comrades have done a first-rate job of illuminating your comprehensive role in history and contemporary life. Perhaps we say too little about it, perhaps we shy away from high-flown talk, but it's the truth all the same, that's the way it all really is. Everyday life furnishes us with dozens of striking examples which demonstrate how Kobaism is constantly penetrating deeper and deeper into the consciousness of the masses and truly becoming a guiding star for all mankind. But, Comrade Koba, here, in the free and open company of friends, I would like to point out yet another enormous talent you possess which your innate modesty prevents you from ever mentioning. It is your literary talent I have in mind. Yes, comrades," he said, elevating his tone and now addressing the entire company, "not long ago I had occasion to read once again Comrade Koba's early poetry,

which he wrote under the pen name of Sosello. And in all
candor I must say that this poetry, like precious pearls,
could adorn the treasure house of any nation's literature,
of all world literature, and if Pushkin were alive today . . ."

At that point Zhbanov burst into tears.

"Hurrah!" said Vershilov, but quietly this time and
without retaliation from Koba.

The tension left the room. Leonty clapped his hands
and the two silent figures by the door vanished into the
air. Comrade Koba wiped away the tear running down
his cheek. Perhaps he did not enjoy such things being
said to him, but he enjoyed it even less when they were
not.

"Thank you, dear friends," he said, though his tears interfered with his speaking. "Thank you for putting so
high a value on the modest services I have rendered for
the people. I personally think my doctrine, which you
have so aptly named Kobaism, is truly good, not because
it's mine, but because it's a progressive doctrine. And you,
my dear friends, have put no little effort into making it
that progressive. So, without any false modesty, let's drink
to Kobaism."

"To Kobaism! To Kobaism!" They all joined in.

They drank down their vodka, knocked their glasses
against the table, then drank again. After the fourth glass,
Comrade Koba decided he needed a little entertainment
and requested Borshchev to dance the *gopak*.

"You're Ukrainian, you'll do fine," he said encourag-
ingly.

Borshchev hopped from his chair into a squat, Zhbanov
accompanied him on the piano, and the rest of them
clapped their hands in time to the music.

At that moment a messenger appeared without making a sound and handed Zhbanov a telegram informing him that his wife had just died in the hospital.

"Don't bother me," said Zhbanov. "Can't you see I'm busy."

The messenger withdrew. Then Comrade Koba personally strode over to Zhbanov. He stroked his trusty comrade's head with his rough and manly hand.

"You're a true Bolshevik, Antosha," said Koba with feeling.

Zhbanov raised his eyes, full of tears and devotion, to his teacher.

"Keep playing, keep playing," said Comrade Koba. "You could have made a name for yourself as a musician, but you chose to devote all your strength and talent to our party, our people."

Koba walked back to the table and sat down across from Molokov, Mirzoyan, and Merenkov, who were involved in a discussion.

"And what are we talking about here?" asked Comrade Koba.

"We were just saying," Molokov, who was sitting in the middle, answered readily, "that the agreement with Dolph, concluded on your initiative, of course, was both wise and timely."

Koba glowered. Because of the reports that had recently come to his attention, there was nothing he wanted to hear about less than that blasted agreement.

"I'm curious," he said, staring at Molokov, "I'm curious to know why you wear glasses, Mocha?"

Another whiff of danger. Zhbanov began playing more softly. Borshchev, still squatting and dancing, looked from Molokov to Koba. Just to be on the safe side, Merenkov and Mirzoyan moved away, each to one end of the table. Molokov, pale as a ghost, rose on legs out of his control and, not knowing what to say, looked in silence at Comrade Koba.

"So, you cannot tell me why you wear glasses?"

Molokov remained silent.

"But I know already. I'm well aware why you wear glasses. But I won't tell you. I want you to use your head and then tell me the real reason you wear glasses."

Shaking a threatening finger at Molokov, Koba suddenly let his head drop into a plate full of green peas and immediately fell asleep.

"I've got to stretch my legs a bit," said Mirzoyan cheerfully and slipped away from the table with an independent air. Then Merenkov, too, slipped away. Taking advantage of the absence of authority, Vershilov and Kazanovich found a corner and started playing cards. Borshchev, who had not received permission to rest, continued dancing to Zhbanov's accompaniment, but he, too, had already begun to slacken off—he was no longer squatting fully, just bending his knees a little.

Aria was sitting by himself, playing mumbletypeg with his knife.

Suddenly this peaceful picture was shattered. Vershilov's hand shot out and slapped Kazanovich resoundingly across the face. This was more than Kazanovich could bear, and screeching, he dug his fingernails into Vershilov's face. They rolled on the floor.

Awakened by the commotion, Comrade Koba raised his head. Catching sight of this, Borshchev sank back into a deep squat with renewed vigor, Zhbanov began playing at a livelier tempo, and Merenkov and Mirzoyan began clapping their hands in time to the music.

"Enough." Koba waved angrily at Borshchev. "Take a break."

Borshchev staggered to the table and polished off a glass of Borzhomi. Vershilov and Kazanovich continued rolling on the floor, which was strewn with their cards. Kazanovich succeeded in grabbing hold of his opponent's right ear; Vershilov kept on trying to knee Kazanovich below the belt. Koba summoned Aria over.

"Listen, Leonty, what kind of people are these, anyway? Leaders or gladiators?"

Aria brushed off his knee and stood up in front of Koba, holding his curved Caucasian dagger, with which, a moment before, he'd been playing mumbletypeg.

"Shall I pry them apart?" he asked darkly, testing the blade with his thumbnail.

"Please. Except do me one favor and put that dagger away. God forbid something terrible might happen."

Leonty slipped the dagger into his belt, walked over to the combatants, and gave them each individually a good kick. They both hopped to their feet and made quite an unsavory sight as they presented themselves to Comrade Koba. Vershilov was smearing blood across his face, Kazanovich gently feeling the dark bruise swelling under his left eye.

"So, so," said Koba, shaking his head. "Our people have entrusted their fate to men like you. What game were you playing?"

Embarrassed, the two enemies looked at their feet.

"Come on, I'm asking you a question."

Kazanovich glowered up sullenly at Koba.

"Blackjack, Comrade Koba."

"Blackjack?"

"Nothing to it, Comrade Koba, just a little game."

"I don't understand," said Comrade Koba, spreading out his hands. "What do we have here? Bosses? Leaders? Or just a bunch of crooks. What was the fight about?"

"That kike was cheating," answered Vershilov.

"What kind of word is that, 'kike'?" asked Koba angrily.

"I'm sorry, the Jew," Vershilov corrected himself.

"You're a stupid person." Koba sighed. "An anti-Semite. How many times have I told you to get rid of those great-power ways of yours. I'm giving you one week to study all my works on the question of nationalities, you understand me?"

"I do."

"All right, go. And you, Kazanovich, you didn't behave right either. You Jews do nothing but furnish anti-Semitism with ammunition by your appearance and provocative behavior. I'm getting tired of struggling with anti-Semitism; at some point I'll get fed up."

Koba was about to develop this thought further when Pokhlebyshev appeared. "Comrade Koba, we've just received a dispatch. Dolph's troops have moved right up to the border."

These words made Comrade Koba uneasy. "Come over here," he said to his secretary. "Bend close to me."

Koba took his pipe from the table and began knocking out the ashes on Pokhlebyshev's balding head.

"Dolph's my friend," he said as if hammering his words into his secretary's head. "It's our custom in the Caucasus to stand up for our friends with everything we've got. We can forgive someone insulting our sister or our brother, we can forgive someone insulting our father or our mother, but we cannot forgive someone insulting a friend. To insult my friend is to insult me."

He threw his pipe to the floor and raised Pokhlebyshev's head, using the one-finger-under-the-chin method. Fat tears were running down Pokhlebyshev's face.

"Oh, you're crying!" said Comrade Koba in surprise. "Tell me why you're crying."

"I'm crying because you spoke so touchingly about friendship," said Pokhlebyshev, sobbing and tugging at his nose.

Comrade Koba softened. "So, all right then," he said with a little more warmth in his voice, "I know you're a good man at heart, you're just severe on the outside. Go rest up a bit and tell the doctor to put some iodine on your head, God forbid you should get an infection."

Comrade Koba then reassembled all the boys at the table and proposed a toast to friendship.

"Comrade Koba," asked Molokov, "may I drink with you, too?"

Comrade Koba did not answer, letting the question slip in one ear and out the other. Molokov continued to hold his glass of vodka, and, unable to make up his mind one way or the other, stayed just as he was.

Next, Comrade Koba expressed a desire to play a little music. He walked over to the piano and, playing with one finger, sang the following well-known ditty:

> *I was up on the hill,*
> *I gave Egor all I had,*
> *Now don't you think I was bad,*
> *It was just my rolling tobacco . . .*

Everyone broke into amiable laughter and applauded. In a short speech Comrade Zhbanov remarked on the high artistic merits of the piece. Vershilov took out a pad of paper and a stubby indelible-ink pen from his pocket and requested permission to take down the words of the ditty on the spot.

"I'll copy them down, too," said Borshchev. "I'll sing it to Zinka tomorrow. She'll get a laugh out of it."

"Sure, let her have a laugh," said Koba, returning to

his place at the table. He laid his head on his arms and again fell immediately asleep.

The earliest dawn of that summer began, the night growing gradually lighter like ink being diluted with water. Everything stood out with increasing clarity against the background of the brightening sky, the golden cupolas sharpened in relief.

No little vodka had been drunk that night, and now the group was beginning to fade. Comrade Koba was sleeping at the table. Aria, his hand still on his back pocket, had reclined on the sofa and dozed off. Mirzoyan was snoring noisily under the table, using Merenkov's cheek for a pillow. Still not daring to budge, his face like stone, Molokov was sitting in front of Comrade Koba. Kazanovich and Vershilov had made their peace and were playing cards again. Zhbanov was standing in the corner, his forehead against the cold wall, trying to vomit. Only Borshchev was still wandering quietly about the room with a look of great concentration on his face, as if he had lost something and was trying to find it. He had apparently sobered up and now a hangover was torturing his brain, which was filled with vague and gloomy thoughts. Crinkling his face in sympathy, Borshchev stood near Zhbanov and recommended the old folk remedy—two fingers down the throat. Zhbanov mooed something resembling words and shook his head. Borshchev then walked over to the card players. He started following their game out of simple curiosity, but Vershilov soon drove him away. Borshchev looked over at Leonty and, convinced that he was sleeping, sat down by Molokov, keeping, however, a certain distance. He sighed loudly in an attempt to attract Molokov's attention. Without turning his head, Molokov looked out of the corner of his eye at Borshchev, who winked back and said in a whisper:

"You should take off your glasses for the time being. Comrade Koba's been a little nervous lately, you shouldn't get him riled up. Later on he'll forget all about it and you can put them back on."

Borshchev grabbed a cucumber from the table, took a bite of it, and spat it right back out. Bitter! He gave Koba a sidelong look and then sighed once again. "Of course it's tough working with him. He's not a regular person, he's a genius. But what am I doing here? I used to work in the mines, drilling coal. Not what you might call the cleanest work, but it was a living. Now look at me, I've ended up as one of the leaders, they carry portraits of me when the people parade through the streets. But what kind of leader can I be when all I've got is a third-grade education and Advanced Party School. The rest of you are all prominent people. Theoreticians. I've heard that you know twelve languages. Now take me, for example; I consider myself a Ukrainian, I lived in the Ukraine, but I couldn't speak their language if you put a gun to my head. It's a funny language they've got. We say 'staircase' and they say 'stairladder.'" Borshchev burst out laughing as if the strangeness of Ukrainian had just struck him for the first time.

Even Molokov smiled. The rumors about his knowledge of foreign languages were greatly exaggerated. The fact of the matter was that at one point, to increase the authority of the ruling body, Comrade Koba had endowed them with merits that none of them had previously even suspected themselves of possessing. Thus, Merenkov became a major philosopher and the theoretician of Koba-ism; Mirzoyan became a man of business; Kazanovich a technician; Aria a psychologist; Vershilov an outstanding general; Zhbanov a specialist in all the arts; Borshchev a

Ukrainian; and he, Molokov, who knew a few foreign words and expressions, a linguist.

Naturally, Molokov said nothing of this to Borshchev, remarking only that his life was no bowl of cherries either.

"There's something I don't get," sighed Borshchev. "Where's your conscience if you can pick on someone because of his glasses. He asked you why you wear glasses. Maybe you just like to. If he talked about me like that," said Borshchev, growing heated, "I'd spit right in his face and not be shy about it either."

At that moment Comrade Koba stirred in his sleep. Borshchev froze in horror, but his fears were groundless; Koba remained asleep. "What a fool I am," thought Borshchev with a sigh of relief. "Like they say, the tongue's loose, it's got no bones in it. But with a tongue like mine, oi, what trouble you could get in!" He decided not to talk any more with his colleague who was out of favor, but he couldn't restrain himself and once again he bent close to Molokov's ear.

"Listen, Mocheslav," he whispered, "what about asking him to let us go? Look, if he's a genius, let him decide everything himself. What the hell does he need us for?"

"All right," said Molokov, "but what would we live on?"

"We'll go to the mines. I'll teach you how to mine coal, it's simple. First you dig down into the bed, then you pull out the coal from the top. The money's not like the money we're making here, but the work's less risky. Of course you might get buried in a cave-in but that's a one-time thing; here you die from terror every single day."

Borshchev shuddered, then straightened up, having heard someone breathing behind him. It was Aria. Rubbing his ear with the handle of his dagger, Aria cast a curious glance from Borshchev to Molokov. "What could you be talking about that has you so absorbed, I wonder," he said, imitating Koba's intonation.

Did he hear or not? flashed through both minds.

He heard, decided Molokov, and immediately found the surest way out of the predicament.

"Comrade Borshchev here," he said with a touch of sarcasm, "was just suggesting that he and I abandon our political activities and join the inner emigration."

But you couldn't put anything over on Borshchev either. "You fool!" he said, rising and smoothing his chest. "I only wanted to feel you out and see what makes you tick. Doesn't matter anyway, nobody's going to believe you. Everybody knows I don't wear glasses. My eyes are clear when I look into Comrade Koba's eyes and into the distance shining with our beautiful future."

"Here's the future for you," mimicked Molokov. "First learn Russian properly, and then . . ."

He never finished his sentence. Fortunately for both of them, Pokhlebyshev came flying into the room, his head swathed in bandages.

"Comrade Koba! Comrade Koba!" he shouted as he entered the room, for which he immediately received a box on the ear from Leonty.

"Can't you see that Comrade Koba's busy with his predawn sleep?" said Leonty. "What's happened now?"

Shaking with extraordinary excitement, Pokhlebyshev kept repeating one word: Dolph. It required tremendous effort to squeeze out of him the fact that Dolph's troops had poured across the border.

An urgent, special, and extraordinary meeting then took place, chaired by Leonty Aria. Comrade Koba, still sleeping in his chair, was elected honorary chairman. The group began deliberations on which course to take. Vershilov said that it was imperative to announce a general mobilization. Kazanovich proposed that all bridges and train stations should be blown up at once. Mirzoyan, taking the floor to reply, noted that although their meeting was both timely and business-like, they should not lose sight of the presence and at the same time the absence of Comrade Koba.

"We can of course make one decision or another," he said, "but after all it's no secret that none of us has any guarantees against making some serious mistakes."

"But we'll be acting as a collective," said Kazanovich.

"A collective, Comrade Kazanovich, consists of individuals, as everyone knows. If a single individual can commit a single error, several individuals can commit several errors. Only one man can reach an infallibly wise and correct decision. And that one man is Comrade Koba. He, however, unfortunately, at the moment is busy with his pre-dawn sleep."

"Why do you say 'unfortunately'?" interrupted Leonty Aria. "I'm obliged to correct Comrade Mirzoyan here. It is truly fortunate that at a time so difficult for us all Comrade Koba is busy with his pre-dawn sleep, building up his strength for the wise decisions he will soon be making."

Merenkov requested a point of order and said: "I totally and completely support Comrade Aria for rebuffing Comrade Mirzoyan for his ill-considered words. It would appear that Comrade Mirzoyan had no criminal intentions and his statement should be considered a simple slip of the tongue, though of course at times it is quite difficult to draw a sufficiently clear boundary between a simple slip of the tongue and a premeditated offense. At the same time I think it would be advisable to acknowledge that Comrade Mirzoyan is correct in thinking that only Comrade Koba can make a correct, wise, and principled decision concerning Dolph's treacherous invasion. However, in this connection, yet another question arises, one that requires immediate resolution, one which I now propose be discussed, namely, shall we wake Comrade Koba or wait until he wakes up himself?"

The comrades' opinion was divided on the subject. Some thought he should be awakened; others proposed waiting, since Comrade Koba himself knew best when he needed to sleep and when he should wake up.

In spite of having just learned of his wife's death and in spite of being ill from alcohol poisoning, Comrade Zhbanov took an active part in the debate and said that, before deciding the question of whether or not to wake Koba, it was necessary to decide a question which preceded that one, a sub-question so to speak, concerning the seriousness of Dolph's intentions and whether this might simply be a provocation designed to interrupt Comrade Koba's sleep. But to decide whether this was a serious invasion or a mere provocation was again something that could only be determined by Comrade Koba personally.

Finally two issues were put to a vote:

1. To wake Comrade Koba.
2. Not to wake Comrade Koba.

The results of the voting on both propositions were as follows: For—no one. Against—no one. Abstaining—no one.

It was noted in the minutes of the meeting that both questions had been decided unanimously and that certain of Comrade Mirzoyan's ill-considered statements had been pointed out to him. After the minutes had been drawn up, Comrade Molokov unexpectedly asked for the floor to make some supplementary remarks. He realized that now his only salvation lay in taking an active role. Molokov said that in view of the developing situation he intended to wake up Comrade Koba at once and take full responsibility for the consequences of his act.

That said, he walked decisively over to Comrade Koba and began shaking his shoulder. "Comrade Koba, wake up!"

Comrade Koba shook his head without yet waking up. His legs twitched.

"Comrade Koba, it's war!" In desperation Molokov shouted right in his ear, this time shaking him so hard that Koba woke up.

"War?" repeated Koba, looking at his comrades' faces with uncomprehending eyes. He poured a bottle of vodka over his head and halted his gaze at Molokov. "War with who?"

"With Dolph," said Molokov, who had nothing left to lose.

"So, it's war?" Comrade Koba was gradually coming around. "And when was it declared?"

"That's just it, Comrade Koba, that's the treachery of it all, war hasn't been declared."

"Hasn't been declared?" said Koba in surprise, filling his pipe with the tobacco from a pack of Kazbek cigarettes. "Interesting. And how do you know it's war if war hasn't been declared?"

"We received a dispatch," said Molokov desperately.

"But if war hasn't been declared, it means there's no war. For that reason we Kobaists do not accept or acknowledge it, for to accept something which doesn't exist is to slip into the swamp of idealism. Isn't that so, comrades?"

Everyone was staggered. A thought of such brilliance could never have entered any of their minds. Only a genius could have resolved such a complex problem with such ease.

"Hurrah!" cried Vershilov boldly.

"Hurrah!" seconded all the remaining comrades.

"And now I want to sleep," Comrade Koba announced decisively. "Who'll give me a hand?"

Molokov and Kazanovich took their teacher under the arm. Vershilov, too, rushed forward but wasn't quick enough.

"You shout louder than anybody else," Koba remarked disapprovingly, "but when it comes to action, you're not quick enough. Next time be a little faster on your feet. And you, Mocha," said Koba, giving Molokov a little slap on the cheek, "you're a true staunch warrior and Kobaist and I'll tell you straight off why you wear glasses. You wear glasses because you don't have such good eyesight. And every person who doesn't have such good eyesight should wear glasses so he can see clearly what's in front of him. All right, let's get going!"

He dismissed his two helpers at the door to his office and locked himself in. He listened for a while until he was sure that Kazanovich and Molokov had walked away, and only then did he crawl into his room, taking the usual route through the safe. Upon arrival, he threw his pipe in the corner, then ripped off his moustache and flung it to the corner as well. He was perfectly sober. He had realized what was happening. He had not been sleeping when Pokhlebyshev reported Dolph's attack and he had not been sleeping during the meeting of his comrades. He had been playing the role of a drunken man asleep and he had played it very well because, of all the talents ascribed to him, he did possess one—he was an actor.

Now, with no spectators, there was no reason to play a part. Comrade Koba sat down on his bed, pulled off his boots, unbuttoned his pants, and sank into thought. Somehow things weren't turning out right. He had never trusted anybody except this once and look what had happened. How could he have any faith in people after this? Still, he had to find some way out. In this country, he thought to himself, it's you alone who does the thinking for everyone and nobody is going to do any thinking for you. What to do? Address an appeal to the people? And say what? Forgive me, my dear people, it seems I've just about fuc . . . Oh, he had almost said a dirty word. Request military assistance from the Americans? Or political asylum for himself? Then what? Settle somewhere in Florida and write his memoirs: *My Life as a Tyrant.* Or maybe go into hiding in Georgia and live there disguised as a simple shoemaker?

"Soso," his father used to tell him, "you'll never make a real cobbler."

Comrade Koba lifted his eyes and noticed a pitiable, moustacheless old man on the opposite wall. Mechanically rubbing his scrawny knees, the old man was sitting on an iron bed, his pants at his ankles. Comrade Koba smiled bitterly.

"So there it is," he said to the old man. "Now you see. You thought you were the most cunning, the craftiest. You wouldn't listen to anyone's advice or warning. You ripped out every tongue that tried to tell you the truth. And the one man in the world you trusted turned out to be more cunning and crafty than you. Who's going to help you now? Who's going to support you now? The people? They hate you. Your so-called comrades? Comrades, that's a laugh. A bunch of court flatterers and flunkies. They'd be the first to sell you out as soon as they got the chance. In the old days, at least jesters and saints were allowed to tell the truth. But who'll tell the truth now? You demanded lies; now you can choke on them. Everybody lies now—your newspapers, your public speakers, your spies, your informers. But there still is one man with the courage to tell you the truth to your face. And he's sitting right in front of you now. He sees right through you like you were his own self. Look at yourself, you who considered yourself a superman. What kind of superman are you, anyway? You're small, pockmarked, you've got aches and pains everywhere. Your head aches, your liver aches, your intestines do a lousy job of digesting what you gobble down, the meat you steal from your hungry people. Why then, if you're such a superman, are your teeth and hair falling out? Superparasite, why did you kill so many people? Mensheviks, Bolsheviks, priests, peasants, intellectuals, children, mothers . . . Why did you ruin agriculture and decapitate the army? For the sake of a brighter future? No, for your own personal power. You like it when everyone fears you like the plague. But you, the creator of an empire of fear, aren't you the most frightened person in it? What is there you don't fear? A shot from behind, poison in your wine, a bomb under your bed. You're afraid of your own comrades, guards, cooks, barbers, your own shadow and reflection. Driven by your own fear, you ferret out enemies of the people and counter-Kobaists everywhere. There's no need to. Just look to yourself—you are the number-one enemy of the people, the number-one counter-Kobaist."

While Koba was speaking, the old man's face glowered and grew increasingly malicious. It was obvious that, as usual, the truth was not to his liking. He fended off the reproaches hurled at him by flailing his arms, grimacing, and crinkling up his face. As he spoke his final words, Koba's hand began moving of its own toward the pillow. He noticed the old man doing the same thing. He had to beat him to it. Koba darted and grabbed the pistol from under the pillow. At that same instant an identical pistol

flashed in the old man's hand. But Koba had already
pulled the trigger.

Gunfire in an enclosed area always produces a great
deal of noise. One shot followed by another and the old
man's pockmarked face cracked into a web of crooked
lines. The room smelled of hot gun oil. Koba's eardrums
vibrated; the old man's nasty face burst apart, flew into
falling pieces, creating the illusion of a living man writh-
ing in the throes of death.

Suddenly everything was silent. The pistol was empty.
Koba looked up—now there was no one there.

"That's it," said Koba sadly, and with significance,
though to exactly whom was unclear. "I have saved the
people from the hangman." And with those words he
tossed away the pistol, which was of no further use to
him.

It later appeared that no one had heard the shots. This
should cause no surprise—the walls of Koba's room were
so thick that even sounds of a much greater magnitude
would not have escaped them.

The old woman who came the next morning to clean
the room saw the slivers of glass strewn everywhere. She
found the master lying on his back in bed. His left leg
was on the bed, his right leg, with his pants caught
around the ankle, was on the floor. His right hand hung
lifelessly, almost touching the floor. At first deciding that
Comrade Koba had shot himself, the old woman was
about to sound the alarm, but then, convinced that the
body on the bed had suffered no harm, she decided
against it, not wishing to be called in as a witness. She
put his arm and leg up on the bed, finished pulling off
his pants, and covered Comrade Koba with a camel's
hair blanket, carefully tucking it in around him. That
done, she set about cleaning up the glass, hoping that

Comrade Koba would certainly sleep off his drunkenness by the next day. But he did not wake up the next day, or the day after; reliable sources indicate he spent the next ten days in a lethargic sleep. They say that it was sometime during those ten days that the old woman retired and brought the note concerning the millet to the Museum of the Revolution. I, however, do not believe that. I believe the note's value would have fallen somewhat during those ten days, then risen back in value afterward. Clearly, the old woman was clever enough to bring that note to the best possible place to sell and therefore would also have waited for the best possible price. Besides, there now exist many contradictory opinions concerning the old woman. Supporters of the pro-Kobaist line in our historical scholarship, while not denying the existence of the old woman, doubt that she actually removed Comrade Koba's pants, which they consider unremovable. These scholars point out that just as Comrade Koba was born in a generalissimo's uniform, he lived his life in it as well, without ever having once removed it. The adherents of the anti-Kobaist line, on the other hand, maintain that Comrade Koba was born naked but that his body was covered with thick fur. From a distance his contemporaries mistook this fur for a common soldier's overcoat or a generalissimo's uniform. Not adhering myself to either of these versions, I admit finding each of them interesting in their own way.

1967

P.S. This story is solely the product of the author's fantasy. Any resemblance of any of the characters to actual people is purely coincidental.

SKURLATSKY, MAN OF LETTERS

According to information whose reliability I will not guarantee, there was, in the second half of the nineteenth century, a certain prominent figure in Petersburg literary circles, a tall thin man whose military bearing was, as he put it, a carryover from years of service in the guards. He had been dismissed from the guards, owing, it would seem, to a duel. If any such did in fact occur, it occurred long before the period described here. He was now approaching sixty, yet he still had great vitality and a most lively interest in all areas of life. Upon being introduced to someone, he would at once hand his new acquaintance his calling card decorated with golden vignettes, beneath which was printed in a severe type face:

SERGEI STANISLAVOVICH

SKURLATSKY, MAN OF LETTERS

Skurlatsky was not known for his achievements in the field of literature (it seems no one had more than the vaguest idea of what they were), but for his personality, and for the fact of his being a constant visitor to all the literary salons, circles, and editorial offices. He could hold forth on any subject and appeared well informed in all areas of human knowledge; he spoke confidently, like a person whose authority had been acknowledged everywhere; at those points in his discourse which seemed especially felicitous to him, he would touch his heart, open his green eyes wide, and suddenly break into a strange croaking laughter which would force his interlocutor to laugh as well.

He spoke of the most famous people by their first name, and if one were to take his words as truth, he had, by his intimacy and counsel, exerted a beneficial influence on many of them, starting with Alexander (Pushkin). Well, as far as Alexander was concerned, he may have been going a bit too far: at the moment of the poet's death, Skurlatsky, even with the most generous of calculations, could not have been more than sixteen. With Nikolai (Gogol) he seems truly to have been closer, at least in age. Rumor even has it that Khlestakov and, to some degree, Chichikov, were modeled on Skurlatsky; however, this too becomes dubious if one compares the dates involved.

Nevertheless, Skurlatsky was fond of recalling his close friendship with the author of *Dead Souls,* both when it was apropos and when it was not.

"So, sometimes Nikolai and I . . ." he would begin and then relate the longest of stories, which was of no interest to anyone, with the possible exception of Skurlatsky himself, who told them solely to be able to use the expression "Nikolai and I."

It goes without saying that, although in his stories Skurlatsky sometimes depicted his relations with the great as friendly, sometimes as hostile, they were always relations between equals. One time this led him to considerable embarrassment. He was conversing with a stranger in someone's drawing room. As usual, the conversation hopped from one subject to another and then turned to Dostoevsky, who was much talked about at the time.

"I'm no longer on speaking terms with Fyodor since he wrote that *Possessed* of his," said Skurlatsky decisively.

"Is that so!" said the stranger in surprise. "And you're acquainted with him?"

"We were friendly for many years, which I now regret." At that point a shadow of doubt passed across Skurlatsky's face. "But allow me to inquire with whom I have the honor of speaking?"

"Dostoevsky," said the stranger, bowing. "Fyodor."

Skurlatsky blushed deeply, mumbled something on the order of "An honor," then made a dash for the cloakroom. One would think this embarrassment would have lasted him some time. But the next day, in another drawing room, he was recounting the story with gusto and only one deviation from the truth—that it was not he who had boasted of knowing Dostoevsky but Dostoevsky who had boasted of knowing him.

"Skurlatsky!" He demonstrated the crucial moment, clicking his heels. "Sergei."

And, laying his hand on his heart, he opened his green eyes wide and began laughing.

But Skurlatsky not only boasted of knowing famous writers. He also hinted that he was an intimate of the court. And when the Nihilists came into fashion he let it be known to all and sundry that he was accepted among them as an elder comrade and even as a sort of spiritual leader. Obviously, no one took any of his statements seriously; everyone knew Skurlatsky was an old fibber, a chatterbox, and an idler, though a completely harmless one. Naturally, it could never have entered anyone's mind that his life would finish in the unusual fashion that it did.

In March 1881, several days after the assassination of Alexander II on the Ekaterinsky Canal, an appeal to the new autocrat from the still secret Executive Committee was issued and distributed throughout Petersburg. Many prominent citizens of the capital found copies of the appeal in their mailboxes or under their doors. Obviously, the Nihilists not only wished to convince the new sovereign of the necessity for urgent reform but they also wanted to elicit sympathy for their cause among the educated public. It was then that the incident occurred which forms the basis of this tale.

Skurlatsky, man of letters, was sitting in his study at his ample desk wearing a dark and ample dressing gown edged with silk cord. In this dressing gown he looked like an authentic major writer; he looked even more authentic than most authentic writers do. That day he had fallen greedily upon his desk, at last able to set to work on the grandiose novel so long in his mind. Up until that point, something had always interfered. Two hours of the morning went for the reading of the Petersburg and Moscow newspapers. Then it was necessary to pay visits to his acquaintances in order to learn what was going on in the world (since newspapers were never to be trusted). Then he had to visit other people he knew and recount what he'd heard from the first group. After that, he was obliged to make the rounds of all the editorial offices, pick up his orders, and then finally spend the evening in one fashionable salon or other. Without such socializing, the life of the writer would be unthinkable. Thus, day after day passed in hustle, bustle, and general gadding about. Skurlatsky would return home weary, annoyed, and dissatisfied with himself. Another day had passed and once again no time had been found for his principal endeavor.

He pulled over a pile of clean paper, sharpened his quill, dipped it in ink, and sank deeply into thought. Why the devil did it happen like that? Why did the most varied thoughts (thoughts sometimes of genius) occur to him wherever they pleased—during a stroll down Nevsky Prospect, when visiting at the office of an editor friend—anywhere but at his desk?

"Tell me, doesn't it terrify you to be all alone with a blank sheet of paper?" one of his admirers had once asked.

Terrifying, that wasn't the half of it. That admirer, Evdokiya, had long since become his wife. But he remained terrified by a blank sheet of paper. While he was pondering all this, the ink on his quill had dried up and he had to dip the quill back in the inkwell.

Skurlatsky knew that a real novel begins with the first sentence. It was enough to write a strong opening sentence and then thoughts would flow one after the other, and the rest was merely a matter of time. But it was precisely that first sentence that kept eluding him. Perhaps it might not have eluded him any further, but just as the sentence began to gleam in his mind, something went crash in the kitchen. "They never let me work!" he thought in irritation and went out to the kitchen. There he found Paska the cook, a buxom country girl, washing the dishes.

"Pelagiya," said Skurlatsky sternly, "stop banging those dishes this minute. You're disturbing me."

"I just have a little left to go, sir," said Pelagiya guiltily.

"You can finish them tomorrow. Meanwhile, bring me some tea in the study, and make it strong."

It is a well-known fact that tea invigorates and refreshes. But that evening it did neither. After his tea

Skurlatsky continued to sit quite some time, paper before him, until someone rang at his door. He glanced at his watch; it was rather late. "Who could it be this time of night," he thought, with both irritation and relief. Drawing his dressing gown around him, he went to see who it was. But there was no one there. Only then did he notice the envelope which had apparently been slipped under his door.

Returning to his study, Skurlatsky held the envelope up to the light, trembling with excitement. Scrawled on the envelope (probably with the left hand) was the following: From the Executive Committee of the People's Will. "What sort of deviltry is this?" thought Skurlatsky.

A minute later, holding a lamp in one hand, he went into his wife's bedroom. Evdokiya was sleeping. Her golden curls, in which the gray was barely noticeable, were spread out across the pillow.

"She seems to be sleeping," thought Skurlatsky. Closing the door carefully, he tiptoed across the bedroom and set the lamp down on the dressing table. He was not about to get undressed in the dark. He positioned the lamp so that it shone directly on Evdokiya's left eye. She began to moan, muttered something, and turned to the wall.

"Maybe she's not sleeping after all," thought Skurlatsky and coughed softly as if something were tickling his throat. Evdokiya did not wake up, and Skurlatsky began coughing again, but this time as if he were in the final stages of consumption. Even this had no effect on her. "She *is* sleeping," Skurlatsky thought, now with a certain irritation. Finished with coughing, he began to walk about the room, scuffling his feet like an old man and bumping into everything. All this came to an end when he knocked over a chair. It fell with such a crash that this time Evdokiya woke from her sleep and sat up in bed.

"What was that? What happened?" she asked in fright, trying to get her eyelids open.

"You're not sleeping, my love?" said Skurlatsky tenderly. "And I was just hoping to read you a little something," he added, not allowing her time to gather her wits.

"Maybe tomorrow?" she asked timidly, rubbing her eyes.

"Of course, maybe tomorrow," he agreed. "But since you're not sleeping anyway . . . Not much to it, just a couple of lines."

"All right then, read it." Evdokiya lay back down and dutifully looked over at her husband.

Skurlatsky sat down beside her on the bed, pulled the lamp over closer, and said, with genuine feeling: "Your Majesty!"

"What?" shuddered Evdokiya.

"It's what I'm reading," said Skurlatsky soothingly.

Your Majesty! While understanding completely the painful frame of mind you are experiencing at the present moment, the Executive Committee would not, however, consider it right for us to yield to that natural sense of tact which would require us to refrain for a certain period of time. There is something higher than a person's legitimate feelings, namely, one's duty to one's native land, to which a citizen must sacrifice himself, his own feelings, and even the feelings of others. In compliance with this universal obligation, we have decided to appeal to you immediately . . .

The bloody tragedy played out on Ekaterinsky Canal was not a chance matter and came as no surprise to anyone. After everything that has happened in the last decade, it was perfectly inevitable; that fact contains

*the most profound significance and it must be grasped
by the person destiny has placed at the head of all gov-
ernmental authority . . .*

Evdokiya continued to look dutifully at Skurlatsky
but, understanding nothing of what she heard, sank off
into oblivion, where only bits and pieces reached her:
" . . . such facts . . . by his own merits . . . the late
Emperor . . . the guilty and the innocent were hung
. . . the process of the national organism . . . Our Saviour's
death on the cross . . ."

Giving up on sleep, Evdokiya propped herself up on
one elbow and tried to concentrate.

"The government," declaimed Skurlatsky, "can still of
course round up and hang a great number of individual
persons. It can destroy a great number of separate revolutionary groups. Let us suppose that it even destroys the
most serious revolutionary organizations now existing. All
this will not change the state of affairs in the least. Circumstances create revolutionaries, as does the people's
universal dissatisfaction and Russia's striving for new social forms. It is impossible to annihilate an entire people;
it is also impossible to destroy its dissatisfaction by means
of repression: on the contrary, this increases the dissatisfaction . . ."

"What is it that he's reading?" thought Evdokiya, unable to make heads or tails of it. "I know he's been intending to write a novel. But that's a very strange beginning for a novel."

"The terrible explosion," continued Skurlatsky, "the
bloody shift of power, the convulsive shock spreading
throughout Russia will complicate the process of destroying the old order . . ."

Sleep had now definitely passed. Evdokiya shook her head and began to listen attentively.

Rejecting all bias and suppressing the mistrust created over the centuries by our government, we appeal to you. We prefer to forget that you are a representative of that power which has so deceived the people, done it so much harm. We are appealing to you as a citizen and an honest man. We hope that your personal feeling of bitterness will not stifle your awareness of your obligations and your desire to know the truth. We, too, can be bitter. You have lost a father. We have lost not only fathers but brothers, wives, children, close friends. But we are prepared to suppress our own feelings if the welfare of Russia requires it. We expect the same from you.

We are not setting you any conditions. Do not be shocked by our proposal. The conditions required to replace the revolutionary movement with peaceful labor are not created by us but by history. We do not set conditions but only remind you of them.

In our opinion, there are two such conditions:

1. *A general amnesty for everyone convicted of political crimes, since these were not crimes but the discharging of civic duties.*

2. *A convocation of representatives of the entire Russian people for a review of the existing forms of state and social life, and a revision of them in accordance with the wishes of the people . . .*

And so, Your Majesty, you must decide. There are two paths before you. The choice depends on you: we can, then, only implore fate that your mind and conscience suggest to you the sole decision consonant with the welfare of Russia, with your own dignity, and your obligations to the country of your birth.

10 March 1881   *The Executive Committee*

"Well, Evdokiya, how did you like it?" Skurlatsky covered his heart with his hand, opened his eyes wide, and began laughing. "Isn't it wonderfully written? What firmness, and yet at the same time what wisdom and restraint. No, this wasn't written by any bomb thrower but by a man in fine control of his pen!"

"Yes, not badly written at all," agreed his wife. "Who could have written it?"

"It must have been me!" Skurlatsky blurted out, surprising even himself.

Evdokiya dropped her eyes. She knew all her husband's weaknesses but had grown used to treating them indulgently. "Go to bed, Sergei. It's late now," she said.

Skurlatsky's wife knew his weakness for fantasizing. However, she supposed that by morning he would have forgotten all about his idea, as had happened more than once before. But she was mistaken. That next morning, forsaking both breakfast and his newspapers, Skurlatsky dressed hurriedly and set off to see his friend Kozodoev, also a man of letters, to whom he read the letter from the Executive Committee. While he did not come right out and declare himself the author of the letter, he did hint that such was perfectly conceivable. He behaved in exactly the same manner in the editorial offices of *The Voice* and the *Saint Petersburg Gazette* and at the home of the writer Gleb Uspensky and that of Dr. Lesgaft.

Soon Petersburg was abuzz with the rumor that the Executive Committee's letter to Alexander III, printed in large numbers on a secret printing press and distributed by hand, had been written by the man of letters Skurlatsky.

Conversations on this subject were conducted in secrecy and whispers, each person swearing not to breathe a word of it to anyone, which only made the news spread faster. Skurlatsky's prestige in liberal circles rose dramatically. He was a sought-after guest in all sorts of homes, where, with great pleasure, he would discourse on general topics. It was said that a certain privy counselor even received Skurlatsky secretly and that a certain retired general of the gendarmes expressed a desire to be introduced to him. (It is a well-known fact that, upon retiring, some police generals manifest strong liberal tendencies.) The rumors concerning Skurlatsky circulated far and wide and eventually reached the police, who are always the last to find out anything.

Late one night, awoken by an odd racket downstairs, Evdokiya Skurlatsky dashed half dressed into the entry hall and found her apartment swarming with policemen.

"What's going on here?" asked Evdokiya. "What do you want?" she addressed the young police officer in charge of the operation.

"Forgive me, madam"—the officer clicked his heels—"but we have orders to search your apartment and to arrest your husband."

Skurlatsky, man of letters, was standing by the wall, his face slightly pale, his hands clasped behind his back.

"Evdokiya!" he roared suddenly, puffing out his chest. "When the police come to this house, Skurlatsky's wife must be properly dressed!"

"Officer, officer," implored Evdokiya, "there's some sort of misunderstanding here. My husband loves to make-believe, everyone knows that's his weakness. If this is about that damned letter from the Executive Committee, I can assure you, sir, I swear to you, my husband had nothing whatsoever to do with it."

"Evdokiya!" Skurlatsky raised his voice. "Get dressed at once!" And when Evdokiya had left the room, Skurlatsky said like a weary general: "Gentlemen, do your duty!"

The police rummaged through all of Skurlatsky's quite extensive library and turned the whole house upside down. The search resulted in a few odd issues of *The People's Will*, a tattered, ten-year-old copy of *The Bell*, and a few random proclamations. The same could be found in the home of any intellectual.

The police then asked Skurlatsky to accompany them to the station. He put on his overcoat, cap, and gloves and walked to the door. At the doorway he stopped and turned to his sobbing wife.

"Evdokiya," he said sternly but tenderly, "take care of the children. Tell them that their father perished in the cause of freedom."

"Officer, officer!" called Evdokiya, drowning in tears. "It's all lies and nonsense. He never had any children!"

That same night, under suspicion of especially dangerous crimes against the state, the prisoner was transferred from the police station to Pre-Trial Detention and placed in a solitary-confinement cell reserved for especially dangerous criminals. The next morning he was summoned for questioning. In a spacious office with a portrait of Emperor Alexander III on the wall, Skurlatsky met with the officer in charge, a lively man wearing a spotless uniform with new epaulettes.

"Lieutenant Colonel Sudeikin, Georgy Porfirevich," the officer introduced himself. "I have the honor of heading the department charged with maintaining public tranquillity in the city of St. Petersburg."

After a few questions of no great significance, Lieutenant Colonel Sudeikin showed Skurlatsky the Executive Committee's letter.

"Are you familiar with this document?"

"I should say so!" Skurlatsky smiled significantly.

"Will you corroborate that you authored this document?"

"Yes, I will."

"Mmmmm, yes . . ." Georgy Porfirevich drummed his fingers triumphantly on the desk top. He then rose and, clasping his hands behind his back, began pacing up and down the room. "My dear Sergei Stanislavovich," he said pensively, "you see the point—by acknowledging yourself the author of this document, you put yourself in a very grave position. After all, this is not merely a letter but a programmatic party document glorifying heinous crimes. Naturally, in composing such a document, a serious organization like the People's Will could not employ anyone outside its ranks. Someone from the central committee, one of the most active members, composed this letter. Thus, by insisting that you wrote the letter, you are as well admitting your membership in the Executive Committee."

"Obviously," said Skurlatsky with an air of dignity.

Even Sudeikin, an old hand in these matters, began to grow excited. "But that's impossible!" he cried. "I have not yet encountered a single person who would admit to being a member of the Executive Committee. Even Zhelyabov and Perovskaya only admit to being agents of the Executive Committee. Zhelyabov and Perovskaya! Are you familiar with those names?"

"They are my people," said Skurlatsky calmly.

Sudeikin returned to his desk and spent a long interval gazing curiously at the prisoner. "Listen, Sergei Stanislavovich," he said sincerely, even ingratiatingly, "your wife and your friends say that you have a certain tendency to . . . how to say it . . . to fantasize."

"Do you mean to say that I am lying?" Skurlatsky paled.

"No, no, not at all. But judge for yourself: our investigations have produced no material, I emphasize, no material concerning the activities of the People's Will Party in which your name figures. You must agree that's rather strange. All the leading party members are known to us. Both those already under arrest and those still at liberty. And now suddenly it turns out that one of the main members of the Executive Committee was completely unknown to us. How do you wish me to understand such a . . . mmmm . . . contradiction?"

Skurlatsky flushed. "My dear lieutenant colonel," he said menacingly, flinging aside his chair. "I find your insinuations insulting. I request that I be returned to my cell at once."

Sudeikin sighed and looked over at Skurlatsky sympathetically. "Sit down, please. You'll return to your cell in due time. I implore you, Sergei Stanislavovich, tell me it wasn't you, that you were just playing a joke, and I will order you set free at once."

"And I am asking you to return me to my cell," said Skurlatsky stubbornly.

"Ach, Sergei Stanislavovich," said Sudeikin, shaking his head. "This is a fruitless venture you've engaged in. Very much so. As you may know, the police and the judicial bodies have received instructions to eradicate all sedition. His Majesty is taking a personal interest in anyone with even the slightest relation to the People's Will and the Executive Committee. All the principal figures on the committee will be punished as severely as possible, and that can include capital punishment. And at a time like this, you insist on your, if you'll pardon me, not particularly clever fantasy."

"Lieutenant colonel, sir," said Skurlatsky wearily. "I once again request that you order me returned to my cell."

"All right, fine," said Georgy Porfirevich, waving his hand in a gesture of weary submission. "I believe you. You are a member of the Executive Committee. I want the names and addresses of your confederates. What can you tell me of the party's activities, its problems?"

"Ha, ha, ha," laughed Skurlatsky sarcastically, covering his heart with his hand. "You, a lieutenant colonel, you're much too naïve for your job. From me you will hear"— he raised his thin index finger in the air—"not a single word. So, my dear fellow, I once again insist that I be taken back to my cell immediately. And if you are unable to order this done, I shall return myself. It was my pleasure, lieutenant colonel."

With those words, Skurlatsky, man of letters, placed his hands at his sides, clicked his heels, nodded abruptly, executed a tight military about-face, and, puffing out his chest, began walking toward the door with a firm stride.

"Back to your chair!" bellowed Sudeikin suddenly.

"What?" said Skurlatsky, turning.

"Back to your chair, I tell you! Sit down!"

"Well, if . . ." Skurlatsky shrugged his shoulders. "I submit to force." He sat down.

"That's right," said Sudeikin, still indignant and growing increasingly heated. "Now listen, you!" He rose. "You're telling nothing but lies! You're lying right and left! But if you keep on insisting on your story, it's going to cost you dearly. You'll be hung! Can you imagine what that means? You'll be led out onto a scaffold knocked together out of rough boards. They'll set a black coffin down right in front of you. A bowlegged hangman will slip a thick rope around your skinny neck. Your legs will twitch in the air, your babbling tongue will come sliding up out of your throat . . ."

"Ach, lieutenant colonel," said Skurlatsky, crinkling up his face and averting his gaze. "Stop telling me all these horror stories, I find it most unpleasant."

"Aha, so you're frightened," said Sudeikin, warming up. "Well, it's all in your hands. Tell me that you were just joking and I'll release you at once."

"No," said Skurlatsky firmly. "Duty enjoins me to walk my path to the end."

"You're an idiot! You're an ass!" Sudeikin 'exploded again. "The devil with you!" He slammed his fist down on the table. "I'm releasing you. Go!"

"Where?"

"To hell! Wherever you want!"

Skurlatsky relaxed in the chair, crossed his legs, and grabbed his knees with both his hands.

"A police ploy." He smiled understandingly. "Easy enough to see through, my good lieutenant colonel. I leave here, you dispatch your spies to find out whom I'm meeting. Order me returned to my cell, let them hang me. I'm not afraid. I spit on you!"

Skurlatsky rose and then truly did spit in Sudeikin's face. Strange as it may seem, Sudeikin reacted with perfect composure.

"Idiot," he said, wiping his face with a snow-white handkerchief.

"You're the idiot!" cried Skurlatsky, opening his eyes wide.

"Madman!"

"You're the madman," said Skurlatsky, growing even more heated. "An animal in a police uniform! I'm throwing down the gauntlet, and if you're a nobleman, tomorrow we duel!"

Sudeikin took a small brass bell from his desk and rang it. Two strapping gendarmes appeared at the door.

"To his cell!" said Sudeikin wearily. "And put him in irons!"

Skurlatsky's subsequent fate is shrouded in obscurity. However, if one were to collect all the rumors that circulated about him, separating the probable from the improbable, one would come up with something like this:

The evidence given by Skurlatsky to Lieutenant Colonel Sudeikin caused a great commotion in official circles. Skurlatsky was questioned by the director of the police department, the prosecutor from the judicial chambers, and by the Minister of Internal Affairs. Skurlatsky was taken to these interrogations exhausted but adamant. His persistent testimony that he alone composed the letter to Alexander III was never corroborated by any subsequent investigation. Nor was his membership in the Executive Committee. Members of the terrorist group arrested around that same time were presented with Skurlatsky at a face-to-face confrontation and assured police that they had never seen him before. When the interrogator demanded that Skurlatsky explain this, he, with his unfailing smile, explained that there exist rules among revolutionaries forbidding them to betray one another at such confrontations. Yet one more strong tactic was used on him. His wife, who, it was said, he loved deeply, was permitted to visit him in his cell. All through the night, Evdokiya implored him with tears in her eyes to renounce his foolishness. Skurlatsky was gentle and tender with her, but after she left, he once again displayed his former firmness. The file on Skurlatsky, man of letters, being exceptional, finally ended up with the Supreme Prosecutor of the Holy Synod, Konstantin Petrovich Pobedonostsev and, through him, was passed on to Alexander III. In his letter accompanying the file, Pobedonostsev wrote that although Skurlatsky's testimony was undoubtedly the fruit of his all-too-fertile imagination, the very direction his fantasies took bore witness to his pernicious cast of mind and the former man of letters should thus receive the same punishment as criminals who were truly especially dangerous. It was said that on the margins of Skurlatsky's file the Emperor himself, in his own hand, had written in bold letters: "Try the wretch and hang him. A."

After this, the Emperor received several communications from representatives of literature and medicine, which, while recognizing Skurlatsky's pernicious state of mind, declared, nevertheless, that his testimony could only be explained as the result of deep psychological disturbance, signs of which had been observed earlier. The consequence of these communications was that the Emperor most graciously crossed out the original resolution and inscribed a new one: "Inasmuch as the laws of the Empire do not permit us to beat up the liar with a birch, he should be sent to a lunatic asylum until he is completely cured, which will not, I hope, be too soon. A." Eventually Skurlatsky was sent to a lunatic asylum, where he made such a powerful impression on the patients that two of the six resident Napoleons began to call themselves Skurlatsky, while another adopted the dual last name Zhelyabov-Perovskaya, after the famous Nihilists.

It is also said that subsequently a new form of mental illness was discovered in that hospital, a collective delusion of grandeur—an entire group of patients declared themselves to be the Executive Committee. Each year, with the approach of spring, the members of this group would begin to experience a strange uneasiness; they would then begin to collect empty tin cans and to dig up the ground in the most unlikely places. Once, on the first of March, a bunch of tin cans, bound together with a sinister-looking wire that led to the wall, was discovered in the hospital director's desk. The patients were evacuated at once, and the police cordoned off the hospital. When the cans were opened, however, they turned out to have been filled with the most harmless of substances—oat kasha, which the patients hated—and the wire led to the next ward, to the cot of one of the pseudo-Skurlatskys. The subsequent fate of the real Skurlatsky has remained, unfortunately, obscure. Having found no information about Skurlatsky in the archives, this author still cannot find his way through the maze of conjecture surrounding this remarkable man.

1972

AUTOBIOGRAPHICAL STORIES

A WORD

FROM THE AUTHOR

At one time, having decided to become a writer, I wanted to begin with my memoirs immediately. I was twenty-two years old and all the events of my short life were still vividly before my eyes. But people who knew better told me that, before writing my memoirs, it was necessary to become famous in one field or another. I decided to win fame as a writer and began writing stories and short novels, sharing my reminiscences with friends, sometimes over a glass of vodka, sometimes not. I told them about being a carpenter, an aviation mechanic, a blacksmith's helper, an instructor at the regional executive committee, and so forth. Once one of my friends advised me to write my stories down and publish them under the title "My Life As . . ." I liked the idea but did not rush to turn it into a reality. Still, in my free moments, I somehow managed to write these four stories. The first story requires no explanation. The next three are about my life as a soldier. The setting is a school for aviation mechanics, in Poland.

UNCLE VOLODYA

In the fall of 1953, after much time and trouble, I finally managed to take up residence in Moscow. Due to a shortage of workers, the construction organizations were permitted to take on workers from other cities, who were then issued temporary residence visas. And that is how I ended up in a workers' hostel not far from Razgulyai.

There were eight cots in our room and eight of us: Uncle Volodya, Uncle Sergei Svintsov, Tolik Chekmarev, Volodka Krikunov, Fedya Utkin, Sashka Peskov, Sashka Shmakov, and me.

At that time Uncle Volodya was fifty-one years old and Uncle Sergei was fifty-three. Each of them was more than twice as old as any of us. They both worked in our construction organization, the former as a maintenance man, the latter as a yard keeper. They were always at each other's throat.

Uncle Sergei could not bear Uncle Volodya because Volodya could not bear him; Uncle Volodya had no specific reasons—he just simply loathed Sergei. Smashing dishes was Uncle Volodya's favorite form of entertainment. After he had a few drinks in him, he would take glasses, plates, and saucers from the the kitchen table in the middle of the room and fling them one after the other, trying to hit the lamp suspended from the ceiling. He never once managed to hit that lamp, though the glasses and plates always did shatter against the wall. Fragments would rain down on Tolik Chekmarev, who slept next to the wall. At first, Tolik would jump out of bed, but then in time he got used to it all and would only burrow a little deeper under his blanket and cover his head with his pillow just to be on the safe side. We were soon out of breakable dishware and so we replaced the glasses and plates with aluminum mugs and bowls. Uncle Volodya tried to use these objects a couple of times, but just as before, the lamp eluded his aim and the metal dishes did not produce the same effect the china had, though they made no less racket against the wall.

But Uncle Volodya was a resourceful man. He thought up a new way to entertain himself. After a few drinks, he'd take his straight razor from his night table and chase poor, puny Uncle Sergei around the table. I don't believe there was any real danger for Uncle Sergei; it was simply that the sight of his enemy hopping in craven fear around the table replaced other of Uncle Volodya's pleasures. When the yard keeper would finally manage to slip out of the room into the corridor, Uncle Volodya would walk over to me, holding his razor, and stare at me for a long while. Then he would take his quilted jacket off the back of his chair.

"I'm going," he'd say to me. "You've seen the last of me. I'm fed up with life. You understand me. These people here . . ." he'd say with a sweep of his hand, "they're idiots. Nothings." Then he'd lapse into thought, seeking another term for them. "Lice. They won't understand. Farewell. My razor's sharp. I'm going."

The next morning he'd return alive and well, and for that very reason, there'd be a somewhat sheepish expression on his face.

Uncle Volodya was tall and heavyset. His face was pale and on the puffy side. His thick, black, bristly eyebrows almost looked pasted on. His head was absolutely clean-shaven. He shaved the little hair that grew behind his ears, at his temples, and at the back of his head, without any help, using that same straight razor of his.

All he owned was one quilt jacket and two suits—one for work; the other for days off. Both suits were made of cotton. One was old and dirty; the other was not all that new either, but at least it was clean and pressed. He also had a cotton service cap with a cardboard visor, a pair of canvas shoes reinforced with leather on the toes and heels, a guitar, and a teach-yourself book.

Our cots were next to each other. Uncle Volodya was not especially friendly to me the day I first arrived with my permit from the superintendent. He was sitting on his bed, his eyes fixed on the sheet music spread on the stool in front of him, plucking the guitar strings one at a time. He'd pluck one string, then look at the music, pluck another, then look again. He paid no attention to me.

I set my suitcase under my bed and opened the night table. It was crammed full of tin cans, bags of groats, sugar, and other such provisions.

"This all yours?" I asked.

"All mine," he answered, glowering.

"May I clear off a little shelf for myself?"

"Please do." Reluctantly he laid down his guitar and began shoving the cans and bags I was handing him under his bed.

"And what post has been assigned to you?" he asked me politely, to let me know that I was dealing with an intelligent person.

To show him that I, too, was no bumpkin, I answered that I had been assigned the post of carpenter but that this was just for the interim until I had gotten myself settled in Moscow and, needless to say, I had not come here to work as a carpenter. I hinted that I had another goal in mind.

"Exactly what?" he asked derisively.

"I write a little," I explained modestly.

"A poet?"

In the literary group to which I belonged at the time, anyone who had ever touched pen to paper called himself a poet. We saw nothing unusual in this, and so I answered calmly: "Yes, I'm a poet."

"A poet, then?" He livened up, anticipating some fun at my expense. "Then I'll test you right away. 'I break the layered rocks on the silt-covered ocean floor at the hour of ebb tide.' Where's that from?"

I knew I was sunk, but it never hurts to try and use your wits. "Sounds familiar . . ."

"Familiar?" He was now totally ironic. "Familiar! That's 'The Nightingale's Garden.' You ever heard of that poem?"

"Ah, ah, Heine," I said, thinking I'd guessed right.

"It's one of Alexander Blok's poems," he said softly, pulling his guitar back over to him again. I had clearly ceased to interest him. Still, five minutes or so later he remembered me again and said: "You're a dilettante."

Now I can admit that at the time I had no idea what that word meant, and with no dictionary of foreign words handy, I did not dare object.

I'll say right off that his attitude toward me changed rather quickly. This may have happened because I worked and read a great deal during that period and was always up on the latest literary events or because I had achieved a certain measure of success—two of my poems were printed in a newspaper, the *Moscow Builder.*

That very first day I learned that Uncle Volodya had recently "hopped out"; that is, returned from prison, where he'd been for some twenty-five years, if not more. Later on, he told me that it was once having been a member of the Socialist Revolutionary Party which had caused him so much grief. I didn't believe it then, and now I think that he'd most likely been in prison on criminal charges, though back in those times anything was possible. Sometimes he enjoyed hinting that he was a gang leader in the camp and that all the criminals groveled at his feet and did his bidding. This, too, may have been true, yet I'm still inclined to believe all this was no more than wishful thinking and that it was he who groveled and did someone else's bidding during those long years in the camps; but to keep his own self-respect he did not want to admit the truth and had someone else in mind when describing himself in the role of gang leader, someone he had long wished to emulate.

For his work at the construction project Volodya received 600 old-style roubles, minus taxes. Once in a great while he'd moonlight a bit, but these were rare occurrences and obviously caused no substantial change in his financial situation. I was surprised by his ability to manage his money. Each time he received an advance on his pay, Volodya would stock up on groats, macaroni, sugar, potatoes, canned borscht, and so on. All provisions were precisely calculated to last until the next payday. He would then hand over fifty roubles to Uncle Sergei to be returned upon demand. I don't know why he chose his enemy to be his treasurer, but that's what he did.

He took very good care of his health, demanded that no one smoke in the room, and opened the casement window at night (and everyone obediently froze, until finally Sashka Peskov revolted). He approached the question of nutrition scientifically: in the morning, fried potatoes or an omelette, tea, bread and butter; for lunch, cold appetizers followed by a three-course meal; and a proper meal in the evening, too. Each of us earned more than Uncle Volodya, but none of us lived as well as he did. If, for example, we cooked up some macaroni, we'd eat it for breakfast, lunch, and dinner, until the pot was empty. This we did partly from laziness—no one felt like putting himself out to cook—partly from a simple lack of money. The most interesting thing was that Volodya also drank better than any of us. On payday, having stocked up on provisions for the next two weeks, he'd buy a quarter liter of vodka and carry it hidden under his quilted jacket, under his right arm, his elbow pressing the bottle against his side. This caused his left shoulder to ride up and he'd start walking strangely, as if one leg were shorter than the other. If we ran into him on the street, there was no problem in telling whether or not he was carrying a bottle. Volodya would hide the vodka in his night table, cook himself a proper dinner, and then set everything out on the table, which he covered with a piece of newspaper. Then he'd get down to business. He'd sip his vodka slowly and linger over his appetizers. The first signs of drunkenness were that he'd gaze straight ahead and start to debate with an imaginary opponent. "Yes," he'd say in challenge. "No," he would confidently refute. "This time, my dear sir, you've gone too far. Yes. No. Pardon me. I didn't understand you."

This phase of drunkenness would not last long. It was quickly succeeded by the next, in which Uncle Volodya would replace the empty quarter liter and the remains of the food in the night table and begin chasing Uncle Sergei. Thus would ensue that spectacle which I described at the beginning of this story. Afterward, he would try to avoid working for one, two, sometimes even three days, a possibility open to him by virtue of his job. Then his pocket money would run out and, with it, the spree. Uncle Volodya would never drink away the fifty roubles Uncle Sergei kept for him. This money would go for bread and butter and last precisely until the next payday. Everything was calculated down to the last kopeck. I cannot remember him ever once borrowing money from anyone, just as I cannot remember him ever loaning anyone money.

Occasionally, Tamara Andreevna Konoplevna, who managed the hostel, would stop by our room in the morning. She was a strapping woman, known for her strength and courage; if a fist fight broke out in the hostel, she'd rush bravely in and reestablish order right on the spot.

"Vladimir Mikhailovich," she'd say sternly, "you behaved disgracefully again yesterday, bursting in on the girls in room 42."

"Really?" Uncle Volodya would smile innocently. "Perhaps your information's incorrect?"

"We don't make mistakes. It's just no good at all, you, an older man, those girls could be your daughters . . ."

Uncle Volodya would stand with his hands by his sides, and lean slightly toward Tamara Andreevna, paying close attention to her words as if trying to understand and memorize them.

"Forgive me. It clearly was the negative influence of the alcohol," he would say in an attempt to explain his behavior scientifically. Having threatened him with every horrendous punishment up to and including dismissal and court action, Tamara Andreevna would leave.

In the intervals between sprees, Uncle Volodya would sit for evenings on end, guitar in hand, gazing into the teach-yourself book lying in front of him. He would pluck the strings, one at a time. Several times I asked him to play me something. He always refused, but then once, without my requesting it, he suddenly began playing. I think the song was called "The Hungarian Polka." I've seen people who play their guitars like balalaikas and hit all the strings at the same time. Uncle Volodya played masterfully by making each string sound separately. His style was like that of the well-known guitarist Ivanov-Kramsky. I remember being struck by the thought that a man with so much talent was working as a maintenance man.

"You ought to try and break into the music world," I said, certain that everyone ought to be trying to break into some profession. "Get to know some musicians . . ."

"I know some," said Uncle Volodya. "Have you heard of Kostenko, the composer?"

"No, I haven't," I admitted.

"We were in prison together. Besides, to be a guitarist and entertain the idiotic public . . ." He shook his head in disgust.

His revulsion for the idiotic public, as I discovered later, was reinforced by his tin ear. It had taken him a year and a half to learn that "Hungarian Polka," and that was all he knew how to play.

Sometimes he would swap insults with Uncle Sergei even when sober. Their arguments made little sense. "Sergei," Uncle Volodya would say, "why are you so stupid?"

"Who's stupid?" Uncle Sergei would roar, not fearing his enemy when he was sober.

"Not me."

"I'm stupid?" Sergei was boiling. "I'm stupid, me?"

"Stupid," Uncle Volodya would calmly assure him. "As a sheep. A log. A club."

Uncle Sergei would begin flitting nervously about the room. "And you're so smart, is that it? You, smart? You spent your whole life in prison. And I'm supposed to be the fool, me. I've got shell fragments right here, in my head, four places. And my nose was broken right here, go ahead and feel it."

"What do I want to feel your nose for?" said Uncle Volodya in surprise.

"For what? In Chita I unloaded medals by the boxful. And I also know how to tell novels."

"Tell novels?" Uncle Volodya looked at him with curiosity. "All right, let's hear."

"You want to hear, huh?" gloated Uncle Sergei. "In 1930 people'd come to me and pay me money, but you want it for nothing. Stand me a hundred grams of vodka, then I'll tell you one."

"You may be dumb but you're tricky. For what a hundred grams cost, I can go out and buy Leo Tolstoy and read him."

"So go read him," agreed Uncle Sergei. "But I won't tell you a novel. Or maybe I'll just tell you the beginning. 'In the year eighteen-hundred-seventy-five, Ivan Semenov Korolev, a merchant of the first guild, traveled with his daughters Sonya and Liza from St. Petersburg to Moscow . . .'" Uncle Sergei broke off at this point and turned away from Uncle Volodya.

"Then what?" asked Uncle Volodya.

"Then what? Buy me a hundred grams and I'll tell you."

Uncle Volodya would never buy him the hundred grams and that would be the end of Sergei's novel. Then Uncle Volodya would take his guitar down from the wall and begin studying one of Chopin's nocturnes, which he'd started on six months before.

His guitar was old and rattly. I heard somewhere that the sound of a guitar is greatly improved if you smash it and then glue it back together. I mentioned this once to Uncle Volodya, who looked over at Sergei and said: "All right, the next time I get drunk, I'll break it over Sergei. Kill two birds with one stone."

Uncle Sergei flared up again and started running about

the room. "Smash it, huh? The guitar, huh? Give away your wife. Find yourself one first, then give her away. Or else—'Come to me, I'll cut his throat.'"

In his fifty-three years of life Uncle Sergei had not learned to express his thoughts coherently, but we still got the point.

Uncle Sergei had taken up residence in our hostel a short while before I had. He had a room of his own somewhere, where his wife and his grown daughter, Larisa, lived. Larisa had not married. She used to bring men home and then turned her father out of the house because he was, as she saw it, getting in her way. She even forbade her mother to see him, but sometimes Sergei's wife would visit him on the sly and spend the night in our room. She was a small, timid woman who looked at each of us in fear, smiling fawningly. One time, when Uncle Sergei was in bed with his wife, Uncle Volodya came back drunk and disrupted everyone's sleep by shouting at her: "Come to me or else I'll cut his throat."

The woman lay there in horror, ready to agree to anything, though she was afraid of her husband as well. Uncle Volodya repeated his demand several times, then fell peacefully to sleep.

Sometimes he would bring girlfriends he'd known since his youth back with him, drink with them and make love with them in front of everyone. He had three or four of these girlfriends, but I recall only one, Shura, who was in our room more often than the others. To us she was just an old woman. Small and gray, she always arrived wearing the same tattered, threadbare coat with the gray artificial-fur collar, always the same soiled black dress.

Uncle Volodya would split his quarter liter with her

and boast of his virtues and his successes in life. And, if there weren't enough of his own, he'd boast of other people's successes. "Even though we're working people, doesn't mean we've got no creative spark. I'm crazy about music. Volodka's our poet. They print his poems in the newspapers. Read her one of your lyrics."

Shura would open her mouth in delight, revealing a single tooth and her readiness to abandon herself to any amusement. She would leave well before dawn, while we were all still sleeping.

On one occasion Uncle Volodya went off somewhere after work and returned around ten o'clock, sober and unusually excited. He straightened up his bed and cleared the pan and teapot off his table and, God only knows why, swept the room.

When I asked him what it was all about, he answered: "You'll see" and chuckled to himself.

A short while later a princess appeared. The elegance of her clothing distinguished her from all his other girlfriends. She wore an expensive but rather shabby fur coat and a dark wool dress. Her mouth was packed with gold teeth.

Uncle Volodya set a quarter liter on the table.

"I won't drink," the princess said decisively.

"Why, Nyusa?" I'd never heard such tender notes in his voice before.

"You know." She looked around, clearly uncomfortable at carrying on such a conversation in front of strangers.

"Nonsense," said Uncle Volodya. "You can drink a little tea, after. Tea kills the smell."

She shrugged her shoulders and smiled at me. I took Tolik Chekmarev aside (none of the others was there) and we left together.

I returned about two hours later. It was the usual story—Uncle Volodya was chasing Uncle Sergei with his razor. Sashka Peskov in his underpants and T-shirt was sitting on his bed, somberly observing it all.

Just as I appeared, Sashka grew incensed. "Ach, you son of a bitch, when's all this going to end!"

Uncle Volodya halted in surprise. No one had ever yelled at him there. Uncle Sergei was standing on the other side of the table, panting like an exhausted horse.

"What's with you?" asked Uncle Volodya menacingly.

"Nothing." There was no less resolve in Sashka's voice.

"I'll show you, you son of a bitch . . ." Uncle Volodya went after Sashka with his razor.

Sashka suddenly rushed forward, slamming Uncle Volodya's arm with the heel of his hand. The razor flew to my feet. I picked it up. Uncle Volodya dashed at me.

"Give me the razor!"

Sashka leaped in between us. "Go to bed!"

Uncle Volodya looked at him and seemed to shrink pitiably into himself. He walked over to his bed, then hesitated.

"I told you, go to bed." Sashka had no intention of giving an inch.

Obediently, Uncle Volodya began unbuttoning his shirt. Sashka took the razor from me and slipped it under his pillow. Volodya Krikunov and Fedka returned from a dance a few minutes later. Then Tolik arrived. Everyone went to bed. The lights were turned off. Suddenly I heard Uncle Volodya's voice: "Sash, hey, Sash."

"What do you want?" Sashka answered heavily.

"Give me back the razor, all right? I'll go cut my throat. I swear I'll cut my throat and that'll be the end of it. I won't be any trouble to anyone any more. Give me the razor, Sash."

"Let me sleep. You can cut your throat tomorrow," Sashka replied calmly.

Uncle Volodya accepted his fate and said no more. Later I heard him wiping his nose every few minutes. He may have been crying.

After that incident he seemed to grow quieter. Whenever he'd start in on Sergei, he'd shoot a quick glance over at Sashka to see how he was reacting. Nyusa never came to our room again. I soon forgot about her and never asked Uncle Volodya about her. It was he who brought up the subject.

One time, chance left us alone in the room together. It was close to payday; no one had any money. Uncle Volodya was studying his Chopin and tormenting his guitar. I was shining my boots in preparation for my classes at the literary union. Suddenly he stopped playing, laid his guitar across his knees, and asked: "Getting ready for classes?"

"That's right," I said.

"I look at you and there's something strange about you," he said after a moment's silence.

"How come?" I asked.

"All you do is write, write, write. There's nothing else that interests you? You should find yourself a girl. Youth doesn't last forever."

"I've got time yet."

"Maybe." He sighed. "And maybe not. Come over here." He took a little three-by-four photo from his night table. "Recognize her?"

It was a picture of a girl wearing the sort of tall circular cap that, I knew from the movies, had been fashionable at the beginning of the thirties. The girl did not look at all familiar, but it wasn't hard to guess who she was. "Nyusa?"

"That's her, all right." He winked at me. "Good stuff?"

"Beautiful," I said. Perhaps I was bending the truth, but what else could I do?

"You know, I was planning to marry her," he said, then fell silent. "And now she's got two grandchildren. Her husband manages a store. Sometimes I ask her: Are you sorry we didn't get married then? She says: No, I'm not sorry. I ask her: Why? And what kind of life would I have had with you? she says. Sitting home waiting while they dragged you from prison to prison. So I say: So what, that's all in the past. I'm a free man now. She says: What's the use. You can't even earn enough money to buy yourself a decent pair of pants. But when she was young she used to say she'd give up her whole life for me. Don't trust women. Never trust them, you hear me."

I can no longer recall how the newspaper, which was either from Piatigorsk or from Kislovodsk, fell into my hands. The last page had a small obituary notice in which the Party Committee and the Local Trade Union Committee sorrowfully reported the untimely death of Chief Engineer Vladimir Mikhailovich Golovin. Everything—the first name, patronymic, last name—was the same as Uncle Volodya's. I showed him the obituary. He grew highly excited reading it, took the newspaper from me and ran up and down the corridor showing it to everyone he met. Then he came back to the room and said to me: "You know what? I just got an idea. I'll give you Nyusa's address, you go see her and show her the obituary. Tell her: Here's all that's left of Volodya."

"She won't believe it," I said. "It's written right there—Chief Engineer. And she knows you're a maintenance man."

"What does she know. Tell her that I hid the truth on purpose, that I didn't want to talk about it. But that in fact I was a chief engineer. I wonder how she'll react. She'll probably feel sorry. This isn't like that store manager of hers. They don't get written up when they die."

He remained excited all evening, imagining how I would go and see her, what I would say, what she would answer, how she would experience his death and her error, how she would weep and what words she would actually say. I thought I should never have shown him the newspaper. Not that I ever went by Nyusa's; finally, Uncle Volodya even lost the obituary.

He loved to boast of his strength, his health, his learning, and even his successes in life. But he also liked to lament his fate: "Here I am, living alone, no family, no friends. My whole life gone up the cat's ass. I'll croak and there won't be anyone to say a good word for me." Though this was the truth, he said it somewhat insincerely, knowing that was what you were supposed to say on such occasions. I'd comfort him the best I could, tell him that he should get married, that then his life would take on new meaning. Sometimes he, too, would start talking about marriage, but then he would start bragging again and say that with all the successes he enjoyed with women it'd be difficult for him to settle down with one.

He usually drank alone, or with one of the girlfriends he'd known since his youth, or sometimes with Volodka Krikunov, to whom he was well disposed for some reason. Volodka wasn't a bad fellow; he was even rather good, except that he was utterly dumb and boastful. He'd brag about absolutely anything.

"Fedya," he'd propose to Utkin, whose bed was closest to his, "let's take them out and measure to see whose is the longest."

He also bragged of his drawing a cat, copied square by square from some magazine, and of his ability to make kitchen tables, which were clumsily thrown together. He was also able to spout rhymed nonsense as if speaking in the third person, and always with the obligatory introductory phrase: And so he says.

And so he says, he came at nine and Nastya's fine.
And so he says, the sparrows fly, though you can die.

He would spout such nonsense at any moment, and I don't know whether he made it up himself or whether it was some sort of folklore.

Once he said to me: "You know, if I'd gone to tenth grade, I could have become a poet, too."

I replied in clichés, saying that it wasn't a matter of grades but of one's general cultural level; that to write, one had to read a lot, and so forth.

"I can't stand reading," he admitted. "It gives me a headache and puts me to sleep."

One evening I returned from the literary union around eleven. The room was dark, which surprised me. As a rule, no one went to sleep that early. I could tell by the noise in the room that no one was actually sleeping. When I asked whether I could turn on the lights, someone giggled. Then Volodka Krikunov answered: "Turn them on!"

I turned on the light and I'm not sure how to put it but I was dumfounded.

Volodka Krikunov and Shura, in full view of everyone,

were engaged in what is usually called love. Her gray
hair was spread out against the pillow; eyes rolling, she
was wildly abandoned to pleasure. Volodka was shouting
out boasts about his merits and measurements and
promised that Shura wouldn't get out from under him
alive. All his shouts were actually addressed to Fedka,
who was standing by the bed in his underpants, weak
from desire, imploring Volodka to let him have a turn.
With a most serious look on his face, Uncle Sergei had
thrust his hand in between the two bodies and was
saying that he had to make sure everything was in order
because he was the superintendent. Tolik was observing
the scene, giggling bashfully, his blanket pulled right up
to his eyes. But it was Uncle Volodya whose behavior
was the most surprising. He was sitting in front of an
empty quarter liter (for which, it later turned out, he
had let Krikunov have Shura) and debating with his
imaginary opponent, paying no attention to what was
occurring right before his eyes. Then Uncle Volodya put
the empty bottle and the rest of his appetizers back in
the night table, waved his hand in a gesture of dismissal
(not at Krikunov, not at Shura, at no one in particular),
and then left the room. I, too, left and did not see what
happened next. Later on, I was told that Shura refused
Fedka. Sashka Peskov, who arrived a little while later,
put her out the door and forbade her ever to return.

Shortly after this incident Uncle Volodya unexpectedly
married Auntie Katya, a supervisor in our hostel. There
was no ceremony at all. Uncle Volodya simply gathered
all his belongings in a net bag, took his guitar, and moved
from the third floor to the fourth, where Auntie Katya
lived. Her son, Stepan, also a musician (he played the
accordion), moved down to our room. Everyone was

satisfied, especially Uncle Sergei and Tamara Andreevna. But their joy was short-lived. Three days or so later, Uncle Volodya moved back.

"Do you know what that bitch tried to pull on me?" he said to me. "She went and got an advance on my pay and wouldn't hand it over. So I wouldn't drink it away, she said. I got fed up with all that a long time ago. In the camps they took everything away from me, too."

Once again the guitar occupied its former position on the wall, and the accordion, along with its owner, returned to the fourth floor.

We lived side by side like this for about a year. Then certain changes occurred in my life. I left the hostel, and although I lived close by (in the next lane), I seldom saw Uncle Volodya. He was always friendly to me and each time I did see him he would ask me about my affairs. It was clear nothing special had happened in his life, and he talked mostly about the others. Volodka, Sashka, Fedka, and Tolik had gotten married, and he and Uncle Sergei had been switched to the small room where the superintendent had lived before.

"You know what happened to me?" he said one time. "A coronary."

"Go on," I said in surprise, sure that his health was going to hold out a good long time.

"That's right. Too much drinking, nearly did me in. I was out flat in the hospital for over a month. I don't feel too bad now. Except my arm aches me here." He rubbed his left arm near the shoulder and then said: "I quit drinking."

"Completely?" I knew him too well.

"Completely. And you know, I don't feel the urge.

I'm happy. It pains me to remember how I used to be. So much strength and health wasted, and on what? On that filth. It's no accident they say drunkenness is voluntary insanity. Now my life is peaceful. I bought myself a hat and a new guitar . . ."

"Another one?"

"Yes. I'm changing it over to six strings and leaving the old one the way it was. I just about know the Chopin now. Come see me in a month, I'll play it for you."

A month later I ran into him again in the same place. He was walking with a preoccupied look and a jerky gait. His left shoulder was higher than his right. I understood at once.

We exchanged greetings.

"Vodka?" I asked.

"Of course not, what are you talking about? No strong drink for me. The doctors have categorically forbidden it. But a little dry wine, that's all I bought." He showed me the neck of the bottle. "Dry wine's good for you. There's a great incidence of longevity among mountain people who drink dry wine."

But even with the aid of dry wine Uncle Volodya did not manage to achieve much longevity. From Uncle Sergei and others I learned that Uncle Volodya had had his second and final coronary.

Uncle Sergei went to the hospital twice and brought him kefir the first time and a jar of honey the second. A week and a half or so later, Uncle Volodya died. His trade union paid for his burial. Tamara Andreevna went from room to room collecting a rouble from everyone to buy him a wreath. The funeral-goods store turned out to have only expensive wreaths—what she'd collected wouldn't cover even half the cost. Tamara Andreevna made up the difference out of her pocket, a significant portion of her earnings. This was the sole wreath on Uncle Volodya's grave.

His property was divided as follows: by right of being his former wife, Auntie Katya took his quilted jacket and new guitar for herself. Uncle Sergei took the old guitar for having visited Uncle Volodya in the hospital. His service cap and his old suit, of no use to anyone, were thrown out. No one in the hospital could be given his new suit, as none of them was his legally registered relative.

1961

MAJOR DOGADKIN

When we were by ourselves we cadets called him Fyodor Ivanovich, though that was against the rules. Later on, Dogadkin was to earn himself the nickname "Dickens," and for that I was partially responsible.

One time he summoned me to his office for an ordinary infraction of discipline. With few exceptions, my infractions were always the same: I had no love for formation and preferred to make my own way to the mess hall or the latrine in the morning. Usually I was successful, but since the main concern of the battalion's entire staff of commanding officers, from classroom supervisor Pfc. Sosik all the way up to Battalion Commander Lieutenant Colonel Kovalev, was the nabbing of cadets out of formation, it's not surprising that I did get caught every once in a while. And when I did, thunder and lightning would come crashing down on my head. Extra duty details would also rain down on me; the easiest was washing the floor in the Lenin Rec Room, and the hardest was a few days in the kitchen. There was no duty worse than that. Everyone had to clean a hundred kilos of potatoes per night. Of course you could clean them any old way you wanted: slice off half, leave in the eyes, but still . . . By morning you couldn't unbend your back, your hands were shaking, and your field shirt, your pants, your boots, everything was covered in potato spume. You felt like collapsing right then and there, for even just an hour or so, but then it would be time for breakfast and they would assign you to dishwashing. And so then two of you have to wash eight hundred bowls and eight hundred spoons, and then there's eight hundred mugs you've some-how got to rinse out, too. It's lucky that soldiers aren't given knives or forks. Naturally, there were never eight hundred bowls, spoons, and mugs available, but there always were eight hundred soldiers; so the two hundred bowls we had on hand had to be washed out four times, and as fast as possible, because no sooner had one com-pany left the table than the next would appear and the duty men would start hurrying us: "Come on, come on, move it!" After breakfast you wash the last two hundred bowls, slack from exhaustion. You're supposed to hurry, but you've got no strength left, and just as you've washed the last bowl and you're rolling a cigarette with stiff fingers, the boots of another company come clattering in with a song ("Invincible, legendary, having tasted the joy of victory in battle . . ."). Lunch. After twenty-four hours of this, you stagger for a week. And all for the one rare pleasure of walking two hundred meters all by yourself.

And so it was for just such a little stroll that I had been summoned by the company commander, Major Dogadkin.

I stood before him almost at attention while he attempted to fathom my soul. "So, tell me, why do you keep breaking the rules of military discipline?"

I stood there without saying a word, unable to explain why I didn't like to travel in a marching formation.

He was honestly trying to get at the truth of the matter—perhaps my lack of discipline was due to a low cultural level.

"Tell me, do you read good literature?"

"Sometimes, comrade major."

That meant I was not entirely a lost soul.

"And just what do you read?"

"Whatever's around."

"But what, precisely? Have you read about Alexander Matrosov?"

"No."

"The Story of Zoya and Shura?"

"No."

"The Story of Liza Chaikin?"

"No, haven't read that either."

Now he'd found the root of my unconscious attitude toward the army and discipline. "So what do you read, then?" he asked sympathetically.

"Right now, the complete Dickens . . ."

Now it all came clear to him. He looked over at me as if at a hopeless case and shrugged his shoulders.

"All right then, you can go."

At evening roll call, Dogadkin explained the company's slack discipline as a result of the cadets' lack of interest in good literature, the sort which instructs and improves.

"Here's a glaring example for you right here, comrades. I asked Cadet Voinovich what he reads. It turned out that he'd read nothing about Alexander Matrosov. Nothing about Zoya Kosmodemyanskaya. Nothing about Liza

Chaikin. So what does he read?" The major prolonged
the pause so that the cadets would have time to imagine
what level of trash one of their fellows had sunk to.
"Comrades, he says he reads the collected dickens knows
what."

2

"Cooooompany! In place, quick march, singing! One, two!"

> *Battle by battle to Berlin the soldier went . . .*
> *Ech!*
> *Time to send a song ringing out, ringing out . . .*
> *Ech!*
> *There's many a song to sing . . .*
> *Ech!*
> *But you can't sing 'em all, can't sing 'em all . . .*
> *Ech, you darling gray-winged sparrow,*
> *dear homeland that we love.*
> *Ech, you darling sparrow of mine,*
> *with your wings of gray!*

One, two, three, the boots of Company One came
pounding down the road en route to a worthy goal—
dinner.

One, two, three. Alongside them, with a fancy step and
a twirled moustache, came Sergeant de Gaulle. We'd
given him that nickname because of his height and a
certain physical resemblance to the French general.

"There's many a song you can sing . . ." But we didn't
even have time enough for this one, the distance from
the barracks to the mess hall was shorter than the song.

Beneath a street light, where the road took a turn in
front of the sports field, stood Major Fyodor Dogadkin

(eighth-grade education, civilian speciality: apprentice locksmith), his dress uniform clustered with medals earned in the war, not just by serving time.

"Karasev!" he called out to the song leader. "Stop singing those thieves' songs."

"It's not a thieves' song, comrade major. It's in our song book."

"Karasev, I'm telling you that's a thieves' song."

"Yes, comrade major."

And Karasev, the choirmaster, who always took part in amateur nights, began singing another song in his powerful voice (though now he was accompanied by Alexandrov).

> *The years of our great victories*
> *roar like a banner above you.*
> *Lit by the sun of glorious battle,*
> *your path is sung in our songs.*

Bam, bam. Then everyone together.

> *Invincible and legendary,*
> *having tasted the joy of victory in battle,*
> *to you, our own beloved army,*
> *the Motherland sends a greeting in song.*

Bam, bam.
Bam, bam, bam, bam, bam, bam, bam, bam, bam, bam . . .

What was that? Automatic-weapon fire. Someone was shooting. But why and at whom? Battalion Commander Lieutenant Colonel Kovalev raced by.

"Sergeant, why are you standing there with your mouth hanging open? Dismiss the company at once!" he said, then ran off.

A formation must disperse under fire, it makes too large a target.

"Disperse!"

A loud, desperate cry could be heard from the vicinity of the warehouse: "Stop, or I'll shoot!"

The battalion commander did not need to hear that command a second time. He fell face first to the road and then shouted, still lying down: "Sentry, this is Lieutenant Colonel Kovalev!"

"Stay as you are or I'll shoot!"

"Sentry, this is Lieutenant Colonel Kovalev. What's happened?"

"I'll shoot."

The first rumors reached us after dinner. Two strangers in civilian clothing had apparently attacked the sentry. The sentry had opened fire. One of the attackers was killed on the spot; the other was wounded and taken to the infirmary. One passerby, a waitress from the officers' mess, was also lightly wounded. A bullet ricocheted off the street and grazed her temple. One millimeter closer and . . .

The next morning they assembled us in the Lenin Rec Room. Major Dogadkin told us what had happened. A junior cadet (it was our second year, so we were senior classmen) was at his post. Suddenly two men in sports clothes appeared, coming right at him from different sides. The cadet had shouted: "Halt! Who goes there?" But they didn't stop. The cadet shouted out again, but they continued coming at him. The cadet fired a round and one man fell. Meanwhile, the other had succeeded in breaking the seal on the warehouse door. He opened the door and vanished inside. The sentry entered the warehouse and spotted the intruder, who came at him again. The sentry aimed his submachine gun at him and pulled the trigger. The gun did not respond. Later they discovered that the bolt had jammed, though at the time the sentry had thought the cartridge drum was empty. Just as the intruder was almost upon him, the sentry whipped out his knife (we were issued Finnish daggers in addition to submachine guns); he brandished the knife at the intruder, who stopped in his tracks. At that moment the sentry heard the sound of boots coming up behind him, and deciding that he was being attacked by yet another man, he began howling wildly: "Stop or I'll shoot!"

Until he finally realized what was happening, the sentry would not allow Lieutenant Colonel Kovalev, the unit duty man, or the captain of the guard to approach him, answering all their appeals to him with "Don't approach! Or I'll shoot!"

One of the attackers turned out to be the sergeant in charge of the warehouse. The sergeant was preparing to go on leave and had to turn over the warehouse. But there were items missing; the sergeant had sold various goods to the local Poles and had spent the money on drink. He roped in a friend to help him. They had a few drinks, changed into sports clothes, and set off for the warehouse. One of them was supposed to distract the sentry while the other broke the seal. The next morning, when taking over the warehouse, the sergeant would find the seal broken and so refuse to sign the bill of transfer; the blame for the missing items would fall on the guard. But it didn't turn out like that. Wounded twice, the sergeant died that night in the infirmary. His friend was in the guardhouse. But the true horror of it all was that the sergeant had not merely been given leave. As a rule, privates and sergeants doing ordinary duty are not given leave except as the highest form of incentive. In Poland, leave, even as an incentive, was neither offered nor granted. Leave was granted only under two conditions, with no exceptions. One was the death of a close relative, and the sergeant had just suffered such a loss. His sister had died during a cave-in at a mine. His mother had sent him a telegram, and now the mother had lost both a daughter and a son.

Major Dogadkin told us the whole story that morning while we were assembled in the rec room. Everyone was shaken. Pfc. Baklanov asked if the sentry was going to be granted leave now. The major's expression changed immediately and he looked over at Baklanov with horror.

"Leave? For what? For killing a man?"

"But he did act according to regulations," said Baklanov, confused. "And they say leave is to be granted in such cases."

We'd all heard that. If you kill someone while serving guard duty, you get ten days' leave plus travel time home and back. This was the second and only other condition under which ten days' leave was granted. It was true that any one of us could have earned that opportunity ten times over. Every night at the end of summer, gangs of soldiers would slip out past all the sentry points to shake apples down from the Poles' trees, or would steal away right after evening roll call and return with their shirts stuffed with apples. If you happened to spot someone slipping back in, you wouldn't make a fuss or go for your gun. You'd quietly ask who went there. They'd answer, "Friend." You'd let them approach until you saw it really was one of your own. A couple of apples would be paid you in tribute and the intruder would go on his way, to treat you just as humanely the next night. But during our second year at the school, fresh recruits arrived, either from Izhevsk or from Saransk, I don't remember. They wouldn't play the game, and from time to time the night would be shattered by submachine-gun fire; so far, no one had been hit. Practically no one ventured out to steal apples when these raw recruits were standing guard.

These particular ill-fated heroics had been the work of one of the raw recruits. Putting ourselves in his shoes, we all wondered what we'd have done if it had been one of us under attack. We'd been told that the local population was hostilely disposed toward us. Sort of strange—a fellow socialist country and its citizens were openly hostile. It had been explained to us that this was Silesia, former German territory, and that in fact the inhabitants were still more German than Polish. But whoever they were, Poles or Germans, they were hostile, if only because not a single decent orchard in town remained untouched. Branches went cracking every night, and the owners of the orchards holed up in their houses, lacking the nerve to come out, though they still would have liked to make their presence felt. To be just, it must be said that we presented no danger to them and it was enough for a door to start creaking open for us to dash headlong through the fence and away—to attack them never entered our minds. But there had been one incident. One brave Pole came out alone with a lantern and started haranguing the harmless apple thieves. Then someone shouted, "Stop or I'll shoot" from up in the tree, which was more than even this bold orchard owner could take, and he fled back to his house. In reality, no one had anything to shoot with, since we never took our weapons with us when we went out apple stealing.

But I've gotten away from the subject. I was saying that everyone was putting himself in the sentry's shoes. Yes, we were a pretty undisciplined lot and didn't have all that much respect for regulations. We'd sleep on guard duty, stroll over to the next post for a smoke, go to the officers' mess and beg a little food or steal a mug or a spoon (always in short supply); we'd let any amount of our fellow cadets past any sentry post, but if one of us is attacked by two men in civilian clothes coming at him from two sides, just what do we do then?

You should fire in the air, shout, repel them with your rifle butt, said Dogadkin. "We're all close by here, we'd come running right away."

"But, according to regulations . . ." Baklanov began again.

"Baklanov, you're a fool," said Major Dogadkin and then added something not to be found anywhere in the regulations. "What do regulations matter if it means a mother loses two children."

3

After this incident I began to observe Major Dogadkin more closely and I noticed that this man, who at first glance seemed the angry type and who'd given me more than one good tongue-lashing, had a distinctly negative attitude toward violence of any sort.

We were having a class on side arms.

"Cadet Kabakovich, what is the definition of a bayonet?"

"The bayonet is defined as a side arm of the thrust-weapon type and serves the function of wounding the enemy in hand-to-hand combat."

Defined as, serves the function of: in technical literature they always say something is defined as such-and-such and serves such-and-such a function. A wing is defined as the carrying surface of an airplane and serves the function of creating the lift force. The ailerons are defined as devices for the steering of the airplane and serve the function of changing the airplane's position relative to its longitudinal axis. First Lieutenant Potapov used to say that the hollow of the shoulder is defined as a small depression and serves the function of bracing the rifle butt.

And so: "The bayonet is defined as a side arm of the thrust-weapon type and serves the function of wounding the enemy in hand-to-hand combat. It possesses a three-edged form with a pointed tip and three grooves to channel the blood."

"Kabakovich." Dogadkin frowned. "Why did you say that?"

"Say what?"

"You know, about the grooves. We're not children, we all know what the grooves are for, so why bring it up when there's no need to?"

"So what should I say, then?" asked Kabakovich, puzzled.

"Just say it possesses three grooves and the function they serve need not be explained, as it's perfectly obvious."

4

I was standing guard duty, finishing off the last shift. A secret room on the second floor of the school building was the object of my protection. More precisely, not the room itself, but the door. Even more precisely, not the door, but the seal on that door. The secrets kept behind that door weren't worth a kopeck. Our abstracts of the construction of the MiG-15 were by that time known in such detail to foreign intelligence that complete sketches of them were published in American military journals. We had even heard that the information taught us in class was lifted from those American magazines. Nevertheless, all our notebooks were sealed, and kept in that room.

This was one of the best sentry posts, second only to the wood yard. Its merits were plain enough. First, it was warm there; second, you could sit on the stairs or on a windowsill, and if you were a light sleeper, you could even catch a nap. If the captain of the guard took it into his head to check up on you, there was no way for him to catch you by surprise. The sentry downstairs at the entrance to the school would hail him. Besides, it was impossible to climb up that stone stair quietly.

So there I was, doing the final shift of guard duty. Officially it ended at six o'clock, unofficially a bit later. The new sentry would usually be delayed a little at the changing of the guard and then again while instructions were issued in the sentries' quarters. I figured on being relieved around six-thirty. At eight o'clock they were showing a film, *Dreams on the Road,* which I wanted to see again. An hour and a half would be enough time to clean and hand in my weapon, polish my buttons and boots, catch dinner with everyone else, and then go see the movie. The changing of the guard took place on time, that I could see from my post. The new duty officer, Second Lieutenant Dobronravov (he was the school Komsomol organizer), instructed those beginning sentry duty and then they all went into the sentry building. And vanished. Six-thirty, no one in sight. Seven o'clock, those without details had formed up and gone off to dinner. Seven-thirty—one after the other, companies went marching and singing to the club. At quarter to eight I caught sight of Dobronravov walking past. I leaned out the window.

"Comrade lieutenant, why haven't I been relieved?"

He stopped, threw back his head, and looked up curiously at me. "And who gave you permission to talk at your post?"

I wasn't about to answer the question. "Talking is forbidden" means just that. But there was a legal means of calling the captain of the guard. I stuck my carbine out the window, pointed the butt down, and shot into the air. Lieutenant Dobronravov, who had been about to continue on his way, stopped to see what would happen next. What happened next was straight from a book. The captain of the guard, First Lieutenant Potapov, the corporal of the guard, and the sentry from the next watch all came running out of the sentry building, into the school, and up the stairs.

"Why did you shoot?" asked Potapov, panting.

"Why haven't I been relieved?"

"I see," said Potapov.

In the sentry building he took away my carbine and belt and had me sent to the guardhouse for an unspecified length of time.

They put me in a separate cell, where there was nothing to sit on—no cot, no stool. They'd taken away my overcoat and it was cold and damp in that cell. I'd stand for a while, then walk around, then squat down for a bit. This warmed me up, but it also made me tired. After all, I'd been standing guard before all this, and now it was more of the same. An hour, two hours passed. I didn't know if I was allowed anything to sit or lie on. The cement floor was cold as the grave. I got up and kicked the door. The guard peeked in.

"What do you want?"

"Call the captain of the guard."

More time passed. Finally the captain of the guard,

First Lieutenant Kolesnichenko, appeared. He smelled as if he'd been steeped in vodka for a week.

"What do you want?"

"Give me my coat."

"Against the rules."

"But it's cold."

"You'll be warmer at the beach."

That night the guard peeked in again. "You want to go clean potatoes?"

"With pleasure," I said. Not one of the greatest pleasures, of course, but just to sit in a warm room was pleasure enough.

I sat in the kitchen peeling potatoes, the guard beside me with his weapon. He was at his post. Unlike me, he did not have the right to sit, eat, drink, smoke, or go to the latrine. He would have to be relieved. In fact, I should have been guarded by a detail consisting of no less than three men—one to guard me, one to keep the guard awake, and one to sleep. And, so that they could in time be relieved, yet a fourth man would be required, the corporal of the guard.

The guard sat beside me, his carbine across his knees. He was worn out; he kept catching his head as he fell asleep.

Major Dogadkin came bursting in at daybreak. "Who's here from Company One?"

"Me."

"Ach, you again, you son of a bitch!" The major shouted, stamped his foot, and even began threatening me. I was ruining everything for him. Our company was first in grades, but now it looked as if it was on its way to the bottom in the discipline department. He promised to have me expelled from school and transferred to the canine corps. He'd have me rot in the guardhouse, have me court-martialed, write such a scathing report about me that I wouldn't even be able to get a job as a shepherd back in civilian life. "Well, all right," he said suddenly, without the slightest transition. "Finish up the potatoes and go back to the sentry quarters. I've given the order for your release."

5

When I returned to the barracks I found no one there except the duty men. The company had left for class. I cleaned my carbine, stacked it on the pyramid, and went to bed. I fell asleep at once.

Someone was shaking my shoulder, demanding that I get up immediately. It took some effort for me to unglue my eyes enough to see de Gaulle's hateful face glaring down at me.

"Who gave you permission to sleep during the day? Go police the area."

"I won't," I said and rolled over on the other side.

"You won't go?"

He stood over me for a minute and then left. Earlier, the idea of force would never have entered his mind, but now, after the incident . . . But, before relating that incident, there are certain details which must be explained. An innovation had recently been introduced in our school: beds were to be tucked in so the lines of the blanket were as straight as the edges of a brick. To help create this effect, we had each been issued two wooden poles, which we stuck under the blankets and which we placed by the head of our beds at night. One time I was late for reveille and de Gaulle rushed in and pulled me from the bed to the floor by my foot. I hurt my elbow in falling, and enraged, I grabbed one of the poles and went after him. And then that swaggering petty tyrant, the terror of the entire company (not to mention his being twice as tall as me), ran the whole length of the corridor, shamed in front of everyone. He took refuge in the supply room. He made no report of his disgrace to anyone, since he would have just ended up a laughing-stock. As a result of this incident, some of the other cadets began losing their fear of him.

But this time the poles remained in their place at the head of my bed. De Gaulle stood over me a little longer, then left the room.

He returned a moment later and announced triumphantly that I was being summoned by Major Dogadkin.

I had to get up. Dogadkin received me very coldly. There I was before him again, I, the malicious transgressor of military discipline.

"Voinovich, why didn't you obey the sergeant's order?"

"Comrade major," I said. "As you know, I was on detail for an entire day, and then I spent the whole night peeling potatoes."

It didn't take much to win his pity. "Tired?" he asked sympathetically.

"Tired, comrade major," I answered honestly.

"All right, go get yourself a couple hours of sleep."

I thanked him, then went off to bed and could barely wake myself up for dinner.

I don't know whether or not the major reproached himself for excessive liberalism and lack of spine or whether he considered his relations with his subordinates humane and normal. When he was angry he would yell, stamp his feet; sometimes he would even spit. But one glimpse of a distraught expression on the face of the person he was upbraiding was enough for him to do a total turnabout, with no transition whatsoever, and begin almost to apologize. From time to time, however, he did try and show his firmness.

This was the case this time, for, having just released me from the guardhouse, he was soon to send me back, and without any apparent reason. This is what happened. The second day after I'd been released, First Lieutenant Potapov told me that if it hadn't been for the goodness of Major Dogadkin, I'd have been in for a good bit more time than one day.

"I'm sure goodness had very little to do with it," I said for the sake of a phrase. "It's just that the head of the school forbids cadets being locked up for very long. Otherwise, they fall too far behind."

Potapov said nothing in reply. That same evening Major Dogadkin appeared at roll call and ordered me to step forward. I did so, somewhat puzzled, as I was not guilty of any new wrongdoing.

"Comrade cadets," the major addressed the formation, "Cadet Voinovich here contends that I, a major, a company commander, do not have the right to send him, Cadet Voinovich, to the guardhouse. So that he should have no doubts on the subject, two days' strict arrest!"

I did not dare make any objections. I was even almost delighted by this turn of events. And I did in fact serve those two days, though that did not help the major change my mind—I wasn't sent to the guardhouse immediately but on Saturday evening and stayed there through Sunday, so as to lose only one day of classes, and not two.

Incidentally, this time I made the best possible preparations for the guardhouse. Reading the regulations relevant to the care of prisoners, I learned that a prisoner is permitted a stool by day and a cot and an overcoat by night. If the temperature drops below 16° during the day, an overcoat is permitted then as well. In addition, prisoners are allowed to read newspapers, the regulations, and political literature. I was even surprised myself at how much you were allowed in the guardhouse.

So, Saturday came. No sooner had we returned from classes than First Lieutenant Potapov appeared, looking quite satisfied with his mission.

"Shall we go, then?" he proposed to me.

"Right away," I said. "I'll just go get my overcoat."

"Overcoats aren't permitted."

"Oh, aren't they?" I said. "And what does it say here in the regulations?"

He read the regulations and was surprised. He, too, had not known that a prisoner had so many rights.

Taking advantage of his confusion, I took the pile of books I'd prepared beforehand from my night table. All four were permitted reading: *The History of Diplomacy*, *The History of the All-Union Communist Party (Bolsheviks)*, some volume of Lenin's, and Stalin's book *The Great Patriotic War*. Potapov regarded me with a certain horror but did not dare make any objections. Only when I took the thermometer off the wall did he ask: "And what's that for?"

"To measure the temperature in the cell. And if it goes under 16, I'm going to demand my overcoat during the day, too."

Naturally, he could have objected that the thermometer was government property, had been inventoried and belonged to the barracks, but he was clearly at a loss and said not a word.

On the way, we encountered Second Lieutenant Dobronravov, who asked Potapov where he was taking me. He was surprised to learn the guardhouse was our destination.

"I'd have thought the library."

Thus I settled down in my solitary cell with maximal comfort and spent my two days with no little profit to myself. Frankly, I even think that for a soldier who is always surrounded by people, twenty-four hours a day, and is never alone, even in the latrine, and who has no better opportunity to be alone with himself, a spell of solitary is not the worst means of calming the nervous system.

After returning to barracks two days later, I was immediately summoned to Dogadkin. He greeted me with some embarrassment and invited me to take a seat. That was highly unusual. When an officer summons a soldier he practically never invites him to be seated.

"So, how do you feel?" he asked.

"All right."

"Here's the thing," he said hesitantly. "Have I offended you?"

"No, please, comrade major."

"You must understand, I had to punish you because you . . ."

"I understood everything, comrade major."

"Well, good then, if you understood. I thought you were offended. You know I didn't do it out of meanness but because . . ."

And then he began yet another muddled explanation of why he had been forced to place me under arrest.

There are certain overanxious types who're always thinking that someone has spoken ill or thought badly of them, or that someone has acted with the intention of offending them. Dogadkin always thought it was he who might have offended someone.

Many years have passed, but I remember him to this day. Though just what do I remember? A few separate incidents, the way he'd grow angry, how he'd stamp his feet in that funny, awkward way of his, how suddenly his expression would change and he'd say, almost in tears: "But I'm like a father to you!"

1974

FIRST LIEUTENANT

PAVLENKO

"Company, attention!" Pavlenko walked along the front of the formation, peering into the elongated faces of the cadets. Then, in his low, soft, sinister bass voice, added: "Straighten it up!"

Pavlenko had the reputation of being the fiercest officer in the school. He had formerly commanded a platoon in the sixth company, but had advanced since then and had been sent to our school to improve discipline.

For quite some time it had been said that Company One had gotten out of hand and that Major Dogadkin had not held the reins firmly enough, that his relation to the cadets was marked by unforgivable liberalism and flabbiness. Removing Dogadkin had been under consideration for some time, but he was approaching the end of his three-year stretch and, for that reason, was tolerated. Then, one day, the three years were up, and Major Dogadkin left for his new service post, in Russia.

A day, two days, passed in peace and quiet. But then someone was late for reveille.

"Cadet so-and-so, step out of formation! Breach of military discipline, five days of extra duty detail."

If someone shined his boots poorly—five days of extra duty detail. If someone was caught smoking in an unauthorized area—five days of extra duty detail. If the top button of someone's field shirt was unbuttoned—five days of extra duty detail. Why not two, or three, or four, or ten? Because five was the ceiling, the absolute limit a soldier could be given for any one breach of discipline. For any such breach, Pavlenko always gave the whole works. There was, however, another scale of punishment—up to twenty days in the guardhouse—but the commanding officers were reluctant to use it, for reasons I will indicate later.

Pavlenko would appear before reveille, that is, before six in the morning, and would leave after evening roll call, which was past 2300 hours. During reveille he would stand in the corridor holding his watch, keeping close track of the time; he allowed us twenty seconds to get dressed and assemble. Anyone who didn't make it—five days' extra duty detail. He watched to make sure no one marched out of step; he set traps and waited in ambush, trying to catch the cadets off-guard. He also acquired the habit, common among sergeants, of suddenly jumping out from behind a corner.

"Why didn't you salute?"

"My fault. I didn't see you."

"A soldier should see everything. Five days' extra duty detail."

One time it happened to me. Pavlenko came jumping out from behind a corner, and to make matters worse, I had my hands in my pockets. I would have saluted him, but I couldn't get my hands out of my pockets in time. And so, at roll call that night, Pavlenko called me out of formation, and it goes without saying, five days' extra duty detail.

"I won't obey," I said.

"What?" He looked at me as if he hadn't understood.

It appeared I had gone too far, something was bound to happen. But once you've opened your mouth, you've got to stick it out.

"I won't obey."

I was standing in front of the formation, looking straight ahead. Pavlenko was looking at me; the formation was staring at him. Everyone was waiting to see how it would end. Regulations state that an order from an officer is law for his subordinate. An order must be obeyed unconditionally, precisely, and punctually. An officer is duty-bound to employ all possible means to influence his subordinate to obey an order, up to and including physical force and force of arms. (During political training we asked just what sort of physical force they had in mind. Did that mean an officer could beat a subordinate? Sometimes they answered us evasively, sometimes affirmatively.) Everyone was waiting to see how Pavlenko would act. Would he give me the works plus a few days of strict isolation punishment? Would he go for his pistol (I had no idea how far he'd go), or . . .

"Cadet Voinovich, return to formation."

I thought he would summon me after taps, but he didn't. The next morning he was out in the corridor, watch in hand as usual, paying me no attention whatsoever. The longer his silence persisted, the more alarming it became. He went with us to mess and then to classes, and still not a word. What was he cooking up? Perhaps while I was sitting in class, struggling with the principles of the jet engine, my fate was being sewn up elsewhere: a special department was assigning me to a disciplinary battalion.

Our first six hours of classes were in the school building, and the last two hours, physical education, took place in the gymnasium. We were leaving the school building and forming up, with Pavlenko standing right there.

Private First Class Sosik, in charge of the class, gave the command: "Dress, attention!" and then reported to the company commander.

"You take over the class," said Pavlenko. "Cadet Voinovich, come here."

The class stepped forward, leaving the first lieutenant and me a little behind them.

"Why don't you want to obey the order?" he asked me in a tone of voice I took to be favorable.

"Because it's unfair. You came from behind the corner. I didn't see you . . ."

"A soldier should see everything."

"Even through walls? Teach me how."

"All right, then," he agreed, with unexpected equanimity. "Wash the floor in the rec room today and we'll let it go at that."

Of course it would have been more consistent of me to stand my ground. But then he would have had to show what he was made out of, too. There'd have been no telling where it all would end. Besides, washing the floor in the rec room wasn't all that hard. Pavlenko needed everyone to see that he had held his ground. I needed him off my back. And since he was ready to compromise this time around, it meant that next time he wouldn't be jumping out from behind any corners. Next time he'd prefer not to notice me. And that meant I'd have won a victory.

I washed the rec room, but without putting very much effort into it. I wet a rag and pushed it around the entire floor with my foot. Naturally, de Gaulle was not pleased with my work and ordered me to do it over again. When I refused he ran off to complain to the new company commander, who, not wishing to get involved in yet another conflict, told the sergeant to keep out of it.

Free of me, Pavlenko continued to make a mockery of the other cadets. They were afraid of him. But, strangely enough, their progress began to slip and breaches of discipline occurred more frequently than they had under Dogadkin. Once it reached the point of total insubordination. This is what happened:

Bursting into the barracks after taps, Pavlenko heard somebody whispering. He switched on the light and asked who'd been talking. No one said a word.

"I'm waiting," said Pavlenko. His eyes stared unblinkingly from under the visor of his cap, which was drawn low over his forehead.

Silence.

"Company, reveille!" he said softly in his deep voice.

No one budged.

"Company, reveille! Alert!" he raised his voice, now somewhat worried.

According to army regulations, failing to respond to an alert is almost tantamount to treason. But not a single soldier's head budged from his pillow.

Wheeling abruptly on his heel, Pavlenko dashed out of the barracks. Returning a few minutes later, he found the entire company gone. A hundred men had vanished. There was only one duty officer, armed with a long knife, standing by a table.

"Duty officer, where is the company?"

"I don't know, comrade first lieutenant!" said the duty officer, making his eyes bulge out as a sign of loyalty to duty.

Pavlenko ran down the corridor, glancing into one room after the other. Not a single soldier to be found. Only abandoned beds. Finally he realized what must have happened and went up to the attic. He stood in the rectangular light of the doorway, unable to bring himself to step forward into the darkness, from which now came the sound of a hundred men breathing as shallowly as they possibly could.

"Company, outside and form up!" he commanded, without very much confidence in his voice, and was himself the first to go outside.

But this time everyone obeyed the order, went outside, and assembled on the parade ground.

In a low voice Pavlenko commanded: "Even it up! Attention! Left foot forward, quick march!"

We went out to the checkpoint. Pavlenko showed the sentry the unit duty officer's permission to take the company outside the camp limits (that's what he had run out of the barracks the first time for). The sentry raised the barrier and there we were, marching down the streets of a little Polish town illuminated by the moon and the faint flickering of gaslight.

Probably Pavlenko was not much of a psychologist. He didn't realize that for us to be outside the barbed wire, even for a short time, even at night, even in formation, to walk past houses behind whose windows a life totally different from ours was following its usual course, for us such an outing was no punishment, but almost a pleasure.

But where was he leading us? We'd already left the little town behind, and now on both sides of the paved road were fields lit by even strips of moonlight.

"Company, halt! Tanks to your right, cavalry to your left . . ." He hadn't even managed to shout "Disperse" when we had already scattered in all directions like peas on a table top, as if we'd been thrown into actual panic by the nonexistent tanks and cavalry. (What cavalry? what kind of cavalry in this jet age?) We lay flat in the furrows between the rows of cabbage.

It was then that Pavlenko realized his error.

"Company, forward and form up!"

We were lying amid the cabbage, observing all the rules of camouflage, covering our cigarettes with the palms of our hands.

Pavlenko stood alone in the greenish moonlight on the road.

"Company, line up in columns of four!"

We continued to lie there, holding our breath, waiting curiously to see where it would all lead.

Pavlenko started running through the field, stumbling on heads of cabbage. Kabakovich was the first to be pulled out and led back out onto the road. Kabakovich was always the first to be caught.

"Stay here!" ordered Pavlenko, and leaving Kabakovich on the road, he dashed back into the field. But by the time he had brought Grachev out to the road, Kabakovich was no longer there. Pavlenko kept running back and forth through the field like that for some time, until we ourselves got fed up with the game. At that point we all walked out to the road, obediently formed up, and then marched obediently back in formation. But our little night excursion cost First Lieutenant Pavlenko dearly—he was removed from his post as company commander. They sent us a new one then and, naturally, he was even worse.

1974

CAPTAIN KURASOV

At first we decided that he had come to us from the navy, because, while conducting our initial get-acquainted evening roll call, he'd said in a soft and homey voice: "Disperse to crew's quarters," instead of the usual "Disperse." Later we learned that such an expression was used at the infantry academy where he had served previously, also as a company commander.

For some reason we also first thought him a civilian by nature, but soon realized our mistake and nicknamed him "Rule Book." It had turned out that the regulations made for his favorite and, most likely, only reading. He had learned them by heart, knew where a soldier's foot should be when given the command "About face!", at what distance from an approaching officer a soldier must switch into parade step, how many centimeters up the soldier's leg his sock should reach, and how many millimeters there should be between his left ear and the edge of a forage cap.

While drumming all this higher wisdom into our heads, he seemed to be savoring its inner meanings.

Early on in our acquaintance, while conducting a class in parade drill, he announced: "Comrade cadets, there's a court-martial waiting down the road for all of you."

Initially we found this quite a startling statement, because it seemed to us that we had done nothing wrong, if you didn't count petty infractions of discipline like not traveling in formation, as I mentioned earlier. But, with the passing of time, we grew used to this pet expression of his.

Unlike Major Dogadkin, Captain Kurasov never grew angry, never smiled, never raised his voice, and never told us stories about his life. His face was always impassive, his fish-like eyes stared straight and unblinking from under his reddish eyebrows, which looked as if they'd been singed. We soon grew to hate him, though he still had not done anyone any specific wrong. We started discussing him among ourselves, with impunity at first, but we soon began to notice that he was aware of our conversations. Suddenly, out of the blue, someone who had spoken ill of him would receive a disproportionate punishment for the slightest infraction. The code of discipline states that a serviceman can complain about the illegality but not about the severity of a given punishment. That is, for unpolished boots, for being late for formation, for an undercollar not sewn in, they can give you extra duty detail and they can even go the limit to twenty days under arrest. Our Rule Book operated on this scale, without, however, ever going the limit.

And so we noticed that Rule Book was aware of our conversations about him. But how? There could only be one answer—a stool pigeon had been placed among us. We began paying closer attention and observed that Cadet Yakhtonov, whom we called Yasha, took no part in the racier discussions, kept his silence, and constantly seemed to have something on his mind. We conducted the simplest of experiments. In the presence of Yakhtonov, and two others in the know, Genka Denisov and Kazik Ermolenko, I said: "He's a beast, though, our captain, isn't he."

"What are you talking about," said Genka. "He's just a real military man; his only concern is that we become good soldiers like him."

"But he's got a nasty face on him, that's for sure," I said.

"Still, he really knows the regulations," said Ermolenko.

"Why shouldn't he, if he spends the whole night poring over them."

"The whole night? So when does he have time to sleep with his wife?" asked Genka.

"Come on," I said. "What wife. She ran away a long time ago. Now he sleeps with his cat."

"That's horrible," said Ermolenko. "They scratch."

"No," I said. "He had her claws removed just for that reason."

The next day Rule Book was unable to wait for the evening roll call. He came running into the barracks right after dinner and slapped three extra duty details on me for sitting on my bed.

After roll call I dropped by Kurasov's office and told him that I would not do the extra details.

"Then I will punish you for attempting to disobey an order," he said, not the least bit surprised by my statement.

"You can't punish me for attempting to disobey," I said.

"Why not?"

"Because I'm not attempting to disobey an order. I'm simply not obeying it."

I have already said that, according to army regulations, there can be no such thing as failure to obey an order. A commanding officer is obliged to exert all possible influence, including force and force of arms, to see that an order is obeyed. A strict observance of regulations ultimately requires that a soldier failing to obey an order cannot remain alive. Those are the regulations. In practice, however, there are many reasons why a commanding officer cannot exercise his right to take the life of a subordinate. In the first place, he has to reckon with the fact that his subordinates are also armed and that their rebellion might also be expressed by means of arms. In the second place, this point in the regulations does not correspond to the criminal code and the commanding officer would definitely be court-martialed. In the third place, even if the first and second reasons did not exist, the next reason would itself be sufficiently grave—this reason is of the career-bureaucratic-baloney variety. In the army, just as in certain civilian organizations, a commanding officer's activities are evaluated on the basis of various indices. If, in production, the principal index is the productivity of labor, and in school, grades, then in the army it is the state of discipline which is evaluated. Naturally, the state of discipline is judged by the amount of punishments meted out. A commanding officer's career depends on the state of discipline in his unit or sub-unit. A commanding officer concerned with his career, even if he is cruel by nature, will, in a private matter, refrain from punishments that will be entered in the record. For that reason, even the guardhouse is rarely employed. (Generous use of the guardhouse is made by city-based commanding officers, who have many soldiers in addition to their own, the disciplining of whom is not reflected in their own service record.) So, just imagine that some officer has shot a soldier! An extraordinary event! Even if he wasn't sent to prison, his company would automatically be shifted to last place in the discipline column. And the same goes for the unit to which his company belonged, and, naturally, for the formation to which the unit belonged. Even if there was no official punishment, the shooting would still make him wish that he had never been born. Neither his duties nor his rank would ever be increased. Every higher officer would try to get rid of him, and steer away from him as far as possible. In the end, he'd be sent to some God-forsaken hole, and that would be the last of him. And the final reason, which could also have been the first, is that naturally there are very few commanding officers who, even without calculating all the unpleasant results of such an act, could bring themselves to shoot a man for next to nothing. I didn't believe that even our Rule Book would have been capable of such a thing.

"So you refuse to obey my order?"

"Yes, I refuse."

"All right, very good," he said ominously. "If it's a court-martial you're looking for, it's a court-martial you'll get. I'll show you. Watch out, I know everything about you. I know every step you take."

"And every word that's said about you," I added.

"Yes, and that, too," he could not resist saying.

"If you're so upset by what your subordinates say about you, try acting better and then no one will say anything bad about you."

"Is that so?" he said, surprised. "Now you're going to instruct me? You're too smart, that's right. Too smart . . ."

On his lips, the word "smart" sounded like "dangerous criminal."

"And aren't you ashamed," I said, "to be trying to find out who said what about you? How can your subordinates think well of you if you're spying on them, if you've hired some rat . . ."

"Don't you dare talk like that! He's an honest Soviet soldier! He's doing his duty!" The captain realized that he'd let the cat out of the bag, but it was too late to retreat now.

I was something of a romantic at the time and loved fine words. "This honest Soviet soldier," I said, "will betray me to you today, you to someone else tomorrow, and the day after that he'll betray the Motherland."

It was after taps when I returned to the barracks. Everyone was in bed.

"Hey, guys," I said from the door, "Captain Kurasov just let slip who's been squealing on us. He's just about the lowest thing you could imagine and his name is just about the lowest on the list at roll call."

That's what I said and I still feel uncomfortable about

my fancy phrasing. No one said a word. I looked over at Yakhtonov, who had drawn his blanket up to his eyes and was waiting guardedly to see what would happen next. Finally, Genka Denisov, clearly upset, asked: "Yashka, is it true?"

Everyone froze. For an instant I felt utterly strange. What if it wasn't him? After all, I had no proof whatsoever. The little evidence I did have had been tricked out of Kurasov.

"It's true," answered Yashka softly, and I felt a sense of relief.

Again no one said a word.

"All right, tell us about it." Genka broke the silence.

Yakhtonov put up no resistance, which in his position was probably the best way out. Besides, I must assume that the role he was playing was also a great burden to him and that he was glad it was over and done with.

"You remember the story about the missing coats?" asked Yashka.

We all remembered it. One morning after reveille there was a rumor going around that two coats were missing from the quartermaster's. The word was that someone had stolen them. We were all a bit surprised—nothing like this had occurred before. The only thing stolen so far was the soap, which lay around in huge quantities in big plywood boxes. Everybody stole soap, and in the evenings, between supper and evening roll call, we'd bring the soap to the neighboring village and sell it to the Poles or simply swap it for wine. But as for coats, nothing of that sort had happened before. After breakfast, de Gaulle announced that the coats had not been stolen, they'd slipped down in back of something which he hadn't noticed at first and now they'd turned up. There was something a little strange in all this, but none of us paid much attention. The coats had been found and that was dandy.

Now Yakhtonov told us that it was he who had stolen the coats. He was going to sell them to the Poles, he'd gotten caught, and Captain Kurasov had offered him a choice—either a court-martial or become a stool pigeon.

Kazik Ermolenko got up and stuck his feet in his boots. "Let's go out for a smoke," he said.

He, Genka Denisov, Oleg Vasilev, and I went out to the stairs. By the unwritten rules of army life, Yashka deserved what we called a "dark job" (a sudden beating under cover of night), but his story had won everyone's pity, with the exception of Vasilev, who demanded immediate retribution, not from malice, but from a sense of justice. But the purpose of a "dark job" was to conceal the identity of those involved, which, of course, in this case was definitely out of the question. Yashka could squeal again. Besides, our training was almost over and we were afraid we wouldn't be certified if there was a scandal.

"All right," said Kazik. "Let's wait till graduation and then we'll give him what he's got coming."

Everyone agreed, with a sense of relief. Only Vasilev grumbled that it was always like this, that when it came right down to it, nobody wanted to get his hands dirty, that that kind of humanitarianism only spawned stoolies and scum.

"All right," we said, appeasing not only his but our own sense of justice unsatisfied. "As soon as school's over, on the last day . . ."

Of course we knew that we were deceiving ourselves, that nothing would happen the last day. But Vasilev would not give up hoping. When the last day came, he walked over to me and asked severely just what was going to be done with Yashka.

I asked him curiously: "What, now you're just going to go up to him in the middle of the night, throw a blanket over his head, and start thrashing him?"

· "And what was he thinking about when he was squealing on us?"

I barely managed to calm him down by explaining that a lot of time had passed since then, that Yashka had kept clean, and that he'd been reluctant to do it in the first place.

This conversation with Vasilev took place on the day before we were due to leave the school. After passing sentence on Yashka, we returned to the barracks and found him waiting, staring at us with fear in his eyes. He realized what we'd been conferring about and what danger he was in. Genka Denisov walked over to him.

"Here's the thing, Yashka, we're not going to beat you up, but you've got to give us your word that you'll stop informing."

"He'll send me to jail," said Yashka in terror.

"That doesn't concern us," said Genka firmly. "Squirm all you want, but you've got to give us your word."

"I promise I won't do it any more." Yashka was barely able to utter the words.

The next day, Yashka (as he told us later on) reported to Kurasov and told him that he would not inform any more and that he preferred a court-martial. Kurasov understood everything and said nothing. Kurasov apparently decided not to victimize Yashka any further. Yashka had already ceased squealing on us, which would have been hard for him, in any case. We no longer said an unnecessary word in his presence, not because we were on guard with him; it was just that our tongues seemed to know what could be said around him.

On the other hand, we did settle accounts with Captain Kurasov, and rather pointedly, too. And again it was Vasilev who distinguished himself.

As departure time grew closer, we all agreed not to shake the captain's hand at the farewell ceremony.

And so, for one final time, the sergeant drew us up on the parade ground in front of the barracks. He then reported to the captain that the company had been assembled prior to departure.

"At ease!" said the captain, tossing off a salute. "Good-bye, comrades."

"Goodbye, com . . ." someone started, then broke off.

The captain stepped over to the first soldier on the right flank, who just happened to be our justice-loving Vasilev.

"Goodbye, Comrade Vasilev," said the captain, offering his hand.

"Goodbye, comrade captain," said Vasilev loudly and, looking Kurasov right in the eye, put his hands behind his back.

"So, shake my hand," said Rule Book in a pitiable, dog-like whimper.

"Not for anything, comrade captain," said Vasilev clearly, without averting his eyes.

The captain wheeled around as if he had heard the command "About face!" and ran to the barracks as fast as his legs would carry him.

While we were driving out the gate, someone said to me: "Look, it's Rule Book."

I looked up and saw our former commander in one of the windows on the first floor. Half hidden by a curtain, he was watching us, probably thinking that he couldn't be seen. And I, weak creature that I am, must admit that my heart was wrenched by a fleeting sense of pity for him.

I thought before, and I still do, that it is rare that a person's character changes under the force of circumstance. But, strangely enough, the cadets who served under Kurasov after us said that the captain had changed beyond recognition and that there was no better officer in the school. Which goes to show that certain lessons leave their mark, even on people like him.

1974

FOUR OPEN
LETTERS

LETTER TO
COMRADE PANKIN

In response to his interview published in *Literaturnaya Gazeta* on September 26, 1973

Dear Boris Dmitrievich:

I must admit that before reading your interview in the paper I was somewhat confused. All of a sudden, one hears of the formation of some kind of council, which in turn is to found an agency concerned expressly with the defense of "copyright."

What on earth for?

After all, our laws provide for the protection of copyright inside the country, and it has indeed been protected in the past, albeit in a rather singular manner. As for copyright abroad . . .

It was specifically this point that had me perplexed. Who, I wondered, would be most concerned about possible infringement of his copyright abroad? Logically, those whose works are extensively published there—for instance, A. Solzhenitsyn, V. Maximov, Academician A. Sakharov, and other such "dissidents," if you will pardon this fashionable term. Consequently, these are the people one would expect to find on your founding council. However, as soon as I learned that the council would be headed by Comrade Stukalin, I immediately discarded my first suppositions. "No," I said to myself, "Comrade Stukalin would never agree to head a council with *that* kind of membership."

Although your interview clarified some points, it regrettably complicated others even further. On the one hand, it is reassuring to learn that the council will be composed of such major creative talents as G. Markov, Y. Verchenko, S. Sartakov, et al. On the other hand, it is not quite clear why these writers in particular should suddenly evince such extraordinary concern for the protection of copyright. I mean, it is highly unlikely that any foreign publisher would want to issue pirate editions of *their* works.

The strangest thoughts flashed through my mind. I even wondered, for a moment, if perhaps, without my having noticed it, these authors had suddenly produced unprecedented literary masterpieces which were in imminent danger of dissemination through *samizdat*, or publication by Possev or maybe even Gallimard. Or perhaps they had rushed to the defense of copyright through sheer altruism?

I spent a considerable amount of time pondering the possible aims of an agency staffed by the above-mentioned authors and headed by yourself.

In your interview you state that the agency's main task will be to "further the mutual exchange of authentic achievements in various fields of human creative endeavor." The word "authentic" was not specifically stressed, but I noticed it nevertheless. The definition of authenticity of achievements in various fields of human creative endeavor would, I think, be a rather difficult task. In fact, this has sometimes taken years, if not centuries. Can we now expect that henceforth the authenticity of a given achievement will be determined immediately and unhesitatingly?

But by whom? By your agency? It would be interesting to learn, in that case, what your criteria would be. Can one, for instance, consider the works of A. Solzhenitsyn to be "authentic" literary achievements? Or will this appellation refer, in future, to the works of, say, Comrade Verchenko?

Further in your interview you point out, very reasonably, that it is both "bothersome and uneconomical" for individual authors to have to worry about matters pertaining to their copyright. Reading between the lines, however, it seems not unreasonable to assume that it would also become extremely "bothersome" for any author whose works were published abroad without the intermediacy of your agency. Presumably, any author acting without your assistance would be infringing the government's monopoly on foreign trade, and this, in its turn, would automatically make him a criminal.

Such a situation is fraught with the most diverse possibilities. For instance, let us imagine the following: having dispatched his manuscript abroad, an author becomes subject to protection. Protecting the copyright together with the bearer of that copyright can be deemed the most efficient method. In consequence of this, it would be quite logical to start immediate proceedings to have both the Lefortovo and Butyrka prisons placed under the direct supervision of your agency. The necessary number of guards and police dogs should also, naturally, be placed at your disposal. There you could intern not only a great number of recalcitrant writers but also quite a few of those who inherit their rights. Moreover, since your agency undertakes to ensure the granting of reciprocal rights to writers of other countries party to the Universal

Convention, this same form of protection could be extended to foreign writers as well.

There is one point, however, which I find rather puzzling. Your agency is, ostensibly, a social organization, and not a government department. But since all forms of foreign trade are within the jurisdiction of the government, and *only* the government, could it not be that your agency itself risks being accused of criminal activity? In that case, how could the agency possibly protect anyone else, being itself, as it were, "subject to protection"? This possibility surely deserves serious thought.

I have one further suggestion to offer. As your agency intends to decide arbitrarily when, where, and on what conditions to allow the publication of a given work or even to forbid its publication, this "legal" aspect of the agency's powers should be indicated in the name of the agency. Therefore, I suggest that in future your agency should be known not as VAAP (All-Union Copyright Agency) but as VAPAP—the All-Union Agency for the Appropriation of Copyright. All this involves is the addition of one little letter—but how it helps the true meaning to come through! Pursuing this line of thought a little further, one cannot but consider it natural for your agency to acquire not only an author's copyright but the authorship itself. I suggest that in future your agency should be named the sole author of the works of Soviet writers, and assume full responsibility for their ideological and aesthetic content.

Wishing to make a personal contribution to such a worthwhile cause, I should like the agency VAPAP to be considered both the author and, of course, the copyright holder of this letter.

Please accept my assurances of the most sincere respect.

October 2, 1973

LETTER TO
THE WRITERS' UNION

To the secretariat of the Moscow branch of the Writers' Union of the Russian Republic

I will not come to your meeting, because it is due to take place behind closed doors and in secret, that is to say illegally, and I have no desire to take part in illegal activities.

We have nothing to discuss and nothing to argue about, because I express my own opinions while you say what you are told.

The secretariat in its present form is not a democratically elected body but has been imposed on the Writers' Union by outside organizations. Neither the secretariat as a whole nor any single one of its members has any authority over me either in creative matters or, more decidedly, in questions of a moral character. There are just two or three former writers among you, but who are the rest? Look at yourselves—you haven't the slightest notion what the man sitting beside you or opposite you writes. And some, we know, are not writers at all.

I am prepared to leave an organization that has been transformed, with your active cooperation, from a union of writers into a union of bureaucrats, in which circulars written in the form of novels, plays, and poems are handed out as literary models whose quality is judged according to the author's official position.

Champions of our land and patriots! Don't you think your patriotism is costing our land too dearly? Some of

you get as much and more for your colorless boring com-
positions as a whole collective farm of the tillers of the
soil you so extravagantly praise can earn with their com-
bined efforts.

You are a union of unanimity. One puts his hand in the
party till, another sold a government-owned summer cot-
tage, a third diverted cooperative funds into his own sav-
ings account. Yet, in all the twelve years I belonged to
the union, I don't remember a single one of you being
expelled for that reason.

You only need to say one honest word (or at times just
to keep silent when everyone else is yelling his head off)
for every possible sort of punishment to follow at once:
the book you have been working on for years is stopped
and the type broken up, your play is banned, and the film
for which you wrote the script is put on the shelf. And
this is followed by utterly prosaic pennilessness. And so
for a year you get not a single kopeck, for two years you
get not a single kopeck, you plunge up to your neck in
debt, you sell everything you possess, and when you are at
the breaking point, provided you haven't let out any
careless words during those two years, they may perhaps
condescend to present you with two or three hundred
roubles from the Literary Fund, so as to be able to complain for the rest of your life: "We gave him some help,
but he . . ." I don't want your help, I'm not a beggar.
I work no less and no worse than you. I have my readers
and viewers. Don't come between me and them, and I
won't have need of your help.

I will not come to your secret meeting. I am prepared
to debate with you at any open gathering of writers—or
even of workers, if you wish, in whose name you are at-
tacking me. Unlike the majority of you, I myself was a
worker. I began my working life at eleven, minding the

collective farm calves. I have had to plow, mix cement at building sites, and tend a lathe in a factory. I served four years as a private in the Soviet army. I would like to see you at an open meeting presenting me as an imperialist shark or an agent of foreign intelligence services.

The lie is your weapon. You have smothered the greatest of all our citizens in lies and helped to drive him from our land. You think the whole crowd of you together will be able to fill his place. You are mistaken! The places in our great Russian literature are not yet determined by you. And not a single one of you will manage to creep even into the last rank.

Moscow,
February 19, 1974

LETTER TO

THE MINISTER

OF COMMUNICATIONS

TOP SECRET
Minister of Communications
of the U.S.S.R.
Comrade Talizin, N.V.

Dear Nikolai Vasilievich,
It is with deep concern that I bring to your attention the fact that an enemy of the Relaxation of International

Tension, the head of the Moscow telephone system, is in hiding somewhere in the field of national economy headed by you.

This is how I found it out.

On the 20th of September of this year I decided to use services rendered by the telephone system to call a personal friend, the poet Korzhavin, in Boston, U.S.A., and have a conversation the contents of which I pass on to you now.

"'Allo," said I to the poet Korzhavin.

"Hallow," he answered.

"How are you?"

"All right, and you?"

"I am fine."

It was daytime in the capital of our Motherland. It was a bright day of the Tenth Five-Year Plan. Our people in a burst of labor enthusiasm were erecting new buildings, running various mechanisms, smelting steel, and mining coal for the country.

At the same time, it was, naturally, night in the city of Boston. Under the cover of darkness, bands of gangsters were running the show; the torches of the KKK were blazing and marijuana was being smoked; the dollar was going down irrepressibly; the unemployed, having lost all hope, were forming lines at the unemployment office, long lines such as we usually have only for carpets and sausages.

Either oppressed by this situation or not yet wide awake, the poet Korzhavin answered my questions listlessly and absentmindedly.

"How is Luba?" I inquired about the health of his wife.

"Luba?" he asked again, with the muddleheadedness peculiar to his backward world outlook. "Luba is asleep. And how is Ira?"

I think you would be happy to know that the system which you head worked perfectly. I could hear the poet Korzhavin as if he were not on the other side of the earth but rather very close by. Our conversation per se, not of any interest to an outsider (or so I thought), was nevertheless a valid proof that we live in the era of relaxation of international tension, when the continents have come closer and the exchange of information (however trivial) has become not only accessible but encouraged by the countries which signed the Helsinki agreement.

Alas, the triumph of the relaxation did not last long. The next morning, picking up the receiver, I noticed with dismay that it was as silent as a fish. "Something is wrong," I said to myself and went to the nearest telephone booth.

"153–28–53?" a charming female voice at the repair service center asked me. "Is it your telephone?"

"Yes, mine."

"Disconnected for hooliganism."

I was quite taken aback and put down the receiver. Then I called again. "Excuse me, maybe I got it wrong . . . Why was it disconnected?"

"Is it your telephone?" I was asked again.

"No, not mine," I answered this time.

"Disconnected for non-payment of the bill."

Despite my reputation for hooliganism, I tried to be polite. "But just a second ago you gave me a different reason. Please think it over and answer more precisely why my telephone has been disconnected."

It seems that she was embarrassed, but who knows?

"Your telephone was disconnected by an order from above."

"From approximately which above?"

"As if you don't know."

"I don't know."

"That's odd." (She evidently does not believe me.) "Call this number, there you'll get the answer."

I called first this number and then that number, and called again and again. The people with whom I talked refused to identify themselves or give their positions. They answered in riddles, hinting at what I should understand, and I had the feeling that I was calling not the telephone office but some secret organization.

With incredible difficulty I managed to find out that my telephone has been disconnected at the order of the head of the Moscow telephone system, Vasiliev, V.F. But for what?

And now, dear N.V., I am sitting in my apartment, cut off from the whole world and asking the same question: For what?

As for non-payment of the bill, it is, of course, a lie. For the services rendered to me by the telephone company I always pay on time. You may hang my portrait in your study or even on the front of your ministerial building without any risk as one of the most exemplary customers.

Hooliganism? But why wasn't the measure of punishment decided by a court rather than by the telephone chief? And what will happen if his example is followed by electricity, elevators, gas, waterworks, and sewerage chiefs? This is not a laughing matter. It could leak to the newspapers. It could become the property of greedy, sensational Western "voices."

And what does my hooliganism consist of? I did not say anything hooliganistic to the poet Korzhavin. You can call and ask him, if, of course, you are not afraid that your telephone might go dead after that. Though I think you have several telephones, and even if one of them turns out to be disconnected, you can temporarily use others. It might be that the mere fact of a conversation with another country is considered to be hooliganism.

Why does the telephone company render such hooligan services to its customers?

The answer "You know yourself" seems to be unsatisfactory also. I do not know, N.V.

Even with my characteristic self-criticism, I cannot see anything hooliganistic in my actions. But the fact that your subordinate Vasiliev eavesdrops on someone else's conversations, lies and makes others lie, and deprives people of the possibility of communicating with each other—this is genuine hooliganism. Well, it is possible to find some other adjectives: lawlessness, arbitrariness, petty tyranny, you name it. I do not know what is more to your taste. It is not, though, a matter of definitions.

The fact is that there are (maybe you have heard) so-called human rights. According to which man has the right not only (as is sung) to "education, rest, and work" but also to various other trifles. In particular, such as to express freely whatever he wants, to exchange information, ideas, and to enter into contacts with other men. I with you or with the poet Korzhavin, or you with the poet Korzhavin, or with anyone else you'd like to, without asking permission of your subordinate Vasiliev.

And these "our with you" rights are considered to be an integral part of life in the civilized world, and their observance is one of the most indispensable conditions for the relaxation of international tension. They are mentioned in various international agreements and solemnly proclaimed in the very Helsinki agreement which was signed, on behalf of the Soviet state, personally by L. I. Brezhnev.

That's why, by disconnecting my telephone, Vasiliev not only disgraced himself but is trying to sow some seeds of doubt on the sincerity of the efforts of the Soviet Union in the development of the process of relaxation and to put Comrade Brezhnev personally in a quandary.

It is not for me to say to you, N.V., that there are still many enemies of the relaxation of international tension. What a terrific assistant they have found in Comrade Vasiliev. After all, not even the notorious George Meany managed to disconnect a single telephone. But Vasiliev managed. And I heard that he had done it many times before and that the telephone terror under his leadership reached an unprecedented scale.

I do not know what you think, but I think that the situation seems to be threatening. After seizing the telephone network, the enemies may go further. And if they take in their hands telephone, post, and telegraph, radio and TV, then . . . you know yourself what could happen . . .

In order to save our country from such unpleasant consequences, I beg you to dismiss Vasiliev from his position without delay and give an order to a new chief to reconnect my telephone.

Sincerely yours

Moscow
October 12, 1976

LETTER TO

THE BRIGANTINE

LITERARY CLUB

A few years ago I received a letter from the pupils of High School No. 7 in the town of Artemovsk, Voroshilovgradsky Province. They wrote me that a literary club called the Brigantine had been established at their school and they asked me to send them one of my books for their club. I sent them two which had recently appeared. They replied at once to thank me and to inform me that I had been elected an honorary member of their club, which included, in similarly honorary status, Sofronov, Gribachev, Permyak, and whose honorary chairman was, it seems, Sartakov. Quite a bunch. I was surprised and I stopped answering the letters from the Briganteeners. But they didn't stop writing me. On every holiday—New Year's, the twenty-third of February, the first of May, the seventh of November—I would receive postcards and letters of the so-called work-report type which are printed in newspapers.

The crew of the Brigantine (this is how they styled themselves) solemnly reported their achievements, dripping with statistics: their museum contained 480 books signed by authors from 87 different cities, 1,550 letters from writers, and so on. Later on, there were declarations of love and devotion: "Come visit us and you'll be convinced how much the Brigantine loves you and your work," followed by unending desires for my "creative success and sound health."

There came a time when my mail was drastically reduced. Some people had stopped writing me, some letters simply weren't arriving, but the letters from the Briganteeners kept coming on every holiday just as they had before. Time passed, all sorts of events occurred in my life, my correspondents from Artemovsk finished school but new "crews" continued to insist on congratulating me for one thing or another, to wish me something, in particular that I "always remain the person they know me to be."

And yesterday, November 1, 1977, a letter, most likely the last, arrived.

Mr. Voinovich, V.N.!
From foreign radio broadcasts and from a collection published by the Writers' Union we have learned that you have been expelled from the Writers' Union for anti-Soviet activity.
We are also outraged by your "creative work" and after this consider you unworthy to be a member of the Brigantine Literary Club, concerning which we hereby inform you.

> Principal, School No. 7 (signature illegible)
> Club Members (12 childish signatures)

It is a known fact that in our country children participate almost as much as grownups in the life of society. They are constantly (and, of course, warmly) thanking someone for their happy childhood, solemnly reporting on the collection of scrap metal and wastepaper, and, when the occasion warrants, wrathfully branding turncoats and demanding blood. Unfortunately, many of them grow up to be just that sort of adult.

It is precisely for that reason that I think the letter from the Briganteers and my reply deserve public attention. I trust that there is no need to explain that the reasoning used in my reply was calculated to match the level of my young correspondents.

To the members of the Brigantine Club:
I received your letter, addressed to Mr. Voinovich. Its tone made it seem that you had already begun in your classrooms to prepare yourselves to be prison wardens. I would not have considered answering your letter had it

been written by adults. But you are children, there's a great deal ahead of you to learn and understand, and, for that reason, I am replying.

You could not have learned of my "anti-Soviet activities" from any collection issuing from the Writers' Union, because no such collection exists. Your principal is a very poor teacher if he forces children to set their signatures to an outright lie. You will be acting justly if you cease to respect him for this.

The only way you could have learned about my activities, which you call, at your principal's prompting, "anti-Soviet," was from the foreign radio broadcasts you mentioned or from other sources known best to your principal.

About four years ago (you were slow catching on), I truly was expelled from the Writers' Union for activities better termed literary and social; that is, for trying to write to the best of my ability, to live by my conscience, and for having frequently stood up in defense of unjustly persecuted people. (Something I advise you to do when you grow up, or even right now. And not at your principal's prompting either, but out of your own understanding of things.) I was expelled because I, among others, attempted to use my limited powers to oppose the rebirth in our country of those procedures characteristic of the epoch now modestly called the period of the cult of personality.

When you grow up and learn more about that time than you now know, it will make the hair of even the most conscientious of you stand on end. You will learn that millions of people (including perhaps your grandmothers and grandfathers) perished, accused of "anti-Soviet activities."

You will also learn that writers like Tsvetaeva, Akhmatova, Mandelstam, Babel, Bulgakov, Platonov, Zoshchenko, and Pasternak were either tormented in camps or persecuted by all and any means, and that grown men and women, either through foolishness or malice, wrote them letters similar to yours. You will learn that now it is precisely those writers, and not their safe and satisfied contemporaries, who are the pride of our nation's literature.

Unfortunately, the persecution of writers (and other honest people) has not been confined to that distant period. If you listen to foreign radio broadcasts (when your principal isn't looking?), then you yourselves can compile a list of writers who better represent our current literature than the honorary members of your club. It is these writers, exiled from the country or subjected to unbearable persecution at home, who are the best of those now living and who sooner or later will be acknowledged by a grateful posterity. Though why say posterity? Even now, their books are passed from hand to hand and make engrossing reading for thousands of people in our country and millions throughout the world.

It was not so long ago that you wrote me that you loved me and my books. One of you wrote: "We want you always to remain the person we know you to be." But now you write: "We are also outraged by your 'creative work'" (putting those words in quotation marks). So who did you think I was, then? Has my creative work changed? And what was your "love" worth (now it's I who use quotation marks) if it vanished as soon as you learned of my expulsion from the Writers' Union?

Clearly, this "love" of yours was just as much a bureaucratic measure as was your later "outrage."

My books have not become any worse because I was expelled from the so-called Writers' Union. They have been translated into more than twenty languages; hundreds of articles have been written about them in the world press, including the Communist press. I tell you with pride that thousands of readers in our country have not renounced me; they safeguard my books, reread them, and sometimes copy them by hand. Those readers are dear to me, but ones like you, you will excuse me, are not.

In general, the true reader is not one who sends holiday greetings to all members of the Writers' Union indiscriminately, checking their names off a list, but the one who does not divide the books he reads into Soviet and anti-Soviet but into the good and the bad, the true and the false. A reader who devours good books either cries or laughs with them and accumulates intelligence, goodness, and compassion for others.

My books are not now published in the U.S.S.R., for which I am in no way at fault.

In the words of Bonch-Bruevich, V. I. Lenin (who may be an authority for you) dreamed of a time (and here I quote) "when we finally reunify the literature which had been created on both sides of the border of autocratic Russia, when we finally are in a position to study it all completely and turn our most serious attention to the fact that, willy-nilly, many authors had to publish abroad."

I hope that Lenin's dream may yet someday come true and that among those now inaccessible books that find their way to you, mine as well will be included. And then some of you will feel ashamed to have signed such a letter written by your principal.

Moscow
November 2, 1977